Table of Contents

SO FAR AND YET SO NEAR
Stories of Americans Abroad

For Patrick, May you enjoy! Michael

EDITED AND PUBLISHED BY

AMERICAN CITIZENS ABROAD

American Citizens Abroad
Geneva, Switzerland

Cover design by Christin Rossier-Scheidegger

American Citizens Abroad

www.aca.ch
info.aca@gmail.com

ISBN-10
2-8399-0109-9

ISBN-13
978-2-8399-0109-3

Digitally Printed

Acknowledgements

American Citizens Abroad was created in the summer of 1978 for a very specific reason. At the request of one of ACA's founders, the US Congress had enacted legislation calling on the President of the United States to prepare a study, for the Congress, of all of the US legislation and regulations that appeared to discriminate against US citizens living and working abroad. It soon became evident that the White House had no knowledge at all about such laws and regulations and their impact overseas, and thus there was no frame of reference by which to carry out such a study.

ACA was created to provide such a background study. ACA prepared a 50 issue paper which the White House officially endorsed as the benchmark for its report to the Congress. The next year at ACA's request, the Congress reenacted even broader legislation, this time widening the mandate to include all US laws and regulations that not only discriminated against a US citizen overseas, but also those that caused competitive difficulties in world markets. When this second Congressional mandate became law, ACA rewrote its original study to include the international competitive dimension and once again this served as the benchmark for the revised White House effort.

As many of these problems were not likely to be easily solved and would require a considerable amount of on-going educational and lobbying work, the founders of ACA decided to maintain the organization and to open up membership to US citizens living all over the world. ACA has grown to encompass members in more than 90 countries.

During the last 27 years, ACA has been one of the leading organizations speaking out on behalf of the millions of US citizens living abroad, by testifying before Congress, and providing information to overseas Americans and to the press. Thanks to ACA, a number of laws and regulations have been changed, improving overseas American rights in the areas of citizenship of their children born overseas, taxation, voting and a number of other issues.

ACA has also created three awards that are given in recognition of exemplary performance and contributions to the overseas American Community by members of Congress, the press, and the State Department. Additionally, ACA has already published two editions of an Overseas American Handbook, as joint ventures with *USA Today.*

With respect to *So Far and Yet So Near,* ACA would like to thank all those who sent in their stories and, in particular, the authors of the selected contributions. ACA also wishes to express its gratitude to the members of the book committee who, together and individually, spent hundreds of hours—all volunteered—in reviewing the stories received, organizing the book and getting it published. The committee members included Jackie Bugnion, Mike Larsen, Jon McLin, Marylouise Musso, Andy Sundberg and Jennifer Wallace. And many thanks to other ACA members who encouraged the effort through their punctual advice and support.

For further information on ACA activities, including how to join, please check the American Citizens Abroad website http://www.aca.ch

Introduction

So far and yet so near. Those of us Americans—more than three million by most accounts and possibly as many as 6 million—who are living abroad know what it is like to experience different cultures. But what does it really feel like to stand in line to buy a tram ticket in a language you not only don't understand but perhaps cannot even read? Ever changed a tire in the stifling heat of Borneo, drunk mare's milk with Turkmen tribesmen or even attempted to register your otherwise safe (if relatively oversized) US-made car in a European country? Ever lived through a coup, survived a tsunami or simply found it more practical to do what everyone else did in your adopted village and follow the local goatherd over the hills when taking your kids to school?

Early in the summer of 2004, sitting in the convivial atmosphere of the dining room of ACA-founder Andy Sundberg, in his converted farmhouse located in the outskirts of Geneva, Switzerland, and guided by an Australian friend who had recently completed a similar project, a small group of us boldly decided that the stories we had all heard and swapped over the years might well be worth publishing. The ambitious goal of the resulting anthology is to give us—that otherwise unknown and unheard of band of several million Americans—a means to communicate a particularly rich and little understood part of our national character. In pieces ideally containing between 2,000 and 3,000 words each, we wanted to hear about the experiences of living in a foreign country or working on a foreign assignment, the joys and the frustrations. How was it to view your country from the outside in and (this one proved popular) how did the writers relate to the United States they left behind?

Our initial flyer soliciting input stated: "We all have a story to tell. Now is the time to tell yours." We added a quotation from Mark Twain: "Travel is fatal to prejudice, bigotry, and narrow-mindedness, and many of our people need it sorely on these accounts. Broad, wholesome, charitable views of men and things cannot be acquired by vegetating in one little corner of the earth all one's lifetime." Timeless.

The results were astonishing. Despite the stereotype of Americans as less traveled than most Europeans and especially our Antipodean friends, the range and diversity of the 130+ stories we received over the subsequent six months proved how that unique American blend of ingenuity, spirit, eagerness, sense of fair play and can-do energy is alive and well. At times serious and introspective, and often humorous, the contributions we received from every part of the globe gave the committee much to work with. Every story was read by each member of the committee and then reviewed jointly. Our appreciation goes out to all those who submitted their stories.

The timing proved auspicious as well. What it means to be an American, in particular an American residing overseas, and how Americans are viewed in the rest of the world have evolved dramatically since the early 1990s. Crucially, how

Americans "back home" view the rest of the world has changed as well. We undoubtedly live in a period that later generations will look back on as one where values that we once almost took for granted were questioned relentlessly and on a global, interactive basis.

Thanks to all the authors for sharing this wonderful collection of stories, which together manifest the ubiquitous spirit of America. Now, settle down for a good read!

Enjoy!

ACA Book Committee

Adapting

In German "I" is pronounced "E" so ISDN sounds like an Ugandan dictator.
Barbara Goodman Shovers

This truth was sobering and heartening. It confirmed that I might always be slightly ill-adapted to the life I lived. Something deep and early in me was indestructibly from another place.
Wallis Wilde-Menozzi

Admittedly, I was nervous. In a place where English is the official language, it hardly seemed fair that I should not understand what the locals were trying to say to me.
Amy Martin-Bombeeck

The reason I left Wisconsin is not because I was unhappy there; therefore, I believe there will always be things that I miss about it.
Margo Renner

The skills I had acquired in a half a dozen years of motherhood served me well overseas: learning to communicate without words, which my children had taught me, was invaluable, especially when I ventured into Eastern Europe.
Lynne-Therese Gilardi

If you have to ask what the rule is, then you are an outsider. It is worse if you don't even know that a rule is in play.
Jan Harrington

Naturally I went to sit beside my husband and this was my first lesson in Kuwaiti culture. It turned out that he was at the men's table and the other table was for the women.
Celeste Snyder

Defeated, again, in my effort to find acceptance, I was scorned by the neighbors of Kypseli (Beehive) District: a respectable married woman would not allow an animal to live in an apartment or permit a poodle to poop on a balcony.
Cristina S. Karmas

1

Trash and T-Com

Barbara Goodman Shovers

Trash

There is no cow more sacred to Germans than that of the *Umwelt* or Environment. This is a noble venture, but like many noble ventures, it often falls prey to unintended consequences.

"What should I do with the garbage?" Liz asks. She has volunteered to be this evening's dinner cleaner-upper, a thoughtful move prompted by my before dinner outrage at the cocktail-sized disposal-less kitchen sink and its companion heat-leaking oven.

I look at the chart Herr Greico gave me.

Cardboard and paper, wrapped in blue bags, will be collected every other Tuesday.

Food scraps and plant materials, wrapped in green bags, will be collected every other Friday.

Metal and plastic will be collected the same day as paper goods but they can be put in the yellow bin outside the apartment building any day before that.

Dirty food containers and other *Restmull* can be thrown at will in the black dumpster next to the yellow one.

Glass must be separated into brown, clear and green piles and deposited by hand in their appropriate neighborhood receptacles. This can only be done during the hours of 7 a.m. and 7 p.m. (19:00) weekdays. Neighbors, I'm told, are deputized to report people who sneak bottles in earlier or later.

Clothing and shoes have their own neighborhood bins.

Oversized trash is collected once every 30 or 60 days.

My kitchen is 64 square feet. With the exception of a small space under the sink there is no place for one garbage bin, let alone seven. Herr Greico's suggestion is that I store trash in the basement *Keller* and put it on the curb the night before its scheduled pickup. Our *Keller* is four flights of stairs down. He's got to be kidding.

Actually it is unusual for an apartment house not to have blue (paper) and green ("Bio") bins. But Herr Greico says there is no space for them. *"Es ist nicht possible,"* he insists when I question why we have to ferment apple cores for half a month. It is not possible. This is the beginning of a pattern. He will repeat these words more than any others during our stay on Simrockallee.

Our apartment starts to resemble a Christo art installation. A bag of plastic bags hangs from the hinge between the kitchen and dining room. A bag of newspapers hovers in the hallway between the bedrooms. Doors are weighed down with beer bottles (brown—the storage room); wine bottles (green—the bathroom); and everything else (Bill's office).

The clutter is overwhelming.

Sometimes late at night, I sneak garbage down the street and deposit it in other neighbors' bins. I have to wash big pots in the bathtub, so it seems natural to flush their scrapings down the toilet. I purposely leave junk in the communal mail box. I can't read it; why should I have to dispose of it?

"What should I do with the garbage?" Liz repeats. I consider the options.

Recycling should help the environment, but at least visually, it has the opposite effect. There are dumpsters all over the place. Most of these are grimed and graffitied. If they fill up before collection day, people leave bundles beside them. Huge pink waste management trucks do the pick-up, their oversized beds blocking the narrow streets, the cars stuck behind spurting plumes of exhaust. Inside the cars, drivers smoke to vent frustration.

Actually they smoke pretty much anywhere, and often. Germans preach unceasingly about Americans polluting their air with fossil fuels and their bodies with modified foods but see nothing ironic about the fact that not only is smoking tolerated in their cities, it's encouraged. Next to many a recycling bin there's a coin operated cigarette machine. Secondary schools are required by law to have smoking rooms for students 16 and older. Instead of smoking and non-smoking sections, it seems like restaurants have smoking and chain smoking sections.

"What should I do with the garbage?" Liz calls. "If you don't tell me I'm just going to throw it out the window."

"Try it," I say.

She does. It biodegrades nicely.

T-Com

An IT guy from my husband's office is trying to get our phone and internet hooked up. On the table by the only phone jack in the entire apartment he messes with cards, cables, modems, and cords. Deutsche Telekom uses cheerful pink in its marketing materials, but getting their stuff to work makes even Germans see red.

Herr Wischerau mutters something about ISDN and DSL. "This shall not work together. The box is needed."

"What box?" I ask, my muscles tensing. This is the third day Herr Wischerau has been my house guest. Each afternoon he leaves saying, "All is good now," and every afternoon plus ten minutes I find out all is not so good. We still can't dial a number or connect to the web.

"From the T-Com," he shrugs and goes into a complicated explanation of ISDN and DSL and the relationships between such. In German "I" is pronounced "E" so ISDN sounds like an Ugandan dictator. "Uh huh," I nod. "Yeah, OK."

I don't have a clue what he's talking about. But over the course of four weeks Bill and I have made multiple trips to the panther pink offices of T-Online and T-Com and T-Mobile where the counter personnel are just as unhelpful as telecommunications providers are in America, except they speak limited English and never even wish us, "Have a Nice Day." We have already invested close to a thousand euros in non-compatible cards, cables, modems and cords. And this doesn't even count all the converters and transformers we've bought to adapt our 120 volt appliances to Europe's 220 current. They're growing spider webs waiting for their entrance cue.

It is hard enough getting your utilities working in the States where people allegedly talk your talk. It's the seventh circle of hell trying to do it in a foreign country.

"So you must get that and I will return back," he says snapping shut his tool box. It is 16:00 on the dot, the time he normally tells me "All is good." I nod my head and see him to the door. But I'll be darned if I'm going to buy something else.

Instead I start to cry. This is something I do a lot my first weeks in Germany. I've traveled six time zones east and regressed 40 years. But an apple-cheeked tearful little kid activates the compassion gene in onlookers. A middle-aged woman with a red nose fails to elicit the same response.

"I'm going home," I tell my husband the moment he walks in the door, "to Toledo."

"Oh come on. You knew this would be rough. You're the one who kept saying you could keep it together. What an adventure it would be. How your emotions would attack your intellect but your intellect would win."

"I didn't expect something out of Dante."

"It's not that bad."

"Oh, it is. All we do is spend money on stuff that doesn't work. I don't know a soul. I can't talk to anyone. I can't even email. Every day it rains. This apartment is dark and depressing, and I hate the carpet. It's filthy. It's gross. I called about it again and all they say is, "Sorry, we changed it for the last tenant.""

"And I got yelled at for driving the wrong way on a one-way street. Which I was only doing because, to go the other way, I would've been on the tram track. And the grocery place I can walk to was closed. They close between 11 and 2. How convenient is that? I hate everything about this place. "

"How's Liz?"

"She's fine."

"You should take a lesson from her."

By now my entire face is scarlet. "She sleeps till one every day. She doesn't have to deal with a refrigerator the size of a microwave and a laundry machine that takes three hours to do a load. You go to work every morning and they speak English to you. She's holding off till school starts and she gets the same. You have no idea."

"Of course I have an idea. I was here four months before you."

"And look what a great job you did with our so-called communications. I don't even have a cell phone. I could be run over by the *S-bahn* and some old lady would wag her finger at me for blocking the tracks and I couldn't even call you."

"Well you'd be dead or seriously injured so it wouldn't make a difference,

5

would it?"

I am apoplectic, or at least purple. I put my hands to my temples and lower myself to the stained carpeting. "I want to go home," I bawl. "You two can stay if you want."

"Barb, I can't get you a cell phone until we're officially registered. You know that. It's the law. We've just got to wait on the paperwork. Maybe they'll give me a loaner at work. I'll see if we can hire someone else to get the computers working. You can come to my office and send e-mails."

As I knew would happen, my intellect slowly gains on my emotion. I stand up and get dinner ready for the grungy heat-leaking oven the landlord also refuses to "change out." I consider a last tirade about this other inefficient piece of German household design but decide the scale has tipped as far in my favor as it's going to go.

It takes several weeks and many euros worth of consultants more, but eventually we have a dial tone. I am so excited I forget about the waiting transformers and converters and plug my equipment directly into the wall. After almost two months without technology, my first act of liberation is to fry both the telephone and computer printer. I cry again.

Barbara Goodman Shovers was born in western New York and now lives in Toledo, Ohio. She returned to the United States in 2004 after spending two years in Germany with her husband and daughter. Presently a contributing editor and columnist for the Toledo Free Press, Barbara's commentary and humor pieces have been printed in publications including American Airline's in-flight magazine and the International Herald Tribune. In former incarnations, she's hawked bug spray for a major consumer goods manufacturer, written jingles for the United Way, taught business writing to college students and (her favorite) introduced school children to the masterworks of the Toledo Museum of Art.

Birdfeeder

Wallis Wilde-Menozzi

Just the word "Yankee" on the cardboard box of the birdfeeder was enough to staunch the melancholy that often overwhelms me, a dyed-in-the-wool American living out my days on Italian soil. Sometimes the ochre and greens and the pale wash on Parma buildings all pay off in a feeling of glorious gratitude for living in this spot, with the foothills inching towards the spiky Alps and humanity's long dramatic adaptation of the Po plain a humbling measure for one's own life. But sometimes I long for a leaner reality, something like Shaker furniture with strict lines, and a simpler one—one that can almost be tasted in the word "Yankee": a clear-headed, feisty soul unafraid of challenging authority and willing to live an individual destiny in an uncertain state of grace.

There is no logic to the difficulties arising from changing cultures; it is like putting on another skin. When I hear myself saying, *"Mamma mia, che disgrazia,"* instead of what I once meant—something more succinct, with more willpower involved—I feel quite surprised, even amused by the hyperbole. But on a bad day a voice inside repeats T.S. Eliot's line: "That is not what I meant at all. That is not it, at all." Anyway, in moments in which I think material objects will reestablish a piece of my invisible English-speaking identity, I often write to my sister with my requests. Thus when the idea of a birdfeeder came to mind as something missing in my daily landscape, I asked her for one.

My sister is an island of understanding and reference for me. She holds my place on pages where I existed not only as a child, but as an adult whose values she shares. I can confide in her without feeling I will send her into a state of alarm. She is not one who rubs in the lovely gilded *Giotto* postcards she receives by insisting that I can't expect to have everything. She understands what I mean when I say that I miss the "great wandering vegetative world," and the messy un-dictated possibilities of American life.

She responded immediately. With a combination of efficiency and care, the box arrived in time for last Christmas. It was accompanied by the usual sympathetic note: the unstated wish that it were easier for us to see each other more often. And then that good old Anglo-Saxon habit of not dwelling on the unalterable: the birdfeeder was a brilliant idea and might do the trick.

I overestimated its effect once in place. Hanging it onto a bare linden branch, I placed a lot of other hopes there: feelings of things I missed, like the creek frozen to dry crackling ice, and long walks with trails of crusty snow prints that couldn't be erased. Unfair baggage, really, because many of those winter reveries were lost while I still lived in America and found myself settled in California, far from my family. The feeder as it went up was definitely festooned with early experiences.

But I also had the birds in mind. I wanted the orange-breasted finches and sparrows and crows (even if I'm not crazy about the latter) to feel welcome to stop in front of our huge thin pane-glass windows and find succor. Given the heaped up mounds of snow which have bewildered these Mediterranean creatures in recent winters, I felt a calling similar to that when, as a school girl, I threaded suet on yarn ropes and felt kinship with those trying not to freeze in the subzero world outside.

Anyway, the name on the box was auspicious. Its Plexiglas tubing and metal perches, while not directly reminiscent of the little wooden houses we used to hang in trees, were appealing, and its transparency was well-tuned to the grey fog and the bare branches of the Po plain.

Where to begin the tale. Perhaps with my Italian husband, who wouldn't hear of purchasing seed. Cost wasn't the issue. But why buy it when bread crumbs were perfect. Bread crumbs conformed to his historical view of the world, the place of animals within that hierarchy, consumerism, human hunger and waste. In short, in the time it took me to open the box, I was up against a set of beliefs as linear as Italian history is long. A foolish consistency is the hobgoblin of little minds, but Italian schooling builds a deeply abstract way of thinking. The mind is alert to logical contradictions, analytical links. It teaches the basis of a good argument, a near fight-to-the death commitment to endless debate.

I was sad. The feeder's definition had been ambushed by this illuminated way of thinking. It's Yankee-ness and English instructions were being impinged upon. They said *seed*. Points like this are difficult to bridge: the in-the-present pragmatist vs. Aristotle and St. Francis. I was uninterested in historical examples. I didn't resist. We filled the feeder with bread crumbs. And I waited without rancor; without a thought that it would not attract a jubilee of birds.

But no birds came. The finches, the sparrows, the crows went about their business, independent of the lovely translucent column we had hung. Of course, my disappointment led me to accusations. "They can't get the crumbs out," I jousted. But my husband insisted it didn't matter; that birds who were truly hungry would eat bread. During January the long tube took on a bleak deserted aspect that beamed out failure. A few rains and the impacted crumbs began to mold.

My sister and I had some telephone conferences about it. "Try seed," she said. The undaunted postman, who like most people on our dead-end street is delighted to shower one with his opinions, rang the doorbell mid-month, first to inquire what the object was, and then to add that it wouldn't work.

"Why?" I asked. He put his index finger to his head in mock suicide. "Don't you understand? These birds are *furbo*. Sly. They know all about traps. That?" he said pointing to my prize, "Would you trust it if you were a bird?"

Yankee that I was, I nodded my head. Yes, I would. But his comments seemed pertinent to me. I looked at the feeder from an Italian bird's point of view. There were metal parts, shadowy reinforced holes with steel perches. The whole Gestalt suddenly became threatening, given that even little birds are preyed upon by the worst of Italian hunters. Sparrows and robins become the better-than-nothing trophies of renegades determined to keep alive, at this pathetic level, what was once sport. The Yankee bird feeder was for Yankee birds.

"Not so fast," said my husband as I worked my idea into a theory. "One's not much of a sample. Too many variables." Yet it was clear to me; here was my problem neatly displayed. The fact of particularity. The great weight of culture in adaptation and identity. The massive transmission of patterns not only through genes but through learning. Selection plays a role in identity's collective social aspects. Italian birds had learned that a free lunch was most likely a trap.

This truth was sobering and heartening. It confirmed that I might always be slightly ill-adapted to the life I lived. Something deep and early in me was indestructibly from another place. It was a positive perception that we exist in far larger, more subtle sets of responses that correspond to a particular reality we learn and never forget. The present-day Italian bird is more street-smart than its American counterpart. Their collective experiences are different.

But the story doesn't stop there; and perhaps won't where I leave off now. A gentle Swiss friend in Florence confirmed that the little chalet she hoisted into a tree as shelter for the birds was never used. She said: "You can add my experience to your evidence that there is some difference as far south as Florence. Swiss birds are not the same as Italian ones. Italian birds, poor things, have suffered and can't forget it."

Describing this fact to another friend in Parma, I was interrupted by her. "The explanation you give is good—as far as it goes. But birds here are not as suspicious as you think. They distrust machines, noises, technology, if you will. And with good reason," she said with a frown. "But don't think you are on to something scientific. Let me show you something," she proffered, with a sweet smile on her face as she opened her kitchen window. "Look," she said as she lifted up her arms and called the birds from the trees. "Come, come," she cooed gently as they tentatively swelled up in a moving cloud before her. "Here, you see, they will eat from your hands."

Wallis Wilde-Menozzi has lived in Parma, Italy for more than twenty years. Her poetry and essays have appeared widely from Granta *to* Best Spiritual Writing 2002. Mother Tongue: An American Life in Italy, *published by North Point Press, is a memoir about identity found and lost by changing cultures. She teaches writing workshops in Parma, Milan and Geneva, and has recently finished a novel set in Florence.*

Aren't They Supposed to Speak English in Ireland?!

Amy Martin-Bombeeck

As we come of age and begin to spread our wings in exploration of this wonderful world, our first inclination is one of excitement. The second is of fear, or at least some anxiety—this is how we know we are human. There are vast differences in every culture and an experience overseas, however long or short, especially to a country where English is not the mother tongue, can give even the most adventurous spirit a bad case of the shakes and dripping palms. Many travelers, when faced with their fears, prefer to head first to locations abroad where English is widely spoken and understood. This is my best guess why there are always masses of Americans and Canadians tripping around Britain and Ireland. But in this life, things are not always what they seem.

It is often said that there is a lush, jade isle to the west of Britain where fairies live, mystical mists blanket the land and surrounding sea, and the people speak English. Lovingly called Mother Eire by those born and bred there, Ireland is inhabited by a wondrous mix of people, all with an excellent sense of humor, quick wit and the gift of gab, whether they kissed that silly blarney stone or not. It is inbred. I had been told that English was the official language. Gaelic, the historical language of Ireland's forefathers, is still taught in schools and frequently spoken by the old-timers across the country, but it was my understanding that speaking to and comprehending the Irish would be no problem. I assumed that culture shock would not be in the cards. Until I actually arrived...

Once I had finished what felt like centuries languishing in university, I was mad for action. I wasn't really ready to settle into something so serious as a career or starting a family. The next choice, and by far the more interesting choice to me, was to throw a on backpack and go on a walkabout through Europe. The thought thrilled me to the marrow and scared the dickens out of me simultaneously! I had read about cultural exchange programs and one in particular seemed to me the perfect fit. I signed up for a HomeStay Program, which was to last for one month with a family in Ireland. I wasn't going to be studying or working. I had just finished doing that and needed a break. I was to be a simple observer, living and breathing in the Irish culture for myself!

After some exploration in Western Europe, I arrived by ferry into Ireland's Rosslare Harbour. Boarding a train north to Dublin, I began to get the first taste of what I was in for.

I had taken a seat across the table from a fine-looking young fellow in hopes of having a nice chat to pass the time.

"How're ye?" he asked. I smiled in reply and was just about to answer when a large, wooly mammoth of a man pushed himself onto the train and half lumbered, half swayed towards us. He looked at me cock-eyed, reeking of some chemical libation that could not have been less than 100 proof.

"Top 'o the mornin' to ye," he roared. I only smiled in response, wary of beginning a conversation that might last the entire journey, yet torn about how to be polite.

"He's pissed and taking the piss," my Irish companion explained, motioning the old fellow on down the car and away from me.

"Why would he be angry?" I asked, after the man was gone.

"Pissed drunk," he smiled. "Not pissed angry. And "taking the piss" means he is making fun of you." Oh. OK. I had to think about it awhile. So many meanings for one little word.

"It can also be pissing rain," my kind educator added, more than a little amused by my puzzlement. He watched me taking in all of this information with pride and then put out his hand for me to shake.

"You're welcome in Ireland! My name is Patrick. Patrick O'Malley," he said winking. "But my friends call me Paddy... and so can you."

I shook his hand, offered my own introduction and we were off. We began a conversation that should've lasted an hour but turned into more than two because I had to keep saying "Pardon me," and he had to keep translating himself. Learning to speak Irish was already proving to be more of a challenge than I had first anticipated. This was a mere beginning.

Embarrassing misunderstandings

The first evening of my stay in Ireland was quite a learning experience in itself. I had already gotten through that initial train journey to Dublin and found myself in Houston Station trying to find someone I could actually understand to explain to me what the booming announcement on the PA had just been.

I stood in this busy station feeling lost and lonely, and more than a little tired just having heard, "Waa waa wa-wa wa Galway wa waa," as audible to me in that moment as the teacher's voice in Charlie Brown cartoons. This was an announcement for the last train to Galway that evening and as my host family was expecting me on this day, I felt panicked to get there. I stopped a gentleman walking past me and asked him what the announcement had been. In a full Kerry accent (Kerry accents being particularly fast and difficult to follow), he explained it. I was fully aware that my eyes had widened and just as I was about to respond in my usual exasperated way, I heard a voice say my name from somewhere behind me.

"Amy?!" as if angels were calling me...did angels have Irish accents? How is it that I am standing thousands of miles across an ocean and someone here knows me? If it were possible, my eyes widened even more and I spun around on a dime, forgetting the kind Kerry gentleman completely and facing that voice.

"Yes?" I said to the fresh-faced lass bursting with energy before me.

"Its me!" she shouted, throwing herself into my arms, as if this was supposed to

11

mean something to me. "Anne! From Galway! Your host mother!"

She stood before me, her big, brown, animated, gypsy eyes practically popping out of her head; a wild, curly mane of dark brown hair and dressed in a dark green hippie dress, denim jacket and clunky Doc Marten combat boots. Everything about her exuded energy and happiness and Thank Heaven for it. My host mother. Mother being the operative word—I needed my mother right about then.

"I don't be-lieeeeve it!" she cried, jumping around excitedly. It *was* a rather interesting coincidence that we should randomly run into each other on the wrong side of the country in a station full of hundreds of busy commuters. We both agreed that it was some great sign from on high.

She steered me to the correct platform, correct train and into a comfy seat, all the while asking a bazillion questions that I was so happy to understand and answer for her. After a small train picnic and some getting-to-know-you chat, she popped a cassette tape of Mary Black, one of Ireland's most famous and talented singers, into my Walkman. I watched green field and dale, castle ruin and idyllic cottage roll by me. Maybe this will be OK after all, I thought, as I began to relax.

Once we arrived in Galway City and I had met the rest of my new surrogate family, they fed me and announced that since it was my first night in Ireland, we were going to do it up properly—none of this getting to bed early stuff! However, by this time, I was feeling better and even up to the task.

We found our way into one of Galway's many lively pubs and I was tasting my first glass of Guinness when a friend of Anne and Paul's sidled up to our table.

"How's the crack?" he bellowed at me.

"Excuse me?!" I asked incredulously. Did I look like I would know the answer to that kind of question?

"Crack!" he roared. "How's it?"

I looked at Anne and Paul, who were suspiciously grinning ear-to-ear awaiting my response.

I looked back at the gentleman and sheepishly said, "I'm sorry, I don't do that."

Everybody burst out laughing at my expense, knowing glances exchanged between them. Good, clean, Irish entertainment—"taking the piss" out of me!

Anne took pity on me and explained, "It's craic. C-R-A-I-C. Not crack, like the drug. Craic is the fun we are having. When someone asks, 'How's the craic?,' you would answer, 'Mighty!'"

More code. I needed a notebook for all of this information. But I smiled anyway, slightly stymied on the inside but laughing good-naturedly on the outside. It was clear to me on my first day in this marvelous country that I was going to have to relax, go with the flow and ask LOTS of questions. With that realization, I gave up trying to control my surroundings and drank my first Guinness with joy and verve. This very experience was, after all, why I came to Europe.

One thousand ways to talk about the weather

In Ireland you know you can always count on the weather to get a lively discussion going. There is a good reason why the land is storybook green and verdant. I had a running joke with friends of mine who visited there that Board Failte, Ireland's Tourist Board, had laid down mile after mile of astroturf across the country and shipped in daily truckloads of fluffy little snow-white sheep to complete this dreamy picture. That greenness just didn't seem real. Yet the rain—and the resulting anthology of daily rainbows—made it so. In Ireland, inclement weather is simply a fact of life, and no matter the severity, life just does not stop.

My first experience with this came one summer day when I got caught in town "brolly"-less (i.e., without an umbrella) in a thrashing downpour of rain. I had tucked into the recessed doorway of a pub and looked to the sky for any sign of stopping—there was none. I decided to pass the storm with one of my favorite pastimes: people-watching. Surprisingly the sidewalks remained busy, all types of folk moving to and fro, and I noticed for the first time that no one else seemed bothered about ducking in out of the weather. For People-In-The-Know, your daily wardrobe must include shoes that can get wet (the favorite being Welly's or Wellington boots), some kind of raincoat (I quickly purchased my own wax jacket) and the infamous brolly. Most months of the year, this is standard gear. Everyone but me was prepared and as the rain beat down, all went about their business without a care in the world. Being wet in Ireland is synonymous with that fairytale beauty, and it is tolerated if not welcomed.

Just as I was making this realization, staring at the street, the pub door behind me opened up and a bartender came into the doorway with me. He nodded brusquely and joined me in staring to the heavens.

"Great day for ducks," he said.

"Will ye come in for the cure?" he asked after another few moments of us gazing silently to the flooded sky.

"The cure?" I asked intrigued.

"The cure for the flu," he offered, even though I had not one single symptom. Perhaps my nose is red, I thought, rubbing it. "Great cure for any of life's other ailments as well," he added with a grin.

"Absolutely." I answered, following him back inside and sidling up to the old oak long bar which reeked of years of heady spilt ale and stale cigarette smoke. The man produced for me my very first, but far from last, hot whiskey (a strong concoction of one shot of whiskey, boiling water, a spoonful of sugar and a lemon slice with cloves poked into it—a proven elixir for the common cold!). I wiled away the deluge on that very spot, nursing the cure and chatting. I had soon chosen my local watering hole and favorite barman, Johnnie Ray.

In Ireland, it is mostly wet year-round. The exceptions are perhaps the months of May and June. Yet the wet can occur at any time of the year and any time of the day. Generally this precipitation makes its appearance as a fine mist or on more gusty days, a heavier vapor blowing in sideways. Known as "a soft Irish day," it is the norm, thus the aforementioned need to have rain gear handy at all times.

During the approach of spring and summer, when the weather is less predictable and can offer everything from hail to sun to hard rain and gusting winds followed by spectacular rainbows, all within half an hour, the winds tend to blow harder and colder air in from the seas. Such days are described as being "fresh" or "crisp." It is these strong, cool winds combined with sunnier conditions that draw such comments as, "Great day for drying!"

The first time I heard this phrase, I sat on a mossy stone wall out in the country waiting for friends to collect me and enjoying the fine weather. A gentleman rode past me on his bike and called out in greeting, "Great day for drying!"

I had no idea what the drying part meant then, so I simply reacted to the "great day" part.

"'Tis," I called after him, proud as Mary that I knew the proper Irish response by then. I was fast learning the local speak!

Later, of course, I asked my friends what the man had meant. It's a great day for drying clothes out on a clothesline was their explanation. Another purely Irish literary perfection expressed about the simplicity of the weather.

Fairytale endings

The Irish have their own way of speaking, their own slang, and their own language within a language. English speakers are sometimes more comfortable knowing that they are visiting English-speaking parts of the world, but the funny thing about counting on feeling a level of security through language, as I learned the hard (but fun) way, is that you can't count on anything anywhere.

My stay in Ireland, although I struggled to integrate in the beginning, turned into half a decade of a very happy life experience. In travel, as in life, having confidence and a gung-ho attitude to be up for anything, and always remembering that every obstacle you come against will teach you something and help you to grow as you roll over it, is vital. We are all tribes in different nations and within nations. Flexibility, adaptability and patience are the keys to comfort anywhere in the world. That—and a mighty good sense of humor!

Amy Martin-Bombeeck is a member of the American Women's Club of Luxembourg and the Federation of American Women's Clubs Overseas (FAWCO), and has been residing in Luxembourg and Ireland for more than seven years. She is from Kentucky originally, but calls Florida home when she is in the United States. Amy has been writing for 23 years and features a monthly travel column in the AWCL's publication, "The Grapevine." She is also co-editor of the 15th edition of "Living In Luxembourg" and is currently hard at work on a novel of fiction, among other journalistic endeavors.

With a Volcano in the Backyard

Margo Renner

It was on the morning of January 23, 1973 that my mother awoke me in my childhood home in Wauwatosa, Wisconsin to tell me that there was a volcanic eruption on the small island of Krakatau off the coast of Iceland.

As a child I had been extremely fond of volcanoes and dinosaurs, long before Jurassic Park and the popularity that they have acquired in more recent years. In the 7th grade I read Jules Verne's *Mysterious Island* and fell in love with the idea of living on a volcanic island. As a high school teenager applying for placement as an exchange student I neatly penned in "near the ocean or mountains" where the form asked to what kind of place I hoped I would be sent. When, as a summer exchange student through the AFS program, I arrived to the tiny four by six-mile island off the coast of Iceland and saw a perfectly shaped volcanic cone in the center of the island and the busy little fishing village in its shadow, I immediately fell in love with the whole place. The trouble was, Jules Verne's *Mysterious Island* was in the South Pacific. This island was in the North Atlantic. I should have paid closer attention in geography class somewhere during those earlier school years.

But as my mother awoke me with the news she had heard, I knew at least enough about volcanoes to know that Krakatau was actually in the Indian Ocean and that if there was an eruption on an island near Iceland, some news reporter had gotten place names confused. I really did not know at that moment whether I should be worried or not. Two years earlier, I had spent a wonderful summer on Heimaey in the Vestmannaeyjar archipelago just 20 miles off the southwest coast of Iceland. The weather in those months was the best that Iceland had had for 50 years. I had come back to Wauwatosa to finish high school and had gone back the following summer, breaking AFS rules about not returning for two years. I worked the summer in a fish factory as all the young people of the town did during those years. Of course there is often a romance behind such a story, and I have to admit that I had met my husband-to-be in the early weeks of the first of these summers. During the second summer on Heimaey we got married. I was only 19 and he was 23. A few months later I returned to Wisconsin for Christmas and was planning on returning to Heimaey in February to move into a tiny apartment with my husband. A month after my arrival in Wauwatosa I felt nauseous and worn out, and I thought I had caught a stomach flu. When it did not clear up within a couple of weeks, I suspected I was pregnant and went to the gynecologist to have it confirmed. Young marriages and young mothers were the norm at that time in Iceland, so my husband and I were looking forward to the baby. I had booked a flight back to Iceland for the first week of February. This was the morning of January 23.

Needless to say, when we finally confirmed that the eruption was indeed on Heimaey, my Irish Catholic mother felt that she was somehow personally blessed at having me at home and not on that tiny erupting rock in the middle of the North Atlantic.

On the other hand, my husband and his family, my AFS family, and all the other friends and islanders whom I had come to know were there on that rock, and I was in Wisconsin, with no internet, no live news and no way of actually knowing what was really happening. Nothing was said of human lives lost, but stories of the island splitting in two and sinking, townspeople being evacuated, and the town being covered in volcanic ash spurted up in sporadic news reports. On the second day I received a telegram from my husband telling me that everyone had been evacuated safely and that volunteer emergency teams were on the island emptying homes that were in immediate danger of lava flows. Emergency workers were also toiling day and night covering windows with corrugated metal to prevent lava bombs, hot balls of glowing lava forced at high velocity from the volcanic fissure, from crashing through the glass panes and igniting the houses.

My husband was one of those volunteers and had been working around the clock in a desperate situation. He was emotionally and physically exhausted. He eventually agreed to come to the States, but feeling that he was deserting the front line of the battle, he cut short his visit. We returned together to Iceland, thus starting the first chapter in my life as an American citizen abroad.

When we arrived in Iceland on May 5, 1973, the new volcano, which had arisen alongside the old one that I had admired so much, was still spewing lava and ash. Four hundred of the twelve hundred buildings and homes on the island had been covered by volcanic materials. Night and day, bulldozers pushed and shoveled tons of volcanic ash, a light cinder-like pumice, to be carted away by trucks to the other side of the island. Pipelines were connected to large pumps borrowed from the American naval base at Keflavik and were placed in front of the advancing lava flows to pump seawater onto the glowing rock to hinder its advance towards the life source of the town, the valuable harbor.

My husband rejoined the battle against nature at her most ferocious. I was now six months pregnant so I stayed on the mainland with my mother-in-law and brother-in-law, who had both gotten jobs there shortly after the eruption. It was a difficult beginning for me. I was pregnant and knew next to nothing about pregnancy, babies or the hormonal ups and downs that accompany pregnancy. During the first month my mother-in-law and brother-in-law were out working. My days were long and lonely. There was no one to talk to and little to keep me busy. There were just two television channels, which broadcast only several hours during the day with the majority of the programs in Icelandic. I voraciously read everything I could get my hands on. When my mother-in-law and brother-in-law came home they spoke very little English and I spoke even less Icelandic. I did the dishes, straightened and cleaned, but knew nothing about cooking and even less about Icelandic food. Though it would have been nice to be able to use time to at least prepare meals, I was not capable.

My husband worked a program that consisted of 11 days on the island with 4 days off to come to the mainland and then he went back to the island. We had both agreed that the island was where he was most needed, that one day we wanted to make our home there, and that we would do our share to make that dream come true as soon as possible for ourselves and others. Meanwhile, I talked to him every few days on the phone. After about two months I had had as much isolation as I could take and though I am not the crying type, I broke into a hysterical sobbing fit during his next phone call. Though I was now seven and a half months pregnant, it was reluctantly agreed that the island was "safe" enough to visit. My mother would have died if she had known, and I could see that my mother-in-law was not very relaxed about the idea either but at this point nothing could stop me. I was finally "allowed" to go.

It was shocking to see the island covered in black ash, the cone of the "new volcano" spewing forth black smoke, the field of lava steaming at its foot, buildings crushed by its force. I was allowed to stay for one week until my husband was ready to return to the mainland with me on his 4 days off. It was only a few weeks until the baby was due and the time passed more quickly. We had moved to a new apartment in Reykjavik and my mother-in-law had quit her job to stay home with me and the new baby. Our first baby, a girl, was born in the beginning of August. I figured I had read so much on childbirth, babies, and childcare (remember all that reading time I had?) that I couldn't possibly be the least informed new mother and would be able to manage. My mother-in-law was a tremendous help and though we lacked a common spoken language, there was another language where communication needed no words.

It was far from easy though. At some point I came across a self-stress test in one of the women's magazines that someone had sent me. There were about 50 different situations that caused various levels of stress and the reader was to mark off and add up the numbers to determine if her life was indeed stressful. I remember that having a baby had a very high scale. There were also items such as moving, abrupt change of diet, losing a friend or family member (I had just simply left them all behind), marriage, new job, etc. No one mentioned new country, lack of language skills, or volcanic eruption in backyard! I scored off the charts despite the lack of these very pertinent items.

Even though my mother-in-law was the greatest of help and I am sure she would have preferred that I stay with her longer in Reykjavik, I was newly married, had seen very little of my husband since our return to Iceland and desperately wanted to be with him. I also agreed with him that as long as we were in Iceland, the island was the place we wanted to be, despite the natural disaster that had so drastically changed our plans, at least temporarily. In October 1973 we were one of the first families to move back to the island. I have been here now on Heimaey for 31 years.

Thirty-one years seems a long time. The island was cleaned of ash and rebuilt; the fishing industry came to life again. We bought our first home four months after our return to the island; we had another baby, a boy, five years later and we have built a life here together on this tiny volcanic island where my husband was born, raised and helped fight a volcano. We still visit the States and went quite often when the children were small.

Living in such a small place has both disadvantages and advantages. For one thing, it is easier to find a niche in such a small place. Just weeks before we returned to Iceland during that spring when the volcano was still erupting, my husband and I were at an art and handcraft exhibition where I saw someone doing flame working, making little glass figures in a torch flame. The next time I returned to the States, two years later, I signed up for a glassblowing course at a university in northern Wisconsin and also found someone in the Milwaukee area to give me private lessons. I became and still am the only glass artist in Iceland that does flame working. I've held exhibitions and participated in handcraft fairs all over the country. At a time when there still were no handcraft fairs in Iceland, I organized my own, finding artists who worked with various art forms. I also organized one of the very first and the oldest remaining handcraft gallery that is still successfully in business today in Vestmannaeyjar.

My policy was that if there was something I really missed or felt was needed, I would initiate it. "If it's not there, make it happen," has been a sort of motto for me. I haven't been able to grow a forest in my backyard, but it's not for lack of trying. Being a foreigner can be an advantage. I am different, not an islander, which means that I am not expected to be exactly like everyone else. I have the wonderful advantage of having the "excuse" to be different and I have kept my American identity because of that. With friends and colleagues who are interested, I have enjoyed sharing my background, my American holidays and my often different way of doing things. Besides, it would never have been possible to totally blend in even if I had wanted to. If nothing else, the language would have given me away. Talking about obstacles, Icelandic is a linguist's nightmare or dream come true depending on the approach. Unfortunately, it has sometimes been a bit more nightmarish for me.

Part of that nightmare involved the struggle to obtain more education after moving here. When I first came to Iceland I had only a high school degree, and I had always planned on further education. In order to enter the University of Iceland I needed what is called a "Student's Degree." It is more or less the equivalent of a two-year liberal arts college in the States, and requires three years of schooling after their compulsory high school. So when the opportunity arose to take that degree on the island, I spent three years finishing a Student's Degree in the department of natural sciences and with a few extra courses finished a lesser business degree in order to add to my job options. It was a long haul which included a lot of language help from my husband, but I accumulated vocabulary that I never would have otherwise. I could now talk about geology, biology, business law, and economics. Grammar remains a thorn in my side, but I can at least usually find the words I need.

The business degree paid off and I landed a job at a union office where I worked part-time for 15 years. During those 15 years I also did a lot of glass art work, ran the gallery and obtained more education, including a BA in English literature and

18

then a teaching degree for secondary school. When I moved into my present job as a career and educational counselor at the employment office on the island, a degree program in counseling was being offered to 16 applicants from all over the country in a first time offer as a long distance course through the University of Iceland. I applied and was accepted. Today I work as a counselor at the employment office and at the college, and am working on a Master's in career and educational counseling.

Sometimes I look at where I am now and hypothesize about what I would be doing if I hadn't moved to Iceland. I rationalize that if I hadn't left Wisconsin at all, I would regret that. I also rationalize that if it hadn't been Iceland, it could well have been somewhere else that couldn't afford free education and health care, somewhere where I would have had to worry about my children and flying bullets. Iceland has become my home and I do love it here. I miss friends and family but have acquired both here. I miss trees and forested landscapes but have come to love the ocean and panoramic views of rugged, volcanic landscapes. I miss thunderstorms, but in an ironic way have learned how to "cozy up" with candlelight and a glass of wine while the wind howls outside and hail batters at the windows. I find it a wonderful advantage not having to own a car, though most of the islanders do. Coming from a city the size of Milwaukee gives perspective with regard to car ownership on an island where everything one needs is within 10 minutes walking distance. Looking out my window from my school office in the morning I look east at the two volcanic cones that now stand side by side. They glow pink in the sunrise. During the afternoon I am at the employment office and look out over the harbor and the high rocky bluffs that tower over the entrance. They glow orange in the sunset.

The reason I left Wisconsin is not because I was unhappy there; therefore I believe there will always be things that I miss about it. On the other hand, it's not where you live, it's how you live that makes the difference. It's looking at life and taking advantage of what it offers you. It's taking disadvantage and turning it around and making it work for you. It's being first on the island to make pizza, it's celebrating Halloween with neighborhood children whose parents have to have trick-or-treat explained to them, or organizing new recreational activities for the local children based on ideas from "back home." Living as an American abroad can be a good experience or a lousy experience. In the end it depends on what you make it.

Margo Renner was born in 1953 in Wauwatosa, Wisconsin. After an AFS exchange student program, she moved 32 years ago to Iceland and made her home on the tiny island of Heimaey off the southwest coast. She is married with two grown children, a son and a daughter. She has a degree in English literature, a post-graduate degree in teaching and is currently working on her Master's Degree in career and educational counseling. She works as a counselor both at the college and within the employment sector on the island. She has also held many exhibitions of her glass artwork and runs a small cooperative art and handcraft gallery on the island.

On Foreign Soil

Lynne-Therese Gilardi

Moving to a foreign country is a lot like having a baby: it's a leap of faith, a willing embrace of the unknown, the chance to forge a new identity. Like pregnancy and parenthood, an overseas move includes lots of waiting, uncertainty, and surprises. It requires adaptability, and carries with it the possibility of heartbreak. Relocation to another land, like motherhood, forces one to explore foreign territory, and forever alters one's interior terrain.

Seven months after moving from Texas to New England, my husband was offered a transfer to Paris, France. Eleven days later we landed at Orly Airport with our infant daughter and six-year-old son, ready to begin our new lives. I discovered immediately, when our oversized American car seat, stroller, and portable crib were too large to fit into a French taxi, that an overseas move is like childbirth: no matter how prepared you think you are, reading is no substitute for reality.

Although I had minored in French in college, I hadn't used the language in years. I had never spent more than six weeks in a big city. I was excited but overwhelmed, troubled by the absence of familiar foods for my children and mystified by the lack of plastic baby bathtubs (I did find one eventually). My children were equally disoriented. My previously happy kindergartener developed a tick, and my infant refused to relax enough to lay down in her crib, preferring to sleep on her knees, her little hand wrapped around the bed rail, for the first month we lived in Paris. I tried to help my children adapt to their new surroundings, but my assistance was definitely of limited value as I struggled with the same emotions I had felt each time I gave birth: a constant sense of fatigue, a fear I would never adjust to my new life, periods of elation followed by great anxiety.

One day soon after my first child was born I found myself panic-stricken about my overwhelming responsibility, sad that I was totally alone. Although I knew that other new mothers had female relatives who were more than happy to provide emergency baby-sitting and camaraderie, I had no such support. My friends all worked during the day. I lived in a depressed city with lousy weather and the largest percentage of senior citizens in the United States; my prospects for socializing with other new mothers were virtually nonexistent. My husband had just started a new job, and had to work many long hours, even parts of Christmas Eve and New Year's Eve. It was an emotionally and physically draining time for me, but I was handsomely rewarded with a jolly fat baby who kept me laughing. Years later, when it came time to move to another city where I would be, at least initially, all alone, I realized that those early days of motherhood had served a purpose. They had made me strong and independent, a comforting piece of knowledge for anyone contemplating a move to an alien country.

Discussing the realities of life overseas is a bit like sharing one's parenting adventures with the childless. Those without sons or daughters can never understand the complete changes in lifestyle and mindset that accompany the arrival of a child, just as I could not fully comprehend life abroad before I moved to France. Young people often think that a babysitting stint prepares them for parenthood, the way some vacationers think that an extended holiday provides one with an understanding of life in another locale. But those of us who have been there know better. And yet, the uninitiated persist in clinging to their fantasies, which, in all fairness, have not been exposed to the harsh light of reality. One's comments about the sleeplessness and lack of privacy that are part of every parent's memory bank are met with blank, sometimes disdainful stares, perhaps even a bit of envy. Descriptive remarks about the new life of the parent are sometimes misconstrued as complaints. The listener sees only the adorable munchkin in Oshkosh overalls, surrounded by colorful toys. The same is true of an overseas move—tell people you are living in Paris, and they do not believe that your life is anything but champagne cocktail parties and walks along the Seine.

The truth is that everyday tasks are difficult in a foreign country, just as they are for a new mother. Suddenly common chores become a major production—every parent knows that the fifteen minute dash to the market for a carton of milk now takes more than an hour because the baby must be bundled, loaded into a cart with an infant seat, soothed in the checkout line. The same is true for the newly transplanted foreigner. I devoted hours to navigating through narrow European store aisles, hunting down Cheerios and the few recognizable foods I could find for my baby. I spent the better part of two years hunched over from the strain of carrying my daughter, her stroller, and our purchases up and down flights of stairs because many French food shops are not at street level and do not have elevators. Despite a lifetime of dreaming of myself sashaying around a big city in sophisticated outfits, I wore the same tatty black boots and ill-fitting plaid denim dress almost every day of my first month in France, simply because I was too exhausted to wear something different. It reminded me of my early days as a mother. Breastfeeding my son had been very rewarding but hard; when he was about four months old, shortly before he switched to solid foods, his nursing sessions left me so physically depleted that there were many days when I just redressed him in a new pair of pajamas to save myself a bit of work.

Of course I eventually recovered my balance as a mother, just as I found my footing in France. The skills I had acquired in half a dozen years of motherhood served me well overseas: learning to communicate without words, which my children had taught me, was invaluable, especially when I ventured into Eastern Europe. Being the primary caretaker of small children had forced me to acquire patience, an absolute necessity for life in one of the most bureaucratic countries in the world. And the unpredictability of my days as a mother—let's just say they were great training for life in a nation prone to unannounced strikes and spontaneous political rallies.

I loved my life in France. Like my years of motherhood, my time as an expatriate

21

opened my heart and my mind. Although I am not an overly religious woman, I know grace when I see it. My sojourn abroad and my children were gifts, not something I was entitled to. One day, however, my free ride screeched to a halt—my husband's business venture collapsed, and we were given one-way tickets back to the United States. Of course this news was nowhere near as devastating as some of the problems we had experienced before and during our marriage, but it was heartbreaking nonetheless. I had, for the first time in my life, felt like I was creating the life I wanted, and now it was gone. I fretted about the transient nature of life, worried that I would lose my children the way I had lost my new life.

After five years in the United States, I admitted to myself and to my husband that my life had to change. Although I had enjoyed my time in a small town in southern New England, I yearned for the big city life we had left behind, for the tastes and sounds of a culture I had grown to love as much as my own. I had an overwhelming longing to return to Paris, a craving so strong that I could no longer pretend, as I had for almost half of a decade, that it did not exist. It was similar to the sensation I had had when my son was five years old and we decided to try to have another baby. I wanted to repeat a pleasurable chapter in my life, but I was secretly afraid that I might not get my wish. I became consumed with the idea of returning to France, a fantasy that my husband, son, and I had all carried in our hearts since the day we left Paris. (Although our daughter lived with us throughout the duration of our stay in France, she was less than four years old when we left, and therefore lacked our insatiable desire to return. She did, however, bear her own reminders of our foreign odyssey. Her initial attempts to learn the alphabet resembled the sounds a French schoolchild would make, and her word order sometimes reflected the inverted subject-object-verb form of the French.)

After six months of negotiations, my husband secured what could charitably be described as a lateral transfer back to Europe. The catch was that he would have to divide his workweek between France and Ireland, and forfeit a significant amount of income because of the much higher cost of living. But I didn't care—I had happily sacrificed career and earning potential in the past in exchange for the chance to spend time with my children. A smaller living space and public transportation seemed to me a tiny price to pay for the chance to relive my dream.

Returning to France has been like having a second child—the setting is familiar but the experiences are new. Before my daughter was born, I worried about whether I could possibly love another baby as much as I had loved my son. In the months leading up to our move, I wondered if expatriate living could possibly have been as fabulous as I remembered. I have found my life in Paris to be even more than I had hoped for, just as the birth of my second child brought me as much joy as the arrival of my first baby. Hope is what led me to marry, start a family, move overseas, and finally pursue my vocation. Everyone who has ever wanted a child has known hope. Those of us willing to take this leap into the uncharted land of parenthood are the same as those of us living on foreign soil; we are making our own paths, exploring and conquering new territory every day.

Some people wonder what kind of person would willingly leave her country. Pessimistic types say that those who abandon their own people are, implicitly, passing judgment on the society which they have left. I don't see my move abroad that way. Leaving the United States has been the same as quitting my parents' home. I do not deny that both my countrymen and my childhood family have some serious problems, that there are aspects of my national and familial cultures that I do not wish to adopt. But I am and always will be an American, the way I am and always will be my parents' daughter. I do not need to look at my passport to remind me of who I am—my identity is firmly fixed, just as I will always be a mother and a Francophile, no matter where I live.

My lives as a mother and an expatriate are complementary. My days as a mother have been influenced by my years in France. I have cobbled together what I believe are the best American and European child-rearing practices, just like I have blended together customs from France and the United States to create new family traditions. My experiences in Paris have been different because I am a mother. I have visited parks, shops, restaurants, and museums I would never have noticed had I not been in the company of little people, and I have ridden some of the oldest carousels in the world. My children have given me an entry into conversation in a country where silent formality is the norm, and provided me with a common bond with all of the other mothers I encounter every day, even if we do not all speak the same language. Although I do not know the shape my life would have taken if I had not had children or moved abroad, I am certain that I have been enriched by these experiences, for I have had the privilege of exploring and inhabiting worlds other than my own.

Lynne-Therese Gilardi is an American citizen and a graduate of Allegheny College and the University of Richmond, Virginia, T.C. Williams School of Law. She lives in Paris, France, with her husband and two children. She has also lived in La Rochelle, France, and Dalkey, Ireland. Her essays and short fiction have appeared in several publications.

The Art of Being Wrong

Jan Harrington

It was a warm day in full July during my second week in Switzerland. The hibiscus tree stretched fragile purple blossoms across the open window. Dutifully I had remained indoors all afternoon unpacking boxes of dishes.

A white toy poodle dashed into the kitchen. She slid to a stop and looked up at me with small black eyes, a pink bow set squarely between her ears.

"*Salut,*" I said, recognizing her as the dog I'd seen tucked under my next-door neighbor's arm as she made her way from her car to her house.

Our new house had no screens on the windows and doors, and no air conditioning. Having just moved from Washington D.C., where much of the year was passed imprisoned within air conditioned spaces, I felt liberated. Each morning I threw open doors and windows and reveled in fresh air. The poodle had probably wriggled under the fence and entered our house through an open door.

During my short time in Geneva I had observed that dogs were not allowed to run free. They waited silently outside the supermarket, slept under the table in restaurants, and traveled docilely in baskets and shopping carts. I assumed that my neighbor would be worried about her poodle's whereabouts.

I scooped up the poodle and carried her to the patio and garden beyond. I stepped over to the low fence and neat row of dahlias dividing our backyard from our neighbor's.

"*Bonjour,*" I called just at the moment I saw my neighbor, a blond woman in her sixties, stretched out on a chaise lounge, sunbathing, topless. We stared at each other. I turned away and held up her dog in explanation. Only the poodle was nonplussed.

"Bring Juliette to the front door, *s'il vous plait,* and ring the bell."

That is how I learned that in Switzerland you never poke your head over a neighbor's fence, not to offer them a bag of homegrown tomatoes, not to invite them over for a drink, not even if you've noticed their roof is in flames. The Swiss live privately behind meticulously groomed hedges. Within a few weeks, I learned other valuable lessons for living peacefully with our new neighbors.

One humid afternoon I was mowing the lawn in front of our house. I turned a corner and found a short, middle-aged man standing in front of me.

"Madame, you are cutting your grass."

"*Oui,*" I replied, shoving the gear in neutral so that I could hear him. I assumed that his statement of the obvious was meant to be a conversation starter.

He stretched out his arm, revealing a big-faced gold watch on his wrist. "It is half past noon."

"*Oui,*" I repeated.

He turned abruptly and walked back to the house cattycorner to ours, pulling the door closed behind him. Pondering the possible meaning of this existentialist exchange, I finished mowing the lawn.

The next day I found in our mailbox a copy of the front section of our commune's telephone book, with Regulation 154 circled in red. One was permitted to mow lawns only between the hours of 10 a.m. and noon and 2 p.m. and 8 p.m.

"There are more regulations than names and numbers in this phone book," my husband John noted. There were rules for everything from how high your hedge could be to what dates you could leave your Christmas tree at the curb to when your awnings could be lowered, and if you live in an apartment building, which day you were permitted to use the laundry room and the curfew for flushing toilets.

How would we ever master so many rules? Fortunately most Swiss people are happy to assist.

One mild morning I was walking to the post office. (One of the things I most appreciate about living in Switzerland is the ability to do errands on foot. During time spent back home in the United States, I notice that my plans to walk to the video store or drugstore are met with suspicion. "Walk?" my parents will say. "Don't be silly. Take the car.") A Peugeot sedan slowed and pulled over to the curb beside me. A white-haired man leaned out the window, staring at me over the rim of his glasses. *"Etes-vous un vélo?"* he asked. Are you a bicycle?

He pointed significantly at the sidewalk which was divided by a dotted yellow line. I looked down and saw that I was standing in the bike path, not in the pedestrian zone. As he drove away, I marveled that he had cared enough to pull over and correct me.

A few days later, during a Saturday trip to the supermarket, John headed toward the check-out lane reserved for eight items or less. I made a quick count of the items in our basket. "We have nine. I'll take three and pay separately."

"No one is behind us." He gave me a look that said "relax" as he emptied our basket onto the conveyor belt.

The man ahead of us had packed his purchases into a large wicker basket and was waiting for his change. He gave our items an appraising glance. *"Pardon, Monsieur,"* his hand swept over our purchases, "you have nine items."

"Merci, Monsieur," John replied in his excellent French. "You are quite right. However, as you can see, no one is in line behind us."

"Is this not the express line?" The man asked the young cashier with the exaggerated eye makeup.

"Bien sûr, Monsieur," she said, and to John, "you must put your things back in your basket and go to another line."

"I'll pay for two items," I reached for a stick of butter and a box of cereal.

John stopped me. "Monsieur, Mademoiselle, as you can see, I have two identical jars of tomato sauce. Surely that counts as just one item, thus reducing my total to eight."

"Mais non," the man exclaimed.

25

"You're ahead of us!" John exploded. "Why do you care? What difference does it make to you?"

You have to admire a country where citizens take their responsibilities so seriously. John and I are not lawless people, yet during our early years in Geneva, and sometimes even now, we kept finding ourselves on the wrong side of a rule, often one that we hadn't known existed. Like most Americans, we had been shaped by the frontier spirit and rugged individualism that still lingers in our national psyche. It required an effort to adapt to a country that valued rules, conformity and the belief that there was one right way to do almost anything. We mostly admired the end result of this zeal and dogmatism: a peaceful, well-ordered, scenic nation with red geraniums in every window box and trains that ran right on schedule.

It is not just the respect for rules that helps Switzerland work well as a nation. It is also the existence of systems. The task for the uninitiated is to remember that there is always a system (a corollary of one right way to do things) and to discover what it is.

On a gray day in February, I drove to Yverdon les Bains with Kate, an Australian friend, to experience the mineral baths we had heard so much about. We wondered if the natural baths were one reason that so many Swiss people seemed to glow with good health. When we paid the entrance fee, we were given two keys. Eventually we figured out the changing room system (you entered a dressing stall by one door, changed into your bathing suit, left your things there, locked the first door and exited through a second door) and found ourselves at the side of a pool with pale clouds of steam rising from the water. Jets of water at different heights were positioned along the sides of the pool.

We splashed into the water, crisscrossing the pool to try out the different jets.

"Oh, try this one. It feels wonderful against your shoulders," Kate called to me.

I joined her just as a buzzer sounded. "What do you suppose that means?" I pushed a strand of wet hair from my eyes.

"Aucune idée," she replied, lowering herself a few inches into the water to position the jet at the nape of her neck.

A man materialized from the mist and said something to us in French.

"I think he wants that jet," I said.

"Well, he can't have it. What, do men come first? He'll have to wait his turn."

"It is my turn, Madame," he said in English. He explained that one was supposed to enter the pool at the far right and move in a clockwise direction from jet to jet. When the buzzer sounded, one moved to the next jet. For the first time we noticed that indeed this was what was happening around us, as the dozen or so men and women in the pool moved silently from jet to jet.

Some systems are more complex than others. My Swiss friend Veronique and I once took the train from Geneva to Lausanne. We reached the platform just as the train roared in. She took my arm. "Just get on. We can buy our tickets on the train."

"I didn't know that." I settled myself beside the window.

She sat across from me. "Not on every train."

"Of course not." I had lived in Switzerland long enough to know that it couldn't be that simple.

She explained that passengers have the right to buy a ticket on board inter-regional trains because inter-regional trains always have a conductor. In contrast, regional trains may or may not have a conductor on board. This is determined by the hour of the day, the number of stops and other factors. As she continued her discourse, I watched the Alps on the other side of Lake Geneva slide past my window and stared at the blue water that seemed to lap at the edges of the track. I decided that Swiss people must be blessed with an intuitive grasp of rules and systems, just as they were blessed with magnificent landscapes.

If you have to ask what the rule is, then you are an outsider. It is worse if you don't even know that a rule is in play. A friend told me that on her first day in her apartment in a graceful stone building in the heart of Geneva, the washing machine and dishwasher stopped inexplicably in mid-cycle. She called a repairman. The concierge escorted him to her apartment later that afternoon, and upon learning what the problem was, informed my friend that the power to major appliances was cut off every weekday afternoon from one to three to save energy. "Why didn't you tell me?" my friend demanded, chagrined at having to pay for a wasted service call. "You didn't ask," the concierge replied.

Over time my husband and I learned that you must know what questions to ask and ask them precisely. John went to the hospital for routine elective surgery recommended by his ophthalmologist, a tall Swiss-German man whom we experienced as a benevolent dictator.

Following the surgery, Dr. Steiner informed John that he could not read, travel or go to the office for eight days. "You must go home and act like a *légume* (a vegetable)."

"I can't be a *légume* for eight days," John sputtered, "I can't miss an entire week of work." He hadn't taken a sick day in years.

Dr. Steiner loomed in his white coat over John's hospital bed. "You must."

"You told me there was nothing to the recovery. That it was easy! You didn't say I couldn't read or go to work."

"You didn't ask," said Dr. Steiner.

The Swiss have trouble with rhetorical questions, and with Americans' need for choices and options. Soon after my arrival in Geneva, I went to the train station to explore schedules and fares to locations I planned to visit. When it was my turn, I stepped up the counter and asked the young woman for the hours of trains to Zermatt.

"Are you going today?" she asked.

"No," I replied. "Not today."

"What day will you be traveling to Zermatt?"

"I don't know. I'm just interested in finding out how I would go, and what it would cost, if I should decide to go. While I'm here, could you also give me the information about Lucerne?"

She wrinkled her forehead. "Are you going to Lucerne?"

"It's possible, yes, I understand it's lovely. Are there days of the week or times of the day when the fare is lower?" As an American, I thrived on choices.

"But Madame, I don't understand. Are you going to Zermatt or Lucerne? And when are you going?"

Looking back, I can sympathize with her frustration. After all, there were people waiting behind me who knew where they wanted to go and when. I was wasting time and reducing efficiency. Today I find it reassuring when I am greeted at the post office by a digital sign that tells me, on average, how long each person had waited in line the day before. I appreciate the signs that tell me how many spaces are presently free in the city's various parking decks, or how many seats are left in the cinema.

Stepping into a supermarket in the United States today, I am overwhelmed by choices. Do we need 234 breakfast cereals or 15 kinds of orange juice—with pulp, without pulp, fortified with calcium, fortified with calcium and magnesium, acid-reduced, acid left as is. Passing through Chicago's O'Hare airport recently en route to my parents' house, I stopped at a Starbuck's in the terminal. I studied the menu: sizes, flavors, whole milk, fat-free milk, soy milk, foam, no foam, dark roasted, regular roasted. I turned myself over to the young woman waiting to call out my order. "I just want a cup of coffee."

Of all Swiss institutions, banks remain both the most mysterious and intransigent. If the Swiss in general are seldom wrong, banks, and the people who work for them, are never wrong. One day I spent fifteen minutes persuading a teller that I had done nothing wrong to result in my bank card not functioning in the automatic teller machine. No, I hadn't pushed the card into the automatic teller machine before requested to do so, nor had I pushed it in too hard, nor had I entered the wrong code. In fact, the bank card itself was at fault.

Following this incident I developed a pragmatic approach. I opened with, "I'm sure I've made a mistake. Will you please help me sort it out?" The response was inevitably warm and cheerful. The teller or salesperson or whomever would proceed directly to analyzing the problem and be determined to solve it.

As my French has improved and my confidence mounted, I have become feistier. At Christmas my sister mailed a box of presents including gift certificates redeemable at a clothing store in Chicago. She had declared a value of $500 on the customs slip. The Swiss *douane* subsequently sent me a bill for 85 francs duty tax. I decided to take issue, reasoning that if nothing else it was an occasion to practice writing a letter in French. I requested that the tax be reconsidered because the gift certificates could only be spent in the United States and therefore the merchandise was not really entering Switzerland.

A week later I received a letter saying that I must pay the tax immediately, however, I could then request a review and a reclamation of the amount. I request- ed a reclamation, restating my case. The customs office responded by informing me that they had acted correctly in levying the tax, in accordance with Regulations 334

B and 632 C. However, they agreed that I had a point and so had decided to refund the 85 francs I had paid, minus 30 francs as an administrative fee.

It was a partial victory. Yet who knows? I may be learning the system.

Jan Harrington first moved to Geneva, Switzerland as an adolescent and resided there with her family for several years before returning to the United States. In 1997 a twist of fate brought her back to live in Switzerland with her husband and her own adolescent daughter. She presently works as news editor for the International Nursing Review. Her poems, short stories and nonfiction have appeared in literary journals and other publications in Switzerland and the United States.

It Has Been a Real Trip

Celeste Snyder

I am an American who has been living in Kuwait for some twenty-one years. I didn't leave America, the country that millions around the world are literally dying to get into, for a job. I moved to Kuwait to be with my husband Abdullah.

We met shortly after he started school at our local community college in Barron County, Wisconsin. I was taking some music classes there during my senior year in high school back in 1979. Later, I followed him to the University of Wisconsin, Milwaukee. We were together the whole time he was in school, but the closer he came to graduating, the more we began to realize that we had to make a decision as to what direction our relationship would take. I knew he had originally thought he would go home and marry a Kuwaiti girl, and we never planned to get as serious as we did. All I knew was that I couldn't imagine life without him.

He tried explaining to me how difficult it would be for me to live in his country, and since he was so close to his family I knew that he would never consider staying and living and working in the States. No one can ever really imagine what a foreign country is like before actually seeing it, but I was especially ignorant. Even though I grew up only three hours from the Canadian border, I hadn't even been there. Sure, I had traveled to most areas within the United States, but I had never stepped a foot outside my own country. I simply had no idea of what to expect.

When we started talking about marriage, I told him that I didn't care where I lived, even if it were a tent. I just wanted to be with him. My father warned me that I'd be called a heathen and I'd have to walk three steps behind my husband. I found the idea laughable; I simply refused to worry about the inevitable problems that lay ahead of us. My mother came up to Milwaukee for our wedding and helped me shop for clothes to wear for the trip. We picked out a modest suit, I packed what I thought were my basic necessities in the two suitcases allotted me for the flight, and off I went to Kuwait and a new life in June 1983.

My first reality check hit before I even passed customs. As we walked down the plane steps and across the tarmac that early June evening, I felt a rush of hot air that I thought was coming from the jet engines. However, the heat didn't decrease the farther we got from the plane, and I soon realized that it was the hot desert wind I felt burning my face. Soon we entered the air conditioned building to meet some of the family that had come to pick us up. I was kissing everyone on the cheek even though I didn't have a clue who they were. All I knew was that this was the first time in our four-and-a-half year relationship that I had met anyone from his family and it was exciting. They were all very warm and welcoming. They loaded us and our stuff up into their cars and escorted us off to Abdul's grandmother's where the rest of the clan was waiting.

Part of the plan was for us to live with his maternal grandmother once we got to

30

Kuwait. According to old Kuwaiti traditions a grandmother often raised a couple's first born, and since Abdullah's mom was only 15 when she had him, it was his grandmother's place that he called home.

The first view I got of my new country was the huge villas we saw along the road. I had never seen such extravagant homes. Unfortunately, the place we pulled up to was neither large nor beautiful. It was a Government Issue townhouse with peeling paint. Still, I forged on.

The high brick walls surrounding the patio courtyard reminded me of California. Walking through the black iron gate, my heart began pounding as I took in the dozens of pairs of shoes littering the doorway. I entered the peeling brown wooden door to see a small living room with not a single window or table. To the right of the door there was a fuse box sticking out like a sore thumb in the middle of the wall, a TV to the left, and the rest of the room had Arabian sofas (long cushions that lie on the floor) lining each of the remaining three walls. Blocking out the shock of my physical surroundings, I rushed on to meet all those happy people that were waiting to congratulate us on Abdullah's college graduation and our marriage. He hadn't been home in over a year so his loved ones were thrilled to have him back. I was introduced to his grandma, mom, aunts, sisters and brothers, cousins and maids—kissing everyone and knowing it would take me ages to learn their names and their relationships to my husband.

They had prepared a huge feast for our arrival and we were to eat out in the courtyard. There were two tablecloths spread out on the ground cluttered with dishes of rice, grilled meats and salads. Naturally, I went to sit beside my husband and this was my first lesson in Kuwaiti culture. It turned out that he was at the men's table and the other table was for the women. I was too shocked to leave his side, but his family accepted it. For the time being, all we could do was smile and nod at each other since most of them didn't speak English and I didn't know any Arabic aside from the few words I had picked up here and there, like *tukalamu Engalazi* (Do you speak English?). I did notice that there were lots of June bugs crawling around the walls of the house, which were common for that time of year in Wisconsin. Later, to my horror, I was to find that those big black bugs were not June bugs, but flying cockroaches—another fact of life in Kuwait that I had to face.

As the evening wore on, I eventually had to visit the bathroom, and I was shown upstairs to see my room. It was decorated beautifully—much better than the rest of the house. Clearly they had tried to make it special for us. Carpeted in a gorgeous dark blue rug and decorated with a beautiful off-white Italian bedroom set, I had never seen anything as extravagant in all my life. The cupboard doors were covered in full length mirrors that made the small room look larger. The bed had attached nightstands, and the headboard had a built-in radio and lights. Very cool, I thought. Abdul's cousin gave us a TV for a wedding present and that was probably the best gift anyone could have given me at that time.

As pleased as I was with my bedroom, the bathroom threw me for a loop. I walked in and saw a sink and shower that resembled bathrooms as I had known them, but the toilet was something else. All there was to it was a ceramic fixture in the floor with a hole in it. "What the heck do I do with that?" I wondered to myself. I had done enough camping in my life to manage to squat down and use that thing but I wasn't very happy about it. To this day I always end up peeing on my shoe when I'm forced to use Arabian toilets. Putting in an American toilet was first on my list of things to do in Kuwait.

The day after our arrival was the first day of Ramadan. In the Islamic calendar, this is the month of fasting from sunup to sundown. Since I had studied Islam and embraced the faith a couple of years earlier, I was thrilled to spend the holy month in a Muslim country. The whole schedule is turned upside down in Kuwait during this time, as people tend to stay up late into the night enjoying the company of friends and family and shopping for new clothes and gifts for the Eid festival that follows the fast.

After waking up to my first day in Kuwait, in my new home with my new family, I told Shamiya, Abdul's adopted aunt who lived with Grandma Bezza, that I had some laundry to wash. I was puzzled when she told me that it would be better to do it in the evening. I figured that they took it easy during the day in Ramadan, but what could be so difficult about throwing in a load of wash? After all, Abdul had told me that they had two washing machines.

Later that evening when I reminded her about the laundry I had to do, Shamiya took me out to the back courtyard, pulled out a couple of metal wash basins, filled them with water and started putting in some detergent. She flipped over an empty Coke crate to sit on and there we squatted on the ground. "What about the two washing machines?" I asked. "Oh, they're broken," she told me, pointing at a Japanese twin tub and an old wringer washer rusting against the patio wall. Once again I learned how naïve I was. My grandmother still used a wringer washer though I didn't think about it at the time, and for some reason, I just figured that everyone in the world did laundry like I did—you throw some clothes in a washer, pour in the soap, turn it on, and voilà, out come clean clothes. You throw them in the dryer and you're done. That evening, however, was kind of fun. Shamiya knows some English so we got to know a little bit about one another while we scrubbed. She was a year younger than I was and already divorced. I liked her and was happy to have an English-speaking friend in the house. Later, as we hung up the wet laundry on a plastic line that stretched diagonally across the front courtyard, a chorus of prayer calls filled the air from several different neighborhood mosques signaling the beginning of our second day of fast. Next on my list of things to buy: an automatic washing machine.

The next two months were an exciting whirlwind as everyone in the very large family came by to meet me, many of them bearing gifts of gold jewelry. They all seemed so nice and accepting even when I made mistakes, like the time an elderly cousin of Grandma's came by and I sat on those floor cushions with my feet straight out ahead of me. Soon someone came and whispered in my ear that it was rude to show people the soles of my feet. I didn't seem to offend anyone, but I guess they figured since I was going to live there, they'd better teach me the social rules. I also learned that we must serve food and drinks with our right hands, and other little things like that.

However, it didn't take long before the reality of the situation sank in. I got culture shock big time about two months after my arrival. My husband found a job and before I knew it, I was stuck in that windowless house all day with nothing to do. I had an encyclopedia in the letter C, and I had read that thing from cover to cover. I knew every fact in the world that started with a C. English TV didn't start until 7:00 p.m., and I was frightened to go far from the house, let alone drive. Thankfully, Shamiya would walk with me to the local shopping center, where I could spend hours browsing the grocery store and other small shops. It didn't take me long to learn enough of the numbers to make out prices.

Unfortunately, Bezza didn't like the idea of us walking to the store every day and she'd yell bloody murder at Shamiya each time we came home, so I was on my own for my little adventures. I guess it wasn't acceptable for women to be walking the streets in those days, but I had to get out or go nuts. Overnight I had gone from being an active college junior with a job and lots of friends to this lonely life. I had yet to meet any other English-speakers let alone Americans. And in addition to the colorless beige desert buildings, trees, and landscape, I began to find that even little things like the differences in electric plugs, light switches, and door knobs depressed me.

To make matters worse, at 23 I had already been on my own for six years and thought I was perfectly capable of filling my role as a wife. Grandma Bezza, it seemed, had different ideas. She didn't seem to think I could do anything right, from washing clothes to serving food. Since I did things differently from them, it seemed wrong. Before I even saw my husband after work, Grandma had already filled him in on what I had eaten for breakfast and what time I had gotten up that day. I began to feel unhappy with the situation.

But just when I thought I couldn't take it anymore and I was ready to hijack an airliner home, God answered my prayers with an angel named Arwa. Shopping in a bookstore with my husband one night, this young woman came up to me to ask if I'd be interested in attending a religion class in English. That was exactly what I had been asking God for with tears in my eyes five times a day. I also found an article on beating depression in one of my old copies of *Reader's Digest,* which helped me get a grip. I had to hide away all the pictures of my family that I had put out in order to focus on becoming happy there.

I grew up in a typical, dysfunctional American family. My parents divorced when I was only six, but my mom, my brother and I formed a blended family when she hitched up with a man who had two boys and two girls from a previous marriage. We were like the Brady Bunch without the maid and the big house. I missed that old gang, so when I was able to bring their pictures out again without bursting into tears, I knew that was a good sign.

I told myself that I had made the decision to move to Kuwait and it was up to me to make it work. I wasn't going to get divorced, as my parents did, and I wasn't a quitter either. Luckily, I made some lifelong friends at that Tuesday evening class. Also, from there, I learned about an afternoon school for foreigners that taught Arabic and Quran studies. Soon I was brave enough to drive to these classes three nights a week and there I made a Ghanaian friend, Miriam. From her I heard fascinating stories about village life in Ghana. Amazingly, they lived full happy lives though they didn't even have electricity. My life experience before that was so limited that I never imagined such a possibility. I was learning more and more about the world.

Through our religion school, Miriam and I found out about an intensive Arabic program at Kuwait University and before we knew it, we were auditing 15 credits of Arabic. I learned pronunciation within a week and could read newspapers aloud (although I didn't understand them) by the end of the semester. During this time my husband was away at boot camp for the Kuwait National Guard, but I was so busy with my classes and homework that the time passed by in a flash. I was also pregnant with our first child and by July, my life was about to change again. The boredom was gone and I was adjusting to life in this far-away country.

I spent the next Thanksgiving through New Year's holidays back home in Wisconsin with my beautiful baby girl, staying with my mom and catching up with family and friends. I have to mention that my moving was especially difficult for my mother. She said she felt like I had died. That was long before cheap long-distance phone calls or the internet. But when she saw how well I had adjusted, and held her very own granddaughter, she was well on her way to accepting the move as well.

Over the past 20 years, life here has gotten more and more comfortable. Satellite TV, English radio stations that play the latest billboard hits, department and grocery stores—all we need now is Wal-Mart. Eventually, I too was able to finish my degree, and since I was in the United States during the invasion of Kuwait I took the opportunity to attend graduate school, which has enabled me to get a good job and improve the life of our family. Over the years our family has grown, but as long as I live here, I'll never truly feel Kuwaiti. The challenges do keep coming. But asked if I'd do it all again, I'd have to say yes, I would. Living in Kuwait has been a real trip.

Celeste Snyder was born and raised in Rice Lake, Wisconsin. She married and moved to Kuwait in 1983. She and her husband have four children, a girl and three boys. During the school year, she teaches English for the Language Center at the College of Arts, Kuwait University. She usually spends her summers at their hobby farm in Wisconsin.

The Dog Will Never Bring You Tea

Cristina S. Karmas

Now, thirty years later, remembering my mother-in-law's words brings me joy—a smile and a tear. Maya, the family poodle, died in Greece many years ago. She was buried there, in a small village by the sea. Now that I am older, remembering my mother-in-law's words makes me humble: no dog has ever brought me chamomile tea. As I write here in America, the Papillion snores at my feet, and the Shih Tsu nuzzles at my neck. And while toothless *Boobooki* (Flower Bud) has pawed open a box or two of cookie treats, and curious *Noelle* has peeled and eaten a bunch of bananas, neither canine has ever demonstrated even a sniffing interest in tea.

Then, I didn't know what to do with the words, "Maya won't bring you chamomile tea when you're old." According to my mother-in-law, parents took care of young children; children took care of old parents—and animals didn't figure into the plan at all. According to my mother-in-law, everything—plant or animal, straw hat or statue, husband or father-in-law—required its proper care, and woe be it to those who accumulated things they couldn't care for. Then, I couldn't figure out the meaning of my mother-in-law's words—not because the language of Greece was new to me, not because the concept of family was foreign to me. Rather, the words seemed chosen to sever the links between me and my happiest memories of growing up in America.

Pets paraded through my childhood like flags on the 4th of July. Cats named Amazon, Belem, Bucaramanga, and Cucuta testified to the South American adventures of my spirited parents and taught me to care for geography. Sputnik purred his way straight into my heart while commemorating a generation's space race and a teenager's science award. Ladybird, who flew left, then right, into the front window, paid political homage to a popular First Lady of the same name.

Dogs named *Podarok, Chaika,* and *Chaika Nova* (Gift, Seagull, and New Seagull in Russian) fed my fascination with the sounds of words and animals alike—as did a quartet of wild birds, *Adeen, Dva, Tree,* and *Chitiree* (One, Two, Three, and Four), nursed at a medicine dropper. Nijinksky, the family sparrow, danced daily across the pages of my sister's textbooks. And Faust, the feline literata, slept loyally beside me for hours at a stretch, curled on a pile of musical scores and paperbacks, dreaming, perhaps, of kittening on the keys by night while I practiced piano by day.

Some of the family pets had names that didn't overstretch the imagination: Blueboy and Babaloo, while alluding to the art world, rarely left the obscurity of their newspaper-lined cages. Only Flea-free (the oxymoronic kitty born with an immunity to all soaps, shampoos, sprays, and powders) occasionally overturned the bird cages. Simultaneously snarling and scratching, she chased the freed parakeets round and round the small living room until, as always, the fleas got the upper paw and she had to turn her attention to the biting vermin. This she did with a catcall that never failed to scare the escapees back into their cages—where, unlike the proverbial nightingale, they sang the praises of their captors.

For the most part, the names of childhood house pets captured my imagination. Even a carefree pair of desert tortoises, Dobchinsky and Bobchinsky, piqued my curiosity. As nosey as their literary namesakes, they could outrun Flea-free when news of a dog reached their nostrils. But when hungry or thirsty, they would lumber to refrigerator or faucet and wait to be served a plate of fresh lettuce or a bowl of fresh water. Come hibernation time, Dobchinsky and Bobchinsky preferred an artistic hideaway, slumbering all winter among the massive legs of the grand pianos.

Life and its grandeur was all around me then—caught somewhere in the lair of catnip mice and the arc of airborne dogs. I wish that I could say I recognized the glorious lessons in living that I recited while holding a car-struck kitty or a sick puppy in my arms. But I'm sure I didn't. I wish that I could say I appreciated the gifts that I received—from Amazon, who denied animal instinct to fill the house with black and yellow butterflies, gingerly transported amid long white kitty whiskers and longer white cat fangs; or from Buckie, who taunted the laws of gravity with dervish-like abandon until, spinning on her fat cat fanny, she stuffed herself into increasingly smaller baskets—filling the house with flying fur and laughter. But I'm sure that I never once stopped to thank the pets for the joy they brought me every day of my life.

Even so, for me it was a given that living with pets was an absolute good. And while I had never paused, even after leaving the absorption of childhood games, to philosophize on the wisdom of animal ways, I could never have imagined a life without pets. And I could never have imagined the need even for thinking about such a life.

When, as a young bride, I followed my Greek husband to Athens, eager to please and be pleased, eager to love and be loved—eager to belong—I could not have imagined that pleasure would entail pain, that love would entail hate, that acceptance would entail rejection. I could not have foreseen that my desire to blend into a new family and culture, to fit into new friendships and customs, would require that I reexamine pet assumptions. But within a few months of my arrival, I began to believe that if I were ever to be accepted as a Greek, I would be required to reject much of what defined me as an American.

Some Americanisms I gave up with ease: a married woman like me dressed and behaved with propriety. The jeans that were *de rigueur* in graduate school were exchanged for dresses. Knee-length hemlines replaced miniskirts; short haircuts replaced long tresses. Like the other females in the extended family, I prepared for mealtime by peeling potatoes or cutting cucumbers to the chants of raised male voices expounding a cappella on the crucial events of the day. And like the other women, I adjourned to the kitchen after meals to wash and dry dishes while the men

36

rose imperiously and called for the keys to the locked living room doors. Once out of feminine sound and sight, they would loosen belts, fondle worry beads, drink ouzo and talk politics until dawn.

Talking has never been a favorite pastime of mine, but I arrived not speaking a word of Greek. So though I learned the language before the end of my first year, I passed many hours in silence. At dinner parties held to introduce the *neefee* (the bride), I smiled and nodded, nodded and smiled as new relatives gestured at bellies to indicate their wish that I soon be blessed with babies. For a married woman like me, expectations were clear: "open a house" and raise a family.

How disappointing, then, for my in-laws when, after about four months in Greece, around Easter time, I announced (via my husband, who did the translating) that I had adopted a baby chick. Left to die by street vendors who peddled sick cottontails and chickadees to tourists, peeping Karma came to life for a short time in our apartment—and so did I. The chick kept me company after Greek school and before mealtime. And during afternoon siestas, we spent many happy hours together. Sometimes, Karma peeped and cheeped loudly while I chatted and prattled, intent on constructing a small chick house of cotton balls and cardboard, complete with a tiny blue and white Greek flag. Other times, the chick slept comfortably in my lap while I listened quietly to the still unintelligible voices of the Greek radio. Karma was destined to a short life—and I cried long and hard when she died.

How devastating for my in-laws: when my husband's favorite aunt died of cancer a few weeks later, it was observed by the extended family that I had shed fewer tears for the aunt than I had for the chick, that I had mourned more for a farm animal than for a family member. Although a retired American friend of the family noted that I had known Karma longer and better than the Greek aunt, my behavior received universal condemnation: For a respectable married woman, it was inappropriate to house a chicken and inexcusable to mourn its death.

I had no reason to know, when I brought a small black pup home on *Proto Maya* (May Day), that what was good for the chicken was also good for the poodle. Abandoned on the bustling Athens streets amid exploding fireworks and backfiring motorbikes, Maya brightened my life like a shooting star—and as I carried her home (with the help of my husband who, as always, did the translating), I wished again and again that no one would show up to claim her in response to the many ads that would surely be placed in all the Athens newspapers. Claim a lost puppy? When I moved to Greece, people didn't have house pets; dark memories of the dog years, of the war, of the occupation, of the dictatorship, still tortured many Greeks. People who had competed with animals for food to stay alive, who had consumed dogs and cats to survive, could not have been expected to pamper poodles.

I had not expected my pleasure in giving Maya a home to bring the household so much pain: my in-laws chastised the son who had brought a *ksenee* (foreigner) into the family. And they wept for the gypsy-like bride who had filled the house with the sounds not of a laughing child, but of a crying bitch. Nor had I expected my love for a stray pup to cause the family so much hate: my four Greek nephews claimed

37

to despise the old ways of their grandmother and grandfather. The boys loved to pet Maya and groom her wooly coat; but, like all Greek children, they had learned to recite the animal catechism, *"Tha se fie."* ("She will eat you up.")

Many tears were shed over Maya—both upstairs, in the classically appointed home of my sister-in-law, and downstairs, in the sparsely furnished apartment of my husband who, Greek-style, generously shared spare rooms with a host of needy relatives. Maya shared the "bridal suite." Every night, before curling up at the foot of the bed, she gently licked my husband's feet. And every day, before seeing us off, she dutifully went out on the balcony to do her doggie business. "People belong inside; animals belong outside."

Like me, Maya must have wanted only a sense of belonging. Like me, Maya must have cried herself to sleep at night—hoping to dream of a way to please the family. How embarrassing, again, for my in-laws: in Athens, where living space was precious, the balcony was regarded as inside, not outside. A room like any other in the apartment, a balcony might house a television, a dining table, comfortable chairs, and even a bed. In fact, during the summer months, the entire Greek population—or so it seemed to me—lived on the balconies, where name days, holidays, and soccer victories were celebrated. Defeated, again, in my effort to find acceptance, I was scorned by the neighbors of *Kypseli* (Beehive) District. A respectable married woman would not allow an animal to live in an apartment or permit a poodle to poop on a balcony.

By early June, I had completed my schooling in the Greek language and had started my training in the clean balcony; my *Kypseli* neighbors noticed how quickly I learned to wash the intricate iron railings, from top to bottom, sponging the scrollwork of the vertical bars before mopping the marble of the horizontal baseboards. Between new buildings and sea breezes, the dusty balconies kept me busy. By mid-June, when the family moved to the seashore to escape the Athens heat, I would be ready to help open the two-story summer place, the largest property in a coastal village of two hundred residents. And by then, too, I would be ready to help close the Maya story. I was expected to abandon the poodle to the good villagers of my husband's birthplace, Paralia.

Instead, at summer's end, Maya returned to the Athens house, where she lived to celebrate almost nineteen birthdays, a well-loved member of the Greek family. But at mid-summer, I could not have foreseen that Maya and I would eventually belong, that we would finally find the acceptance we longed for.

In early July, my husband's work took him back to Athens for a short time, and I stayed in the village to help, as best I could, with the cleaning and cooking required in a family whose number fluctuated daily between ten and thirty relatives. During the afternoon siestas that followed the mid-day meals—and after I had washed and dried dishes, removed tablecloths and linens, and moved chairs and tables—I picked a cherished paperback (an overpriced luxury purchased at the only existing English-language store in Athens), roped a problematic poodle, and headed out for a walk into the hills behind the summer house. There, not far from the madding mutt, who

38

lived for the time when she would be free of her makeshift leash, I found a shady spot under an olive tree and lost myself in a precious world of words, an intelligible world created of concepts from my own language and culture.

By the time my husband returned to Paralia, the word had spread. The foreign bride had gone mad! She had been seen, on many an afternoon, by many a villager, to roam and read under the trees—she had been seen, again and again, to shun the fellowship of living men and women for the suspect company of a dead book and a mad dog.

Yes, many tears were shed over Maya, whose death, so many years later, was mourned both in Athens and in Paralia. I can't say how or why it happened, but, like me, Maya finally became a member of the family. And I can't pinpoint an incident that changed everything from one day to the next. Things didn't change overnight. But on days when the boys stayed home from school to fight the varied illnesses of childhood, Maya licked away their worries and listened to their tales. And on mornings when I helped my mother-in-law hang the pails of wet laundry on the terrace line, Maya watched for dropped socks, and I watched for spilled tears. The secrets shared and stories told while feeling warm foreheads or folding dry sheets were transformative.

So, as I said, there was nothing in particular that changed everything. Rather, there were little things, little things here and there. Eventually, Maya learned to listen for the heavy tread of my mother-in-law, who came downstairs every afternoon not with a cup of steeping chamomile tea for the *neefee,* but with a dish of steaming food for the dog. And eventually, my mother-in-law learned to watch for the wagging tail between her feet, to care for the adoring canine at her ankles.

In the last thirty years, many pets have shared the homes and transformed the lives of the children, grandchildren, and great-grandchildren of my in-laws. But I remember best the pioneering poodle, the first pet of my Greek family. Thank you, Maya, for the smiles, the tears—the joy.

Cristina S. Karmas holds a Ph.D. in English, a M.A. in English and a M.A. in Philosophy from The Ohio State University. Her interests are foreign languages and music. She is now teaching at Graceland University, Iowa in the Division of Humanities

.

Life Events

So on a cold, sunny day we drove up to the snow-covered Alpine village on a musical mission. We decided to make a day of it, starting with a nice lunch in a gemütlich chalet-restaurant with a good bottle of wine. Then off to Carmel's.

Jon McLin

When I look back on that night, it seems like something out of a movie: I had barely stepped through the door, when a cheerful voice greeted me, "Put your bags down and c'mon!"

Sharon Victor

I had watched "eccentrics" swimming in the freezing winter weather. After Jason's birth, I started thinking a daily swim wasn't such a bad idea.

Laurel Mantzaris

Herr Thiessen was our car's inspector that day. He paced pensive circles around our car like a shark, apparently taking in its distinct and unusual non-Europeanness as he mentally kicked the tires.

Scott Williams

The Return of the Expatriate Piano

Jon McLin

"I know somebody who has a Steinway B over there that he wants to sell".

The speaker was my brother Jim. He and I had been having regular transatlantic telephone conversations—he in Florida, I in Geneva, Switzerland, where I live—about pianos. Like tens of thousands of others, I had studied piano for a few years as a kid only to give it up when more important things came along, like chasing girls and playing football. And like some of those, I had decided much later, in my case around age 50, to take it up again. After testing the water with an electronic piano, I decided to take the plunge with a "real" acoustic piano. I hankered after an instrument that felt like the Steinway I had played on as a child.

It was natural to seek big brother's advice. Jim's life had revolved around keyboard instruments. Playing them, especially, but also selling them. He had a sense of what I wanted and needed. It was he who had taught me how to remember the Steinway model designations: *"'B' is for 'Big'. 'D' is for 'Damn Big'."* The piano on which I played as a child was his; I was drawn, not to say pushed, into learning the same instrument as a way of amortizing the parental investment.

By coincidence, but through a different logic of events, he had also recently returned to the piano in a serious way. A child prodigy, he had been shown off by our stage-mother and by his Memphis teacher as little Mozart had been trotted around Europe by his father, Leopold. At 12 years of age Jim had played the Grieg concerto with the Memphis Symphony. Other triumphs followed. But along the way, the realities of adult life diverted him from serious music. He stopped playing the piano seriously and sold the Steinway of our childhood. He then put his talents and energy into the music instrument business, especially in the design and sale of electronic organs.

He continued this work for most of his adult life. Then a series of business and health misfortunes had the effect of concentrating his mind. In his words, he "wrestled successfully with the demons" of his youth, and began to play serious piano again after something like a 20-year hiatus. He enrolled in the music program at Florida State University to pursue a doctorate in piano performance. As he approached 60 he recovered the old repertory and added to it, performing feats of memorization that I found daunting.

"What do you mean 'Over there'?" I asked.

"In Switzerland, not far from you. Doesn't want much money for it. It used to belong to Anita, an American pianist living in Leysin. She died and left it in the care of her Dutch lover. But the lover has a wife and family and couldn't very well take it home and explain how he came by it. So he sold it for very little money to Don, a colleague at the overseas American college where she taught. In the meantime Don has moved back to the States. He's my next-door neighbor and a fellow student in the FSU music department. He has the piano parked with a friend up there in the Swiss mountains, but he's eager to get the thing off his hands and would be happy to sell it for what he paid for it, which was only 3,000 francs."

This news seemed too good to be true, but I was ambivalent. Perhaps a Steinway B was too much piano for me, too powerful for my small apartment, too unforgiving for my skill level. Nevertheless I took note of the name of the technician who had looked after the piano, and went to see him at his shop in Vevey, just up the lake from Geneva.

Monsieur Genet turned out to be full of colorful piano lore. As a young man he had worked in New York, where he had tuned pianos at Carnegie Hall for Glenn Gould and other pianistic stars of the 1950s. "I would still be there but they tried to draft me into the army during the Korean War. So I returned to Switzerland and am still here."

Yes, he remembered Anita. A nice lady, good musician, too bad about her early death. Yes, he remembered her Steinway. You don't want to buy that one. It's in terrible condition. You'd have to spend a small fortune to put it into shape.

So it was too good to be true, a Steinway grand for 3,000 Swiss francs, or about $2,000. I decided to do a second check with Beat, a Swiss who is an old friend from my Alabama days decades ago. He worked at the college in Leysin where Anita had taught. Yes, he had known Anita, remembered the instrument, and had heard her play it. He did not recall it as being in bad condition, but that was some time ago; perhaps through neglect it had deteriorated.

Given my ambivalence about the suitability of the piano for my needs and the reports about its condition, which were mixed at best, I dropped the idea of buying Anita's instrument.

I decided on a short-list of two instruments. It was with some regret that I concluded the search, because it had uncovered a number of absorbing human stories and thereby taken on a life of its own. Pianos have a way of evoking strong associations and emotions. Owners who had come on hard times, families that had split, musical careers that had taken unexpected turnings. I postponed a final choice until the Christmas season, when I expected a visit from Jim and his wife Jane. Then he would be able to actually put his hands on the short-listed instruments and give me a considered recommendation.

When he came and tried them, he confirmed my instincts (including my hesitation about an instrument that was too powerful and unforgiving) and the deal was done. The piano I bought was of Czech manufacture, a Rösler baby grand, 30 years old, owner short of money, her daughter—the one who had played the piano—long since departed from the family home. He helped me place it in the apartment and try it out. It sounded and looked fine. The story seemed to be over.

One evening during Jim's Christmas visit, Beat and his wife came to dinner. Jim played, we sang, much fun was had by all. Over dinner, we discussed the Steinway

44

B, the one that got away. Jim marveled at the series of coincidences: that his Florida neighbor Don had come there from Switzerland, where I was living; that Don knew our mutual friend Beat, a discovery that was made accidentally; and that I was looking for a piano. All this had led Don to mention that, whaddyaknow, his piano in Leysin just happened to be for sale.

We spoke that evening of Anita, who had been a friend of both Don and Beat. While Jim and I had grown up in a small town in Arkansas, she came from a small town in Texas; Jim and Anita were both born in 1933, only a few months apart. She was part Comanche. They both came to Europe for advanced piano studies, Jim to Brussels, Anita to Paris. They both then returned to the United States, although Anita later moved back to Europe to stay.

On the freighter which brought her for the first time to Europe, she had met Jan, the Dutchman who was to become her lifelong companion. He was then a merchant seaman, the second in command of the ship. When she moved to Europe permanently, Jan arranged to ship the piano from Texas. It was also he who looked after the piano following her death, and who sold it to Don.

Don was later to tell a remarkable story about Anita and the piano: When Anita died, and I decided to buy the piano from Jan, he also gave me several boxes of her music. A lot of it was too difficult for me, but I managed to find some Mozart sonatas that I could play. One night, I was working on one of the later ones ... using Anita's fingering. It was very odd to be playing her music, on her piano, with her fingering. After I had been playing for a while, I got the feeling that she was trying to tell me something. I'm not usually into metaphysical things, but I did have the feeling she was trying to communicate with me. But soon, I dismissed the thought and got up and turned on the television. When I did, Vladimir Horowitz was on playing exactly the same sonata, starting with the second movement, exactly where I had left off. Perhaps it was just coincidence ... or a Carl Jung synchronicity.

We also spoke that December evening of 1992 of the technician whom I had consulted. Beat knew Monsieur Genet and was responsible for hiring him to tune the grand piano belonging to the college, the one used by Anita in her teaching. Beat was familiar with this piano from doing the college inventory and knew it to be in terrible shape.

And then the other shoe dropped.

"Could it be," asked Beat, "that Genet was confusing the college piano which Anita used for teaching with her personal piano?" If this was the case, my decision not to buy the Steinway, following Genet's warning, was based on false information.

We all agreed that this was quite possibly what had happened, but the question seemed of only theoretical interest. I had chosen another piano and was no longer in the market for one. The deal was closed. We were not in the business of trading used pianos for commercial purposes—although the idea did cross our minds that there was money to be made here.

During the Christmas celebrations of the ensuing days Jim and I continued to

45

rehash the story and to marvel at the fortuitous, "small world" aspects of it. It was full of the interwoven experiences of several people whose lives had been enriched by long periods of residence abroad. Some of the experiences were joyful, some banal, some poignant. But all had a special quality characteristic of the bonding that occurs among those who are or have been expatriates.

It became clear that the issue of Anita's piano was nagging at him, that he wanted to know for sure what it was like. When I asked if he would like to go to Leysin to see it, he readily said yes. Don had given custody of the piano in his absence to Carmel, a secretary at the college. We telephoned her. She said yes, it was in her apartment, and gave us directions. So on a cold, sunny day we drove up to the snow-covered Alpine village on a musical mission. We decided to make a day of it, starting with a nice lunch in a *gemütlich* chalet-restaurant with a good bottle of wine. Then off to Carmel's.

The Steinway was in her kitchen, on the linoleum-covered floor. A more unlikely setting would have been hard to imagine. She recounted the difficulties the movers had had with it in negotiating the stairs. But it was there. Jim, still weak from recent cancer surgery, proceeded to try it out. Scales. Arpeggios. Bach's Chromatic Fantasy and Fugue. A Beethoven sonata. Prokofiev's Toccata. Much of this, I later learned, had been in Anita's repertory.

It met his standards. For the next day or two he considered whether or not to buy it. Was it crazy at that stage in his life to invest in a 75-year-old instrument that would have to be moved at great expense and at some risk from a cool Alpine village to the hot, humid Florida plains?

Of course he bought it. And so it was that in a modest kitchen in the Swiss mountains a Steinway of American manufacture, after a long sojourn in Europe, passed between two artists from the American South, one already dead from cancer and one who was soon to be. I arranged shipment by airfreight and it arrived in Tallahassee within days. There it was checked out and lovingly reworked into a high-performance, valuable instrument by the piano technician of the Florida State School of Music. It was Jim's professional instrument for the remaining few years of his life.

En route to Tallahassee it re-entered the United States through Jacksonville, the same port it had transited some 30 years before when Anita shipped it from Texas to Europe.

Jon McLin, a native of Arkansas, has moved across the Atlantic several times since 1960, when a Rhodes Scholarship first took him to England. His university education was at Washington and Lee, Oxford and Johns Hopkins. In Europe he has worked for the American Universities Field Staff, Royal Dutch/Shell, and the International Labor Organization. His European residences have been in Brussels, Rome, London and, since 1984, Geneva. One of his (grown) children, as well as his grandson Liam, lives nearby in Switzerland; the other is in Houston.

Why I Stay in Israel

Sharon Victor

When my friend sent me a copy of the advertisement about the literary competition "Why I Stay in Israel" and suggested that I take a shot at it, I laughed. I told her that I couldn't possibly write such an article because I have absolutely no idea why I have stayed in Israel for so long (21 years!).

Oh sure, there were lots of reasons why I came. I was a young and enthusiastic Zionist, the product of an ardent Bnei Akiva background. To me, Israel represented everything that was inspiring, meaningful and romantic; the mythological Israelis were heroes and the stories I heard fired up my imagination. How I wanted to be one of them, to be part of it all! The short visits I had spent in Israel only confirmed these impressions. But, of course, visiting a country and living there are two very different things, as we new immigrants all learned the hard way. Why I have stayed is often a mystery to me, a cross somewhere between sainthood and insanity. Most of the original reasons why I came quickly became obsolete. Idealism won't keep you company when you're lonely and patriotic folk songs won't pay the grocery bill.

On a cold night in December 1976, I left New York, where I was born and bred. I lived there with my mother and sisters in a six-story apartment building in a city housing project. Our building was located inside the block well off the street and the path leading to our building was always exposed to powerful gusts of wind in the winter. I remember standing by the window that day, looking down at my mother as she walked home on that same route I'd seen her walk hundreds of times. Was this the last time, I wondered. I saw her struggle against the wind looking small and dejected. She had battled that wind so many times, but that day she carried an additional burden: her daughter was leaving home. I felt plagued by misgivings. Was I making a terrible mistake? How would she manage? How would I?

Later that night I sat huddled on the plane, feeling as cold and hard as a block of ice. I remember not taking my coat off the whole way, not talking to anyone, feeling miserable, isolated, almost in a state of shock. At the airport in Israel I was treated to the usual fare for new immigrants—the processing of my paperwork and the wait for a Jewish Agency driver to take me to my destination took over four hours! Although New York had been freezing when I departed, Israel was having one of its winter heat waves, which only added to my sense of bewilderment. What was I getting into?

And then at last, I was delivered to the Beit Brodetsky Immigrants' Hostel in Ramat Aviv. When I look back on that night, it seems like something out of a movie: I had barely stepped through the door, when a cheerful voice greeted me, "Put your bags down and c'mon!" The voice belonged to Peter, who had arrived from New Zealand two months earlier. It seemed almost as if he were a one-man welcome wagon, standing on guard, waiting to grab up any newcomer who should happen to come along. Before I knew what was happening, he whisked me off to his room, made me a cup of tea, and began talking a mile a minute. Soon Daniel from France joined us and the two men began to play chess, leaving me at last to catch my breath and collect my thoughts.

And that was how it all began. During the next few weeks, I met other young adults like myself, all equally alone and baffled, yet all determined to make a go of life in a strange new place. There was Lil from Australia, Tzvi from South Africa, Debby, Gary and Benny from the States, Ruth from England, and many others from an assortment of places. Each had his own story to tell, each his hopes and dreams.

There was one guy in the hostel who was always staggering around in a daze, muttering, "What am I *doing* here?" partly in jest but partly in earnest. His words echoed just how a lot of us felt.

Maybe it was because we were all on our own, maybe it was because of our shared experience, but a powerful bond developed among us. We became a close-knit group of friends, sharing meals, celebrating Shabbat and holidays together, roaming the streets of Tel Aviv, sitting up until all hours of the night screaming with laughter over things that only we "Anglos" could understand. We gave each other endless support as we ventured out into the "real" world of work, cried on each other's shoulders when things got too painful and spent hours immersed in soul-bearing conversations. We were trying to maintain control of our lives in sometimes impossible situations but the vitality of youth was on our side and, all things considered, I had a marvelous time.

Eventually it was time to move out and move on; after all it was a hostel and merely the first stop in our journey. I rented an apartment with one of my newly-found friends. We took a deep breath and plunged into life as real Israelis. Occasionally I felt miserable and down, but often I was deliriously happy. New friends drifted in and out of our group. In the absence of family, friendship moved in to fill the vacuum. As my circle of acquaintances grew, both socially and professionally, I felt more and more at home. Life had a lot to offer an eager young woman and I lived intensely, trying to taste as many new experiences as I could. Maybe I was unaware of it at the time, or too busy to notice, but roots were beginning to take hold.

Time went on. Soon, to my astonishment, *I* had become one of the seasoned veterans and I basked in the admiration of the newcomers, trying my best to ease their way. I watched Dizengoff Center and the Boardwalk being built, realizing that the charming little city that had become my home would never be the same again.

It wasn't all carefree fun and games as I might make it sound. Life in Israel is never easy and there were always new situations to cope with. I was very much on my own, close friends often moved away and there was a kind of loneliness under the surface that even the most well-meaning friends couldn't always assuage.

From the original crowd, more than a few returned to their countries of origin. The rest of us settled down. Although we are now scattered around and some of us no longer in touch, others have remained close, our relationships having survived the tests of time and separation.

Today I am married, have two children, and my life bears little resemblance to that early period, which, despite the hardships, I fondly remember as the "best years of my life." Time seems to have rushed by in a blur. It hasn't been easy. The original dreams have faded, to be replaced by the often tedious routine of everyday life. It's been sad and frustrating to witness the moral erosion of Israeli society, along with the appalling absence of national unity, something that was once considered almost sacred. The possibility of peace seems to be slipping away through our fingers. Money problems have been overwhelming at times.

But most of all, the yearning for loved ones far away has never dissipated, even with the passage of so much time. Maybe it's because I've grown up a little and become more sober. Maybe becoming a mother reinforced my concepts of family life. Today I face problems I didn't dwell on much in the past: for instance, the all-too-familiar dilemma of having aging, ailing parents on the other side of the world. Is there ever a way to resolve that one? And then there are my dear sisters and their families, and the precious, devoted friends I left behind.

Nothing can make up for all the years I lost with them. Whatever I had here can always be measured and balanced against something I missed out on "there." For even after 21 years in Israel, I still sometimes feel torn between my two homes, and the one absolute truth I have learned here is that you can't have it both ways. You can be here or you can be there but you can't have them both. Why did it take me so long to figure that out? Everyone else seems to have known that all along.

When I visit the States, each visit is an intensely bitter-sweet experience, an emotional roller coaster. Saying good-bye to everyone there, no matter how many times it's been done, never gets easier.

But now when I return to Israel from such a visit, there is no longer that sense of culture shock and displacement. Because as the old saying goes, time really does its own. I am as at home here as I am there. I have accumulated as many memories from my life here as from there. And when I gaze down from my window now, I no longer see my childhood, but rather a scene from the present, reflecting the sights and sounds of the life I have created here, for better or worse.

Yes, sometimes I still stagger around asking myself, "What am I *doing* here?" I guess in a way I always will. And yet I still find it hard to answer that intangible question. So why *have* I stayed? I have often thought about leaving. What force holds me here? Is it the comfortable lifestyle, or some abstract need to share the destiny of the Israeli people? Is it habit? All of these offer only a partial glimpse into the puzzle of my ambiguous existence here.

Maybe I just like it here. After all, some places have a way of getting under your skin. I know it also has a lot to do with the friends I made here throughout the years. Today I lovingly salute them. For it was those close personal ties from the period shortly after my arrival in Israel that gave me the sense of belonging and security so vitally needed, and that allowed me to feel connected enough to put down roots. And the friends from the present have helped sustain me.

Sharon Victor was born in 1952 in Brooklyn, New York, in an orthodox Jewish family. She was educated in religious schools and also attended religious youth movements. In 1974, she received her BA from Brooklyn College, where she majored in English literature. At the end of 1976, she emigrated to Israel, where she lives today with her husband, Yosef, and their two daughters, Efrat and Nataly. She works at Bar-Ilan University as an English secretary and language editor. She tries to visit her family and friends in New York once a year and—even after all these years—still considers both New York and Israel her homes.

Swimming in the Winter

Laurel Mantzaris

There's a bitter taste in my mouth when I wake—I've dreamed that someone (maybe my friend Gerrie, who traipsed around Europe with me after college, or maybe my younger daughter, or maybe Jason's girlfriend Sophia) has veered recklessly into heavy Athens traffic, bisecting a busy highway just in the nick of time and then disappearing. When I find her, I pick her up and she's as light as paper.

I brush my teeth, washing away the dream, grab a towel, and run out into the cold drizzle towards the sea. I sit down as always on the rough slabs a sinewy old fisherman has piled up Cycladic style to create a low bench against the wall. Aptly, heavy grey clouds lie like a huge dirty dust rag, the dark swelling water looks like unpolished gunmetal and the mountains of Aegina are faint in the mist. I remove my sneakers, stash socks, keys and glasses, peel off a worn blue tracksuit, and make my way over the mosaic of wet pebbles. It's Jason's birthday today.

The beach is deserted, strewn with purple seaweed, sponges, a tire and plastic bottles from the recent storm. Up on the road, a man in black leather watches me navigate large flat rocks carpeted in underwater growth and step down into the murky water. At first glance the motorcyclist resembles Jason, and I'm startled by the masculine planes of his face, the geometrics of his straight nose and black sunglasses. But no, he isn't tall enough, not big enough by a long shot. He tugs at a muffler. Jason would probably be wearing a T-shirt, oblivious to the cold.

If I step on a broken shell or a sea urchin, this time I understand no physical pain. My mind is back on Jason's birth and its difficulties. The doctor thought he was making things easy for me by coming straight to the labor ward in his tweed jacket, breaking my waters and jabbing me with a drip to speed things up. We couldn't communicate very well. My Greek was still minimal. I almost walked out of the hospital with Jason still on the way.

Involuntarily, the plunge into the cold water thrills my whole body as some tight knot in the middle of my stomach loosens. In spite of myself, my shoulders relax into the briny smell and my skin itself becomes a wet suit in protection against the icy water. The motorcyclist is still watching. I swim further out, feeling smug that those on shore are bundled against the cold. Gulls fight the wind and swoop near me; I'm glad for their company.

I have lived in Greece a whole lifetime—Jason's whole lifetime. He was born just a year after we set up housekeeping here, after being married and starting our family in England where my husband had finished his studies and embarked on his career in shipping. Happy as I was to be back, for I had fallen in love with Greece and my husband in the sixties while traveling with my friend Gerrie, to my surprise our return brought me severe culture shock. I remember my husband's look of concern. "Aren't things better for us here than in London? My family is helping.

What do you want me to do?" I groped for a solution: "I wish we could have another child. Alexi needs a brother or sister."

Jason had come quickly, as the doctor had promised, and I had torn. They left him crying on the table while they stitched me up. He was a good feeder, vigorous, his little body tense and strong, but I remember being depressed and stuck on problems. A voice in the back of my mind constantly whispered, "Maybe I'll just go home." Not yet belonging, tentative acceptance by the in-laws, loneliness, assaults on my beliefs, I felt threatened by the traditions of blue stones to keep away the evil eye, the 40 days a new mother was housebound till she had the blessing of a priest and the virtues of chamomile in fighting colic.

As I swim, I think about Jason's baptism and my agony as the priest pushed him under the water. I think about the little blond boy Jason became, crawling into the shallow waves of a sandy beach on Zakinthos before he could walk, swimming under water to sneak up on his sisters, imitating his brother's prowess on the windsurf and needing our rescue across the bay. I see him protecting his little sisters with swagger and bombast or practicing Tai Chi on the beach with Sophia or guffawing in his hearty infectious belly laugh. I see him in his Boy Scout uniform guarding the flower strewn bier in the church at Easter or dressed up as Dracula for Carnival or wearing a cape for the video productions cast by all the kids in the neighborhood which Alexi directed.

And now in the sea I become something primitive—a squid or an agile star fish, an animal who moves from its solar plexus—arms crawling, legs kicking, head just a more sensitive extension of sensation and breathing and hearing. My swims used to be as quick as a coffee break or a telephone call. But, I'm lucky. My husband has arranged that we live a block away from the sea. So it is easy for me to be loyal to it, to make it a priority.

I had watched "eccentrics" swimming in the freezing winter weather. After Jason's birth, I started thinking a daily swim wasn't such a bad idea. Not that I ever forced myself. Each day as I hung the laundry that first winter, I'd hold up my finger and ask myself whether I could put my body into the sea. Each day I decided I'd try. Each day I found my body responding to the thrill of the cold water. And before I knew it, the winter had passed and I was still swimming. On a busy day I'll still get up at six and run down as the rosy sun rises behind black trees.

Babies don't provide solutions, they complicate life. The nurse dropped Jason's cot as we walked down the steps leaving the hospital after his birth. He wasn't hurt, didn't even stir. As I had been determined not to let the new baby affect the close, intelligent relationship with my first son, I'd asked my mother-in-law to arrange for Alexi to be away when we arrived home so that we could get settled and avoid awkward situations.

But *yaya* hadn't seen fit to respect my ideas. Perhaps it was mutual, this lack of respect, for I found myself glad my first son had been born in the United Kingdom where I'd had a chance to form my own ideas. Yet, I found myself in debt to my mother-in-law when four months after Jason's birth I went under the knife for an emergency appendectomy and she weaned the baby for me, which gave us even more opportunity to clash over simple mundane chores of child care. I felt torn from my child, in excruciating pain. Our problems didn't dissolve themselves till the kids were grown and launched and I could once more appreciate her wit, her sensitivity, her proficiency in five languages,

With Alexi in nursery school, our integration into Greek life sped up. Except for his bringing colds and measles and chicken pox home to baby Jason, and except for the fact that *yaya* wanted us every Saturday and every Sunday for dinner, life slowly got better. We were a bi-lingual family, but the kids attended Greek school, which submitted them to vast amounts of homework assigned even to first-graders, to the emphasis on handwriting, repetition, parroting of lessons, memorization. Long division was taught doing one step in your head rather than writing it down.

My Greek wasn't good enough to help and despite the apparent need for parental supervision or private tutors, as the schools operated on half-day shifts, my children learned to do their lessons on their own. And they learned very well. On family visits to the States, I found they were far ahead of their peers in US schools. People used to ask me all the time, "Where is better—Greece or America?" I began to be unsure.

As he grew, however, Jason often seemed to be listening to a different drummer. He was the child who tumbled down the steps chasing his carriage as soon as he could walk, who stuck a screwdriver in the socket (luckily the electricity was turned off), who swallowed a two-drachma coin and had to be turned upside down and slapped on the back, who swelled up with allergy when he found a June bug and ended up in the hospital, who swelled up with a kidney infection and ended up in the hospital, who suffered acute appendicitis and ended up in the hospital.

His first-grade teacher told me he was the first one in his class to learn to read, but by 4.th grade he was changing his report card to give himself a better grade so that his father would let him go to the States that summer. He once got in trouble for putting his fist through a wall in high school. When he was about 14 and his father was off on a business trip, I came home to find the family car missing. Jason had taken his sisters for a ride and stripped the gears on the next street! But his time in the Navy settled him down a bit. He got his Bachelor's in shipping, following in his father's footsteps, and then went on for a further degree in computers, his passion.

An old fisherman in a yellow slicker has come out on the rocks. Since I can't see whether he is looking my way, I don't greet him. I don't see well since my unsuccessful retina surgery several years ago. I, too, had ended up in the hospital. Recuperating, I found myself in bad shape, with no prognosis of healing, a big black hole in the middle of the vision of my left eye. This time, Jason was the one who propped my pillows, cooked for me, told me jokes, took my calls, phoned my friends, rushed home from classes to be with me, anticipated my needs while the rest of the family went about their business. And he was the one who, sitting companionably on the edge of my bed, tried to talk me out of my rage at the unfairness of losing an eye whose vision had steadily improved over the years. "Go for a walk,

Mom. Do some yoga. It's not worth it."

The water is colder than I'd thought. I feel the chill in the arches of my feet and on my forehead as I start reliving that Sunday morning, just a week after Jason's birthday two years ago. Instead of swimming, I found myself outside the emergency room. Not a lot of chairs. Sophia sat sometimes and I sat sometimes. My husband went to find out what was happening. Sophia said she felt better being there. She had been Jason's nurse after the accident. A minor cycle accident, he seemed to have veered out into traffic at the wrong moment on his way to work. He wasn't speeding; he was wearing his helmet. He'd broken a rib. Sophia had been taking such impeccable care of him that I hadn't wanted to interfere, feeling like a nosy mother-in-law whenever I suggested maybe Jason ought to move around a bit. They would be married soon so I just left them. Then that morning, five days after the accident, Sophia told me he'd been spitting blood.

We had my blue bag with a change of underwear for Jason, some Kleenex, his medicine, his toothbrush, who knows what else. Down a long silent corridor, our footsteps echoing up some stairs. Someone asked if we belonged to the man they'd taken into surgery. My husband said things were bad. I couldn't think, couldn't pray, couldn't move. A white-coated figure started down the stairs, and we asked him about Jason. He came back up and disappeared. They called us into an office, asking each of us what we were to the patient. They told us to sit down. I knew then. I'd been expecting to be told it was serious, but I knew then.

A tall doctor started explaining how Jason was half-dead when brought in, how they'd done everything they could, how he hadn't responded. "He's dead?" asked my husband. "He's dead." The doctor looked at us and then away. From somewhere remote I heard my feebly shouted "no" and put my head down on the desk. "I'll go away. That's the only thing I can do—go away. I give up."

I can see my breath this morning as the sun slants like a knife and cuts it, just as the beaten steel sea tries to steal it. So I mete it out to see how far I can swim across the bay on one breath—eight strokes, ten, twelve, twenty to the exhalation—kicking till I explode. God, they say, took man's rib, a spare, breathed on it, created Eve. So when Jason's broke, I touched him, bid him inhale slowly, deeply, tried to breathe for him, just as I moved for him, teased him: Didn't he feel better now I'd had a swim for him, found fresh air he couldn't for the pain. "Don't make me laugh," he'd said, "It hurts."

I can't dawdle. I race the dark clouds, push my limits to feel what he felt, pain turning to ecstasy as he left his body trying to catch his breath, while the wind whirled only silence. I race, struggle to catch it—the breath I can't see now—catch it, hold it, save it. My body refracts into the water and loses its shape, my legs disappearing into the depths.

But I'm still here. I stayed for the huge funeral up on the mountain where my husband has had a family tomb built of white marble, and we fill it with flowers, icons, Jason's picture and poems. It is overlooking the sea, a place Jason would love. I stayed through all the rites, the memorial services, the offerings of wheat and pomegranates, the burning of oil and incense, the wearing of black, the keening, the grief that doesn't end.

Somewhere along the way I decided to ride out the waves that keep rolling in. Something like the way some Greek music is full of such hurt and passion but is tamed, contained, determined to finish out its needs. Relationships, I've found, don't end with distance or death. Out to sea now, breaking through the cloud cover, there are shafts of white light—like those El Greco painted with ascending angels. There would be a rainbow if it were still raining; beauty as light and ephemeral as a piece of paper. And as fragile.

My husband has papered one wall of Jason's room with diplomas, certificates, medals, pictures from Boy Scouts, Kung Fu and Tai Chi, sailing, school and university. A Greek way of dealing with death, like a tomb dating from the age of Pericles, uncovered this year when they were preparing the Olympic venues, containing a young athlete's prizes, an urn depicting his exploits. Jason's bookshelves and his huge computer are as he left them. But we've put away the extra monitors and cables and spare parts he was always fiddling with. What could we possibly do with the technology? Jason was our connection.

I had counted on Jason being here and he isn't. The other kids are in the States and I can't fault them. They have to live their own lives, just as I did. We get together as often as we can now, despite the tension created by trying to squeeze a year into a week or two. I remember feeling the same when I took the kids to the States to visit my mom and dad. We're trying to close the hole Jason left. We baptized Alexi's little blond son, who reminds us so much of Jason. But it's not that we belong to Greece or belong to the States. We seem to have moved beyond such loyalties.

As I climb out on the beach I find a piece of marble—is it fluted? The rocks feel polished, no longer foreign under my feet, as I walk up the spiny ridge where my clothes hang. I towel glittering pearls of sea off my back, pull on my tracksuit and wipe the coarse sand off my feet. I fold my towel into a tidy roll.

The heavy clouds have broken up. No more shafts of white light or ascent of angels, but the sea is filigreed like a silver icon. Suddenly, I am up the steps to the road without the sensation of having used my legs. I head home.

Laurel Mantzaris *was born and raised outside of Chicago. Equipped with an English degree from Beloit College and some high school teaching experience, she set off to see Europe with a friend in the mid-sixties. When her friend returned to the States, she stayed in Athens, teaching English as a second language. She married a Greek citizen and has been in Greece since—raising her family, teaching, learning, writing, and, of course, swimming.*

Eurosaturn

Scott Williams

We like our little car. It's not a commuter car, but more of a weekend-mobile. It therefore represents physical freedom, fun, and leisure. Most often the cargo it carries includes cross-country skis, bikes, and backpacks. The most important roadside emergency items are always at the ready in the glove box: a pair of compact 10X binoculars and a copy of Peterson's Guide to Western Birds, in case we spot one of our feathered friends in the distance while on the road.

As humble as it is, this car's a luxury for us. It's a four-door Saturn wagon, made with pride in Spring Hill, Tennessee. As a model year 2000, it is by our standards still essentially new. It's seen a lot in its young life. It was purchased in Utah. It dutifully dragged a U-Haul trailer, packed full, all the way from Salt Lake City to Anchorage. It's been ferried from Alaska down the west coast, through the Panama Canal, across the Atlantic to Hamburg. It even got to ride in a big transport truck trailer down the length of Germany to our former dwelling in Switzerland.

We still marvel at all the details that one must sweat when moving house, especially for an international move. Having learned through our previous moves, we try to stay on top of all the regulations pertinent to customs, taxes, licenses, registration, identification—everything. This is why, after our move from the hills between Geneva and Lausanne up to Stuttgart, but well before our Swiss vehicle registration expired, I had gathered as much car-relevant documentation as possible into a folder, and whistled a happy-go-lucky tune as I drove down to the *Stuttgart Technische Überwachungsverein* (TÜV) to get our car inspected for its registration in Germany.

Herr Thiessen was our car's inspector that day. He paced pensive circles around our car like a shark, apparently taking in its distinct and unusual non-Europeanness as he mentally kicked the tires. I stood aside, ready to field any questions Herr Thiessen might throw my way.

In my hand I clutched my folder full of documentation. Inside this folder was our growing collection of any and all forms that could be even remotely useful to today's exercise; a product of natural habit reinforced by time spent in rule-loving Switzerland. As I watched Herr Thiessen circle our little station wagon, the folder in my hand was reassurance and empowerment on paper to me. I could almost see it glow.

Our car straddled a large trench from which various questions and comments emerged as Herr Thiessen tapped on this, and jiggled that from beneath the chassis. His words were soggy with a thick Schwäbisch accent. Nothing he said or asked during the inspection led me to think we'd have to correct much beyond a few thin brake pads. Indeed, the whole process in the TÜV garage was panning out in a manner quite similar to our successful experience at the station in Lausanne, where my wife had elegantly dealt with the inspector's questions in French just a couple years prior. This would be a cinch.

When Herr Thiessen had finished, I was told to park the car around back, and return inside to wrap up some paperwork. I sat down and began to leaf through some back issues of TÜV's monthly magazine. Nearly two hours passed.

Finally Herr Thiessen emerged with papers in hand. He apologized for the time spent waiting, as he'd been busy researching potentially helpful telephone contacts for me that might help me solve all the problems with our car.

Problems?

He produced an 11-point list of things that required attention before we could proceed with our car's registration process in Stuttgart. Some items were simple and logical:

-REPLACE TIRES (ALL FOUR)

-REPLACE BRAKEPADS (ALL SETS)

Good. This we could do, and it's always nice to have new tires and brakes. No problem.

Other items, however, were seemingly pointless:

-REMOVE TRAILER HITCH COUPLING

This would involve the laborious extraction of the rather large, yet nearly invisible black bar that had been bolted, welded and otherwise irreversibly annealed to our car's undercarriage. Not wishing to appear argumentative with this TÜV inspector with whom I'd so far built good rapport, I tactfully inquired why, but was unable to coax an answer from him that went beyond "just because." Another item:

-EMISSIONS KEYING REQUIRED, ENGINE HAS NO KEY NUMBER

The first two words were my translation of *Abgasschlüsselung,* and I have yet to find a more appropriate term; there seems to be no single English word that embodies this idea. Herr Thiessen explained that all cars registered in Germany must have a two-digit key number for their engine. Our car posed a particular problem, as no such key number exists for our strictly American automobile. He gave me the phone number for the TÜV station in Böblingen, just southwest of Stuttgart. I was instructed to call to schedule an appointment for an Abgasschlüsselung there, as apparently these tests were not done at the Stuttgart TÜV. Herr Thiessen explained that the engine needed to be removed from the car, quite an undertaking, usually taking about two days and costing about €750. The list's final point stated:

-HEADLAMP LIGHT DISTRIBUTION TEST DATA ERRATIC

Another yellow slip of paper in Herr Thiessen's handwriting gave the phone number of a certain Professor Gärtner at the Institute of Light Technology at the University of Karlsruhe. I was told to call the professor to arrange an appointment for a headlamp test, as the TÜV instrumentation that day had given inconclusive data. Data regarding just what, I did not know. The test itself would cost €100. If the headlamps passed, then we'd be given a certificate of some sort, and an all-clear on this particular issue. If not, it might be possible for the team in Karlsruhe to fix them for about €600–€800 maybe—Herr Thiessen didn't really know.

Herr Thiessen wished me good luck before I drove our car off the parking lot of the TÜV station, where I had just witnessed the most colossal vehicle inspection failure conceivable. The 11-point list contaminated my otherwise empowering folder of official documents, receipts and clearances. The glow was gone.

Undaunted, I began the long process of ticking items off the list. The most expensive batch of repairs cleared several of the 11 points in one fell swoop. They were easily handled by a local Opel garage, and for the most part, were easy for us to accept in our hearts and minds: new brake pads, new tires. To address some rather bizarre, but no less mandatory items, two additional red reflectors were installed on the back of our car, along with a *Nebellicht,* a type of fog light, which in this case is just a little red lamp beneath the rear bumper. Our car came away with new tires, new brakes, and an abominated backside that would make an ambulance appear modest by comparison.

I drove out of the Opel garage lot €1,300 lighter. In the meantime, I had scheduled a two-day appointment at the TÜV in Böblingen for an Abgasschlüsselung. They'd be able to take me in about three weeks' time. Three weeks? How long was this car-registration project going to last? I began pining for the reasonable simplicity of the US and Swiss auto inspection regulations.

Out of concern and curiosity, I asked the technician in Böblingen what this test would involve. His answer was sadly the same as that of Herr Thiessen: the motor would be removed, tested, and re-installed. Almost desperate to avoid such a ridiculous fate, I pressed on, asking what kind of information one gets from an Abgasschlüsselung, and how it differs from the results of a normal, reasonable, rational, and earthly 10-minute standard emissions test. I was told that removal of the engine allows one to detect and quantify the same gasses as in a standard emissions test, but with more detail. Having lost the will to press further, I simply thanked the man for his help, said I'd see him in three weeks, and concluded with a meek and gravelly *"aufwiederhören"* before hanging up.

I'd heard stories about the strict rules that are the foundation of modern German car culture, but somehow thought our nearly new set of wheels would comply with no more than a few tweaks here and there, and maybe a little spit-shine. Was all this really going to make our car more roadworthy? The inconsistency is what really ate at me: our car was perfectly legal in Germany with its current Swiss plates. If we were able to somehow renew our Swiss registration, we'd be able to drive our car in Germany as-is for the foreseeable future. How could this be?

Over the next few days, as I cooled off, I kept ringing Professor Gärtner's number daily with no answer. When I finally managed to get through, he explained that he'd been on holiday, but that he would be able to conduct my headlamp test the following day. Excellent! Another little step in the right direction, and although we were definitely not yet in the clear, the 11-point list from TÜV was beginning to seem a bit less insurmountable. After all, some of the more expensive points had been checked off already, hadn't they?

As per the professor's request, I arrived at his office at the Institute in Karlsruhe with an entire headlamp casing, lens, bulbs and all. I had parked the car on a street just off the university campus, and had endured the suspicious and prolonged glances of passers-by as I extracted the passenger-side headlamp from its socket.

Wet with rain, hands smudged in road grit, I followed Professor Gärtner down two flights of stairs to his headlamp testing laboratory in the building's basement.

We entered an elongated room with desks and tables upon which sat at least 50 headlamps of various shapes and sizes. Each one was tagged with its respective auto year, make and model, and what appeared to be the last names of their owners. I put two and two together right away: these tables were full of €600–€800 fix-it jobs! This is where our headlamps would end up, and for God-knows-how-long.

Professor Gärtner clamped our car's extracted headlamp to a large, computer-controlled positioning stage and connected a pair of leads from an electric supply box to the bulbs. He aimed the light toward a square opening in a large panel across the room, and after about ten minutes of fine-tuning its position just so, he killed the room lights, and turned on the power box. The headlamp's beam splashed across the panel's white surface. Another ten minutes passed as the professor fiddled with parameters in his computer's software. At last, a little sigh from the professor. He told me that there was unfortunately nothing that could be done about our headlights; the way the lenses were distributing the light simply did not conform to EU standards. It would even be impossible for them to try to make the requisite adjustments.

My parting question to the professor: What should we do now? He told me that if I could manage to find headlamps from an EU-approved car that just so happened to fit well enough into the light sockets of our own car, then we'd very likely be in good shape. I was told to search auto parts stores, or even better: junkyards.

It took a minute for all this to sink in. I had visions of a pair of headlamps from an old VW secured to our car's sockets with duct tape and twine to meet the exacting standards of the TÜV. This would be a fitting supplement to a complete engine removal and replacement, the holes and gashes left from the bolted/welded trailer hitch coupling having been torn away, and a Nebellicht. If our car wasn't roadworthy before the TÜV, I sure couldn't imagine it being any better in its post-TÜV days.

And if we couldn't find appropriate replacement headlamps? The professor smiled sadly and shrugged, saying that we'd simply not be able to register our car in Germany. As a sort of consolation, he waived the €100 testing fee. That was kind, but it increased my fear a bit. It was a gesture that said, just save what cash you can, my friend—you're gonna need it. We promptly canceled the Abgasschlüsselung appointment at the Böblingen TÜV, pending success with the jury-rigged headlamp project.

My initial plan of attack took me to the auto parts stores. Lots of auto parts stores. I had expected to see aisles flanked with shelves chock full of new headlamps yearning to be browsed. Instead, most of the stores seemed to operate by special order, with only a marginal selection of lights off-the-shelf. For any normal human with a normal car, who knows exactly what kind of headlamp they need, this system works, and saves a mess of shelf space and stocking costs. But I was the owner of a very abnormal car, and was beginning to question my normalcy as a human. Each clerk at each store was rearing to type our car's make and model into their computer system to see if they had the right headlamps available to ship in.

None wanted to believe me as I explained they wouldn't find it in their databases, and I obliged them by playing along. How many times I've spelled out S-A-T-U-R-N in German, I cannot tell. (Yes, like the planet...) I gave up on the stores.

My heart quickly regained its weight. Interestingly, however, Professor Gärtner's hunch was right: the Stuttgart area junkyards came much closer to providing a solution to our problem, and my sense of encouragement returned a bit. I was told of one place in the southern part of town that had an extensive supply of used and restored headlights. They were even open Saturdays.

The following Saturday came. Indeed the junkyard about which I'd been so enthusiastic just a few days previously was quite well-stocked with a wide array of headlamps, all of which were EU-approved. None, however, would even come close to fitting our car's headlamp sockets.

I finally snapped.

But did I fly into a rage? Did I laugh hysterically? Did I fall to my knees, bury my face in the thick fur of the junkyard dog and cry shamelessly? Nope. It actually felt good. It was the moment I knew this Quixotic quest was ... well ... Quixotic, and therefore over.

So it was official then, at least in my mind. No more chasing down elusive car parts. No more technicians or appointments. No more paperwork, and thankfully no more telephone calls. I gave the old German shepherd a little pat and left the junkyard lot in surprisingly good spirits. Within a span of just a few seconds, I had managed to reach the plane of acceptance toward this situation with no more than a second or two devoted to denial, fear, frustration, and anger. (This was no small feat in on-the-fly self-psychotherapy, especially for a stereotypical car-loving American male accustomed to having a set of wheels at his disposal.) I suppose I'd been experiencing a sufficient mixture of those emotions over the previous several weeks that near-immediate acceptance of failure was the next natural and automatic step to take.

I accepted the fact that we'd have to ship the car back overseas, and somehow that seemed the best solution. Our car would simply be deported. My wife and I had our work/residence permits, but our car would be kicked out of the country. It's a Saturn. It belongs on North American soil. Furthermore, it would be spared the humiliating fate of jury-rigged headlights and an engine extraction that still, in my opinion, defied all notions of rational thought.

And what would become of our deported car? Surely, some (possibly still-disbelieving) family member or friend back in the States would get some use out of a car freshly equipped with new brakes, new tires, new reflectors and a handy little Nebellicht.

Scott Williams is a native of Boulder, Colorado. He and his Canadian wife met in graduate school in Utah. They made their first big move together to Anchorage, Alaska. A year later, they crossed the Atlantic and moved into an old farmhouse in the Swiss Jura Mountains. Their most recent move was northward, across the Rhine River to Stuttgart, Germany, where both currently work as scientific editors.

The Importance of Home

My tears in the movie theater reflected the momentary loss of this center. It takes time and care to tend the hearth fire.

Susan M. Tiberghien

Not long after signing on to Swiss life permanently, my enthusiasm started to crack. Little fissures of homesickness and displeasure marred my perfectly molded life. I sought out company for my misery and found plenty. All I had to do was take a French class.

Catherine L. Hayoz

As I sat on my parents' deck in Marin County, I could fix myself a bowl of chicory coffee (a bowl, not a mug!) and have the Proustian madeleine moment of believing that I was back in my Parisian apartment.

Shelby A. Marcus-Ocana

Seeking a Hearth and Finding a Home

Susan M. Tiberghien

Recently in colonial Williamsburg, I watched the film at the Visitors' Center on early life in the colony. At the height of the movie, the Virginian leaders initiate the roll call for independence. Each person must choose between America and England. An older statesman announces his decision to leave Virginia: "I am going home," he says to a friend. The younger statesman looks at him and replies, "I am home."

Tears welled up in my eyes. I had left America close to forty years earlier to move to Europe with my French husband. We were now on vacation at my mother's home in Williamsburg. In that small movie theater I asked myself, where was home? On one side of me sat my mother—representing my roots, my country and language. On the other side sat my husband—representing my present life, my adopted country and language. Which way was home?

I was lost. I had lived in many homes, in America and then in Europe—France, Belgium, Italy, Switzerland. I was rich in the memories of homes, so why was I crying? I thought of Hestia, the mythological goddess of the hearth, the symbol of the home. Hestia's role was to keep the hearth fire burning. In the middle of each house there was a hearth, and if ever the fire went out, the house was no longer a home. And likewise in the middle of each Greek city, there was a hearth in front of the temple. And if ever the fire went out, the city was no longer home to its citizens.

As a modern day Hestia, I needed my hearth fire. It had not been easy to leave my home and country. At first Pierre and I lived in his parents' home. There was a hearth, but it was not mine; it was my mother-in-law's, in her house, in her living room. When Pierre left for military service, the house felt cold. I was lonely and far from home.

When we moved to a furnished apartment in southern France, there was a pot-bellied wood stove between the kitchen and the one other room. Pierre was often at the air base, and I had a hard time heating the apartment and keeping the wood fire burning. When our first baby was born, in the middle of winter, my next-door neighbor tended the fire for me. Each morning she came and poked the pieces of wood around until they glowed warmly the rest of the day. I was finding a home.

Pierre's next job took us to Belgium, where we found a large unfurnished house in a suburb of Brussels, close to a quiet street corner. It was summertime, people were on vacation, there was no traffic. But after the holidays, the people came back, and the cars and trucks came back with them. The busy traffic seemed to drive right through the middle of our house. We tried to filter out the noise, closing the windows and doors, lining the curtains, closing the shutters. The house still didn't feel like home.

In the spring we moved into a smaller place, a ground floor apartment on a small narrow street. There was a little courtyard in the back, with a circular path, where the children played happily. And inside, there was a coal furnace. We brought up a pail of coal every morning from the large bin in the basement. It was easier to keep a coal fire burning evenly than a wood one. The apartment was warm and it felt like home.

When we moved to Italy with three young children and settled into an apartment overlooking Lago Maggiore, I learned about the ritual of house-blessing. Early one Saturday morning, the parish priest, dressed in his black robe, arrived and asked if he could bless our new apartment. He walked from room to room, sprinkling holy water and chasing evil spirits. Each of the four years we lived there, Don Francesco came to bless our apartment, to help us keep our house a home.

From Italy we went to Switzerland, to a fifth-floor apartment in a new high-rise building near the airport in Geneva. There were no house-blessings. We tried instead a house-warming party to warm the entire building. Our children distributed the invitations. Everyone came but no one gave another party. We never called the apartment home.

After our sixth child arrived, we moved into a house near the Jura mountains, on the other side of the border in France. The house dated back to the sixteenth century, with an immense open fire and stone seats on either side of the blackened chimney. We lived there during most of the high school years of our children. The fireplace was in a large open room between the kitchen and the living room. We put our dining room table in front of it, and from September to the end of the school year in June, we kept a wood fire burning there—in the center of our home.

With each move, I learned better how to care for a new house. When we returned to Switzerland, we first put in place our dining room table, the antique oval table with enough leaves for family and friends. The table had been with us since Belgium. I then collected a bouquet of wild flowers, some daisies and butter-cups, and put them in a pewter vase in the middle of the table. We were home. The dining room table had become our hearth.

Now that our children have grown up, the table is smaller, the leaves are stored in the hall closet, but it is still the center of our home. It's where Pierre and I first sit down in the morning, where I read the newspaper and the mail, where I have a friend for lunch or eat alone, surrounded by windows and rose bushes and trees. It's where Pierre comes home in the evening, and we sit down to listen to one another and have supper. And when all the leaves are put back in place, it's where we welcome back our children and our young grandchildren for Christmas, for a holiday, for a weekend, for an anniversary.

My tears in the movie theater reflected the momentary loss of this center. It takes time and care to tend the hearth fire. After my annual visits each summer to my mother in Virginia, when I return to Switzerland, the house will at first feel cold and full of shadows. I will pull back the curtains, open the doors, dust off the shelves and books and photographs. I will cut some flowers from the yard, a few pink roses or some of the last petunias, and arrange them in the vase on the table, making my offering to Hestia. Soon our house will feel like home again.

Without this feeling of home around me, I still grow homesick. Then I know it is time to look within. It is time to find the hearth fire inside me and take care of it. And so I sit quietly and close my eyes. I go for a walk in the woods and watch the autumn leaves turn gold. I listen to music. I write at my desk. When the bouquet of fresh flowers becomes a prayer of the heart, then I can say, wherever I am, that I am home.

Susan M. Tiberghien, an American writer living in Switzerland, has published three memoirs, Looking for Gold, Circling to the Center, Footsteps—A European Album, *and numerous essays in journals and anthologies in the United States and in Europe. She teaches workshops for the International Women's Writing Guild, C.G. Jung Centers, and the Geneva Writers' Group and Conferences on both sides of the ocean.*

Finding Home

Catherine L. Hayoz

I have a pot of edelweiss growing on my balcony. I have four boxes of brownie mix in the cupboard. I have an American flag in the kitchen and a Swiss one in the dining room. I have a husband, a daughter and a cat. I have an apartment in Geneva. I have a room in the States. But I don't have one single place I call home.

"You'll like him." Nathalie shoved a small picture at me, one that was dark and underexposed. The man in the picture wasn't more than a smudge of pale peach, his black shirt and hair blending in with the background.

"Umm. I don't think so." I gave the picture back to her and rubbed my eyes for a minute, suffering from jet-lag. I gazed around at the unfamiliar kitchen, with the pale yellow tiles and a refrigerator smaller than my nightstand. We were in Nathalie's aunt's apartment, in Geneva, Switzerland. Nathalie was here for a year. I was here for two weeks.

"The picture's bad. When you see him you'll like him. I know you." She was talking about her cousin, Laurent. I wasn't interested: I lived in Racine, Wisconsin. He lived in Geneva. I didn't care to have a long-distance relationship.

But when he walked in the door I changed my mind.

We could barely speak to each other, yet when I got home we started writing. First letters, then e-mails, passed over the ocean. We visited each other, never saying we'd commit to an intercultural relationship for life. But five years, four French classes and several long visits later, we decided to get married.

When I said, "I do," I knew nothing would be the same again. I knew that living in Switzerland would be a challenge. I knew that I would miss my family. I knew that I would miss my country, with the 24-hour grocery stores, the chocolate chip cookies and the big yards. I knew but I figured it would be fine, because Switzerland, Geneva especially, had many good trade-offs, like four-week minimum vacation time, shopping within walking distance and zillions of parks. But I knew all this in the same way that you know having a child will change your life: you have absolutely no idea.

I started off a zealot. I *loved* Geneva; I *loved* Switzerland; I *loved* Europe. I loved, I loved, I loved. I bought anything I could find with the Swiss flag on it. The red background and the white cross took up residence in my closets, my cupboards, my bookshelves. I praised the public transportation, the apartment living, the closing of businesses on Sundays. I was on a high. I soared, drunk on my decision to live on Swiss soil. But as they say, what goes up must come down.

Not long after signing on to Swiss life permanently, my enthusiasm started to crack. Little fissures of homesickness and displeasure marred my perfectly molded life. I sought out company for my misery and found plenty. All I had to do was take a French class.

My cracks opened to crevices with prodding from my new foreign friends. We all took the same class, Monday through Friday from nine to twelve. Among us were a Spaniard, a Brazilian, a Mexican, two Japanese, three British and a German. We sat around a shiny Formica table at break-time, sucking the cream from éclairs and complaining about the Swiss, and most of all, the Genevois. They were snooty. They couldn't form lines. They were too damn punctual. Even the things I had loved only weeks before became cause for complaint: the buses were crowded; the neighbors were cold; there was nowhere to buy fancy boots on a Sunday.

It didn't take me long to hit bottom. My first public breakdown came only three months into my Swiss adventure. All the complaining about the Swiss got me thinking of how great things were back home in Wisconsin. I missed my life there. I missed my family. I missed the newspaper being thrown onto the front porch with a thud; I missed wide streets and huge parking spots; I missed the squeak of the back screen door in the summer; I missed my youngest nephew's pudgy hands and my oldest niece's jokes; I missed Stove Top Stuffing and Cool Whip and Oreos. I missed it all so much I'd gone to the American grocery store and spent the equivalent of twelve dollars on a box of cinnamon graham crackers and one can of Dr. Pepper.

I was grasping for things to remind me of home. So when Laurent suggested going to the cinema I agreed right away even though the film would be in French. It wasn't the movie that interested me, it was the movie popcorn. I hadn't had it for months, since I had left Wisconsin, and just the thought of getting it made me miss home a bit less.

It was all I could think about as I slipped on my eyeliner and spritzed on perfume. I could remember a lifetime of Friday evenings at the cinema, my fingers greasy with butter, my lips parched with salt.

We'd decided to go see some film that was only playing in the small theater near our apartment. We left early so we could get there with enough time to buy popcorn. We kissed on our way, Laurent glad to see me happy, me happy to be getting a slice of home. It was the perfect night: newlyweds out on a date, ready to share a huge tub of popcorn in a darkened theater. But then we stepped into the foyer.

Laurent paid for the tickets and eyed the small lobby. He turned to the man ripping up our tickets and asked, "Do you sell popcorn?"

"No." The movie guy shook his head and pointed to the freezer in the corner. "But we sell ice cream."

"What!?!" I screamed. "Ice cream! They don't sell popcorn?!? What kind of *#/&! theater is this?!?"

My disappointment crushed me quickly and noisily, like a candy wrapper. No popcorn at the cinema? Where the hell was I, anyways? God, I missed home. I started to gasp and ran to the rest room, where I sobbed. I let my emotions pulverize me right there in the cramped bathroom of the tiny theater. When I finally opened the door and walked back into the lobby, I fell into Laurent's arms. An ache in me shifted a bit and opened wider, like a fault line. I loved my husband, but I wondered what I had done moving to Geneva.

After the movie incident, my zeal for all things Swiss was replaced by sudden American patriotism. I told my mom to send me a red, white and blue t-shirt. I decorated my bathroom with Green Bay Packers paraphernalia. I bought a US flag and hung it in the dining room. I learned the words to Stars and Stripes Forever.

That first year Laurent and I went to the Fourth of July party put on by the American International Club. We climbed the stairs to the bleachers and sat down to watch an American marching band perform on the soccer field. At the first thud of the drums and the first swirl of the baton, I thought I would fall apart. I silently wiped the tears from my eyes, but my body shook violently. Red, white and blue ribbons swirled on the turf below me, brass instruments bleating proudly under the Swiss sky. Twenty-five years of picnics by the Root River and fireworks on Lake Michigan were packed into the notes of The Star Spangled Banner. Twenty-five years that would soon seem distant to me as I was already becoming someone I didn't recognize. Someone who changed with every minute spent across the ocean. I continued to cry and when I looked around I saw I was not alone. A middle-aged woman one row down from me was wiping her eyes with a mangled tissue; a young couple to my left clung to each other: his eyes open too wide, unblinking, her face hidden by the folds of his shirt. I imagine there were several of us whose hearts broke with the music that day.

Time passed. I still wasn't sure I could call Geneva home. I was pregnant and just the thought of raising my child away from my family and my country terrified me. I grew up with crickets singing me to sleep in June, carved pumpkins on the front stoop in October and a life-sized snowman in the backyard in January. How would my child survive in a city and an apartment building without these things? How would I?

After giving birth to my daughter, I decided it was time for another trip back to the States. It had been more than a year since I'd been there. I was ready.

The night before we left I shoved three more pairs of socks into my suitcase and asked Laurent, "What would you think of moving to the States?"

He'd had a can of Coke to his mouth. Now he stopped drinking, but kept it by his lips, until slowly, slowly he brought it down to the coffee table. Just as slowly he said, "Because you want to move there?"

"I just want to know, that's all." I feigned nonchalance as I squeezed a pair of underwear into my carry-on.

"Well, you know I will if it's what you really want. But you need to be sure. There's too much to lose." He said it calmly, but there was terror in his eyes.

I nodded. Yes, there was a lot to lose if we moved: his job (which he loved), a great relationship with my in-laws, all that vacation time and the peace of living in a neutral country. Not to mention the chocolate. But I just wanted to go to the States with a different eye this time. With the idea it could possibly be home for me once more.

The next day I hugged my daughter close as the plane circled Chicago, the lake and the Sears tower shining brightly in the afternoon sun. "This is where Mommy is from, baby. This is where Mommy really feels at home," I whispered into her hair. I was back in the States. Back to the land of movie popcorn and big cars. Back to life under the stars and stripes. Back to where I knew who I was.

But only hours after our landing, I realized that something was wrong back in Wisconsin, too. We ordered a party pizza from my favorite restaurant. I scooped up a huge piece and bit into it greedily. And I was disappointed. The rest of my family raved about it. I chewed the spiced rubber and thought how much better the pizza was back in Geneva. I set it down in its pool of grease and picked off the mushrooms to eat instead.

The next day I was to meet a friend at the mall, but the car wouldn't start. My dad was at his art class with the other car and the bus system in our town wasn't exactly efficient.

"No big deal. I'll walk. I do it all the time at home in Geneva."

My mother studied me, assessing my mental state. "Are you crazy? You could get killed out there. There are no crosswalks. There are no sidewalks. You aren't supposed to go there on foot!"

She was right, of course. My hometown, and most of the United States, I assume, is not pedestrian friendly. Throughout my trip, I found myself going from car to building to building to car, barely walking at all. I could feel the pounds slathering themselves all over my hips and thighs. In Geneva, I drove maybe three times a month. In the States I drove three times a day, or more. In Geneva having to walk more than ten minutes to get to the stores seems outrageous. And more than five to the grocery store means you live in the boondocks. But back in Wisconsin I needed the car to go just about everywhere. My life was dependant on the state of my engine.

Things like that began to irritate me. The perfect image of my country that I had built up in my mind began to fade. Things that used to seem normal now struck me as weird or even unthinkable: I couldn't believe the size of servings in restaurants, I felt lost in the homes with twelve rooms for two people, the constant commercial breaks on TV gave me a headache and the violence in the schools worried me. Was I sure I wanted to call this place home again?

We went back to Geneva. Soon after, I met an American friend for lunch at the *boulangerie* beneath my apartment. She was debating whether or not to marry her Swiss boyfriend, whether or not they would live in Geneva.

"Oh, God. I can't live here. The people are so rude. Can you believe the clerks at the stores? And there's no place to shop on Sunday. And what about the parking? I circled around almost 45 minutes just to find a spot by the library." She picked unknown ingredients off her sandwich. "Eew! What kind of cheese is this?"

I knew something in me had changed because I wanted to tell my friend to stop whining: if she didn't like the life here then she should go back. I wanted to tell her to stop comparing Switzerland to the States because there was no comparison—they were two different cultures—and if she ever wanted to be happy here she would have to stop complaining and start enjoying. But I didn't. I just nodded and checked the amount of cream in my éclair. I'd been in her place, and I knew that the whining was a phase to go through, one that, hopefully for her, wouldn't last too long.

It was then that it hit me, immersed in the delicious scent of just-baked bread, the thick, sweet cream of the éclair on my tongue: I wasn't going back to the States. I liked it here in Switzerland. I liked my in-laws, the Sundays spent outdoors, the buses, the food. I was going to enjoy my life and accept being here. I still wasn't sure if it was home, but it was where I would most likely spend the rest of my life.

A few months later, Laurent and I stood in front of a bonfire for the national Swiss holiday on August 1st. Heat pushed against our cheeks, foreheads and upper arms. I held a ceramic bowl in my hands, the gift for buying the traditional vegetable soup. Children had just come back from parading around the block with their lampions and were now waving them in the air, the thin red and white paper glowing in the darkness. My daughter pointed at them in delight. As the first fireworks shot into the air, I felt my chest constrict and tears sting my eyes. I felt this memory graft itself to my brain, thinking twenty-five years from this moment I would not only remember a childhood of picnics by the Root River and fireworks on Lake Michigan but an adulthood of soup among a crowd and bonfires in the summer heat.

I realized I would never know where to call home. I laughed, but wanted to cry. I belonged to nowhere and at the same time to two countries.

I know this is responsible for my feeling like a see-saw at times; my affections for one country change place with the affections for the other on a regular basis. I feel embarrassed at the lingering talk of the Swiss gold scandal and I consider putting my American t-shirts in storage with Bush winning a second term.

But I know that I can love both Switzerland and the States. And at times I can hate them both as well. But they will both be a part of me always.

I have a large bed with a Swiss duvet and an American quilt. I have a schedule for workshops on how to play the Alp horn and another for classes on country line dancing. I have a husband, a daughter and a cat. I have an apartment in Geneva. I have a room in the States. I don't have one single place I call home; I have two.

Catherine L. Hayoz was born in Racine, Wisconsin as the youngest of six children. Always a homebody, she surprised everyone (especially herself) when she married a Swiss man and moved away to Switzerland in 1998. She lives in Geneva with her husband and daughter. She writes short stories, essays and poems and is currently working on a novel.

Nostalgia

Shelby A. Marcus-Ocana

The presence of yet another icon of American consumer habits on French soil—joining the ranks of Gap, Esprit, McDonald's et al—has me reminiscing about the days when we Americans-in-Paris were hard-pressed to find anything from our native land over here in our adopted one.

I expatriated myself in 1980. Global marketing was in its infancy and the internet did not exist as we know it today. A few American companies had made inroads in getting their product to market in France: one could find Coca-Cola (although the mix was tailored to local tastes, i.e., less sweet and never served on ice), and McDonald's was just setting up on the Champs-Elysees (later to be fined for allowing dogs on the premises; they shut their doors for a bit but reemerged with a new policy). I would always take an empty suitcase on my trips to America, with the intention of filling it with all that I missed and could not find an adequate substitute for in Paris. These items fell into two categories: foodstuffs (peanut butter, Reese's Peanut Butter cups, Hershey's Kisses, Lucky Charms) and health and beauty products (Crest toothpaste, Vidal Sasson shampoo, deodorant).

For my longer stays in the United States, I would do the same in reverse. I would leave France with a suitcase filled with everything I could not find in the States: again, the comestibles (Ricore coffee, 80 percent chocolate cooking chocolate, Carambar candies), and the rest: Dim stockings, Klorane hair supplies, French lingerie.

Oddly, once I had the foreign product in hand in my "other" homeland, I would often refuse to use it for fear of running out, or hoard it for so long that I would surpass the expiration date and have to toss the thing away!

I no longer drag local goods back and forth. I realized after a time that it was not the actual product that I longed for when away from either country, but the country itself. The product was merely a talisman which served to conjure up a memory or illusion of something about that "other place." As I sat on my parents' deck in Marin County, I could fix myself a bowl of chicory coffee (a bowl, not a mug!) and have the Proustian madeleine moment of believing that I was back in my Parisian apartment. And upon my return to France, I could pop a Hershey's Kiss into my mouth while riding the métro and conjure up a memory of sitting in Candlestick Park with my Dad, watching the Giants play ball.

I also realized that I savored the specialness of the separate country/separate product paradigm. Kraft Macaroni and Cheese belongs in America! Runny and ripe Camembert belongs in France! Having access to all goods in all places produced such a pale feeling of sameness. There is a beauty and soul to regional goods. Something that strip malls and ubiquitous branding have left behind.

71

So while I applaud the opening of the Starbucks at the Place de l'Opéra (I like my decaf nonfat latte as much as the next suburban yuppie bitch), I also relish the fact that I can still patronize the little merchant down the street that sells nothing but sea salt from the Guérande. And he has no idea how to export it nor interest in expanding his market share.

Shelby A. Marcus-Ocana has lived and worked in Paris for over twenty years. Born in Marin County, California, she continues to spend her summers in the Bay Area, where she makes it a point to introduce her two bicultural daughters to the joys of Reese's Peanut Butter Cups and Hostess Cupcakes.

Impressions of Youth

What fools the boy's father and I had been! If only we could have kept at bay his black skepticism and my white guilt we could have actually accomplished what we both wanted.

June Appel

I experienced undisciplined children, splintering desks, and cultural confusion everyday…but, you know what? I loved every minute of it, even though every single day I couldn't help but wonder, "What in the world am I doing here?!?"

Chantel Sloan

I was not one or the other; I was both German and American.

Elizabeth Holmes

"Mom, I've got a situation here. I was just riding by the school and I saw Micha with a group of kids. They were smoking. What do I do when she comes home?"

Linda Eisele-Lockett

The perspective that living in Europe and Mexico gave me is one of infinite possibility, open to anything and surprised at nothing.

Liza Monroy

Choose Your Enemies Carefully

June Appel

I was searching for my eight-year-old daughter through the glass doors of her school's lunchroom. A boy approached. I stepped aside waiting for him to pass. He pushed the door open and came out, but he did not pass. Instead, he squared himself in front of me, introduced himself as Aaron and asked, "Are you Aria's mother?"

Aaron's mature and gentle demeanor narrowed the difference between his ten and my forty years. Without rage but with intensity he stated, "I want you to know that Aria said some things to me today that I don't like."

"What did she say?" I asked.

"She called me a black boy."

Adrenaline raced to every 60's-nurtured cell in my flower-child, bleeding-heart-liberal body and silently cried out "Oh my God! My daughter is a racist." But I kept my composure, since this was not the first time Aria had been falsely accused of being a bigot.

The first time, two years earlier, was shortly after we arrived at my husband's new post here in Cairo, Egypt. We were at the American Club when an agitated man appeared, quickly coming to the point. To my horror I learned that Aria, then six, had asked his son, also six, what it was like to pick cotton. When the boy feigned ignorance (in her opinion) she persisted, citing the fact that he was black, therefore a slave, and all slaves knew how to pick cotton.

In a blind-sided act of contrition I disowned my daughter, telling the man I didn't condone her behavior. He, not satisfied, demanded an apology from Aria to his son, in his, the father's, presence. I immediately retrieved Aria from the sandbox and had her comply in trusting confusion.

At home I sat Aria down for a serious talk. My goal? To uncover and uproot her racism. I asked where she'd learned about slaves. "At school," she said. I asked if she knew what a slave was. "Black people who pick cotton on big farms called plant-somethings." Luckily, her naïve enthusiasm wrinkled my brow; something was amiss. I backed off and asked if being a slave was a good or a bad thing. "Oh, Mommy, it's wonderful. There are so many animals on a farm. That's where I want to live when we go to America, but I can't until I learn how to pick cotton."

Immediately the irony of the situation crystallized. What fools the boy's father and I had been! If only we could have kept at bay his black skepticism and my white guilt we could have actually accomplished what we both wanted. But, put to the test, we abandoned lofty goals and considered only how we felt at the expense of our children's color-blindness. I was sorry, but Aria didn't let me off easy.

"Why was my friend's daddy sooooo touchy?" Struggling, I told her slavery was a touchy subject. "No it's not," she reported, confessing how during Passover, she, the only Jewish kid in her class, didn't mind telling her classmates about the Jews who were slaves in Egypt.

I took a deep breath. "Because your friend is black," I said. But she didn't buy it.

Impatient, she recalled her visits to the slave castles in Ghana, West Africa, where black people talked to her about slavery all the time.

Quizzically, head cocked, I added, "and perhaps because they are American?"

Aria, never having lived in the United States, accepted my observation. I, still puzzled, considered the insight half-baked. That is until Aaron, another black American, turned up the heat with his complaint outside the lunchroom.

When Aaron confronted me, I was nervous, but I was also rehearsed. I had the presence of mind to tell him Aria had grown up being called the "white girl" in Ghana, a country where nearly all of her role models, teachers, TV personalities, doctors, politicians, and yes, even her best friends, were black.

I recounted the American Club incident two years earlier and asked Aaron to consider how it would have been if the little boy had said, "I don't know how to pick cotton. Let's go ask my dad." And what if the dad had seized the opportunity to say something like, "Slavery doesn't exist anymore, kids. Machines do that work now. Things are much better. Now run along." But, instead, the dad scraped at the scab of a still-healing historical sore, freeing it to bleed into a current event.

Aaron was intrigued. The idea that it was he, not Aria, who'd made assumptions based on a person's skin color was—well, I wish you could have seen the look on his face.

And I wish I could tell you this story has a happy ending. Sure, in part it does. Aaron and I exchange knowing smiles whenever we cross paths—a narrow intimacy culled from one profound encounter. And this is good, very good.

But alas, Aria's innocence was mortally wounded. And how did it perish? It was the truth, I'm afraid, that did it in. It couldn't survive the knowledge that it's seen as "just teasing" when a black boy calls her a freckle-faced girl, but it's not the same when she, a freckle-faced white girl, calls him a black boy. Aria used to ask, "What's the difference?" Now she "just knows" that there is one.

June Appel is a tourist. Wanting to fulfill her every dream without going bankrupt, her husband, Bob Wuertz, joined the Foreign Service. Over the next 18 years they traveled the world while raising their three children, Halley, Aria and Matt. They have lived in Saudi Arabia, Ghana, Cairo and now the Philippines. June writes for Inklings, the American Women's Club magazine and is completing work on a book, Emails from the Velvet Trenches.

Charting a Path Along
Those Cobblestone Streets

Chantel Sloan

When I first set foot on American soil after having spent two years of my life in a little country called Bulgaria, I remember quite clearly how over-stimulated my poor eyes were. The first time, after my return, that I went into a "Target" store, my entire body shook with anticipation and my eyeballs began to spring right from my head as I took it all in: "It's so ... RED!" I exclaimed deliriously as I took off like a madwoman. "Look, Ma, look at all the colors and the pretty signs ... oooh, oooh! That man over there is actually taking a picture with his phone!" It really is amazing how much technology can progress while you're living the unhurried life in a tiny Eastern European country that struggles to keep up with this fast-paced world; I am still in awe over all of the color and vividness in America after living a life nearly void of color. To this day, a year and nine months later, I am still astonished by all of the choices I have every time I walk into the grocery store: "Wow, look at all of the cheese ... more than two options and they're not all made with goat's milk!" I look upon my experiences as a Peace Corps Volunteer in Bulgaria with humbled fondness, through all of the joys and frustrations, and I don't think I would trade those two years for anything.

As I prepared to board the airplane in June of 2001, I lifted my chin in stubborn determination and gazed into the uncertain and concerned eyes of my parents and brother. "C-c-c-come and v-visit meee," I sniffled to my parents with one last meager wave. I dawdled my way down the boarding ramp wondering, "What in the world have I gotten myself into?!? Where in the world am I going and what awaits me there?!?" I was absolutely clueless as I made my way to my seat, a lump the size of Mt. Everest forming in my throat. As I climbed nervously into my seat and prepared for take-off, that was when the floodgates really broke loose. Have you ever had the misfortune of sitting next to a crying child on an airplane? Well, try sitting next to a crying adult! "Honey, are you okay?" the old woman next to me asked cautiously. "I just joined the P-P-Peace Corps!" I blubbered inconsolably. "I'm moving to B-B-B-BULGARIA for two years! Waaahhh!!" She nodded sympathetically as she handed me a Kleenex to catch the salty tears and the strings of snot dribbling from my erupting nose. "What in the world have I gotten myself into?!?" I questioned with a sob. I was so uncertain about what truly lay ahead, considering that just a few months before I, the ever-clueless American, barely even knew where Bulgaria was on a map.

As I entered into my service as an English teacher, I cannot deny my lonely tears, my exuberant laughter, my anguished frustrations and adventures at the hands of a society that still struggles to progress and be accepted. I trudged determinedly through my ten weeks of pre-service training, embracing my new culture and its people with gusto. I quickly became an intricate part of my host family as my little host sister Iva took me (and my Bulgarian language training!) under her wings. Every day, after hours of language, culture, and job training, I would trudge to my new home engaging in deadly arguments with my gurgling stomach. *"Toughen up!"* I'd chastise with a vicious glare. *"You know you're going to have to slurp down some more grease-intoxicated meatballs and seizure-inducing rakiya (gin) as soon as we get home anyway! Come on, be a "man," I think we could live without yet another trip to the toilet again today!"*

My mind would be mush as I'd make my way up that steep hill home, the hot sun beating down upon my wrinkled brow and my feet wondering if we would ever get there. I was always certain that my brain couldn't handle an ounce more of the Bulgarian language, but I knew I would get home and my host family would want to speak in nothing BUT until I would cry out in mercy! During many of those long walks home, pounding sneakers on the rutted, cobblestone street would interrupt my thoughts. "Chantel! Kako (Big Sister)!" a little voice would cry as two little arms would fly around my waist. Then, I'd take a little hand in mine, all else forgotten, and Iva and I would trek the rest of the way home together, hand-in-hand.

One of my favorite activities while in Bulgaria was hanging out from a balcony that overlooked our street with my host sister (and sometimes my host mom), watching the neighborhood pass us by. Often, we'd fill our mouths with fresh sunflower seeds, which literally came straight from the sunflower, and spit them onto the cobblestone street below with ferocity. As we chewed and spit, spit and chewed, a goat herder usually walked by with his herd on their evening walk, and we would see who could spit a slimy shell onto a goat first. The goats would hobble along, oblivious, stopping regularly to do what goats do, and they often stopped to nibble at whatever looked tasty on the side of the road, whether it was hay, grass, other goats, or small, defenseless children. They would nibble until a determined herder would nudge them with a sharp stick. The sights, the sounds, and the smells ... these are all things I will never forget about my Bulgarian adventure.

As my training came to an end and my adventures as an English teacher began, the roller coaster of emotions that they had informed us about during training strapped me in for a wild ride. I struggled to get acquainted with my communist-block apartment, my new town, and those unruly Bulgarian students. Every day, I meekly made my way through the corridors of that worn-out structure called my school and it seemed as if every child and teacher would stare at me as if I were a flea under a microscope. My sixth-graders were all taller than I was. I could barely understand my colleagues, the students' books were old and the teachers' books were all in Bulgarian. I didn't have any resources, and I taught in whichever classrooms were free during my class periods. Kids ran and screamed wildly through the hallways unsupervised, teachers were continually at least five minutes late for their classes while students went crazy in the classrooms. The schedule changed everyday and nobody ever had a clue what was going on or where they should be. I experienced undisciplined children, splintering desks, and cultural confusion every day ... but, you know what? I loved every minute of it, even though every single day I couldn't help but wonder, "What in the world am I doing here?!?"

After a week of exposing the youth of Bulgaria to the wonders of the English language, the weekends were always a blessed event. I would strap on my hiker's pack for a weekend of visiting friends around the country, settle in with the comforts of a good book, or merely spend an entire day or more washing all of my laundry by hand. Oh, how I truly appreciate washing machines and dryers these days!

And then there was the Bulgarian winter. As I am an Arizona native, Bulgarian winters were definitely my biggest challenge. There was something magical about that freshly fallen snow and about that first White Bulgarian Christmas. However it does get a little bit old by, say, mid-April. To me, getting around in the snow and ice was a hairy amusement park ride that I didn't even have to wait in line for. With or without snow boots, kneepads, protective padding, and a bicycle helmet, I constantly slipped this way and that without any control throughout two long Bulgarian winters. I would walk like a toddler just learning how to walk to prevent slippage, as Bulgarians whipped past me in 12-inch spiked heels; I toddled along with my arms outspread on either side of me, as I kept one eye on my out-of-control feet and the other on the Dyado (grandpa) with the cane and hunched-back pushing me out of his way, or the Baba (grandma) running over me with her little milk cart. My arms would flail in a hundred different directions as my 20-minute walk to school often turned into 4 hours or so. I envied the little Bulgarian toddlers that sat as happy as pie on little wooden sleds as their mothers pulled them through the mess with ease.

During all of my many experiences and adventures in Bulgaria, I also came into contact with a host of interesting, enlightening characters—Peace Corps volunteers, expatriates living in the cities and host country nationals alike. My heart was saddened as I stepped over Roma (gypsy) children huddled together in the cold streets of the capital with one ratty blanket covering their shivering bodies. I was upset by Roma mothers begging for money to buy milk for the baby balanced on their hips and I was sympathetic for the little Roma kids pleading for a better life. I listened intently as older Bulgarians relived memories of a communist regime and as the very people whom I was trying to help became woeful about their dire situation in Bulgaria and their lack of finances to adequately support their families. Often, Bulgarian friends were seeking a "better life" elsewhere and I became increasingly grateful for all of the opportunities I have as an American.

Peace Corps volunteers in Bulgaria are often asked to help with Green Card and work applications, as many of those with whom we come into contact seek the opportunities I have always taken for granted. Once, I met a young girl named Tania, who needed my help with an application to become an *au pair* in America. I went with Tania to her home and, as is customary, I was immediately given slippers to warm my feet and was ushered into the kitchen for soup and tea.

Once Tania and I were finished with what would hopefully be her "key to opportunity," we went into the living room for more food and fun. The wood-burning stove crackled, the TV blared and Tania talked a mile-a-minute in rapid-fire Bulgarian. Tania's father is an international truck driver, so he proudly displayed his collection of currencies and souvenirs from all over Europe (the currencies tucked neatly beneath a glass table top). "My dream," he told me conspiratorially, "is to drive a truck across America." Truly, Bulgaria is a land full of dreams.

As the sun set upon my two years living abroad as a Peace Corps volunteer, I spit my final seed onto a straggling goat and gazed into the distance, the orange sun falling lazily behind the glimmering mountains, with my little host sister planted firmly by my side. I closed my eyes to stamp the picture into my mind forever—the rutted cobblestone streets teeming with livestock, neighbors, and children running wild and free, the ramshackle homes with their clay tile roofs, the soaring church steeples that reach toward the heavens, the hunched-over Babas pushing milk carts and homemade items-for-sale through the streets. As the sun fell behind the mountains, the town was aglow with swirling reds, oranges, and pinks. My grand tale became a cherished memory. Bulgaria, through all of the frustrations and the joys, had taken a special place in my heart. At that moment, I breathlessly whispered to Iva, "*Az Obecham Bulgaria*," ("I love Bulgaria"). She merely nodded her head with a warm, coy smile, which radiated the pride of a typical Bulgarian. There were many times that I had wondered, "What in the world am I doing here?" but now, it seemed, my answer was clear.

Chantel Sloan lived in Bulgaria as an English-teaching Peace Corps Volunteer from June 2001 until June 2003. Currently, she lives in Arizona and works as a kindergarten teacher, spending her days tying shoes, pushing swings, healing booboos, and wiping away tears. However, as any American who has lived overseas, she maintains that "hunger" for overseas adventures and often feels the "pull" towards once again serving overseas in the future.

German or American?

Elizabeth Holmes

In the German election of 1998 the long-ruling Christian Democratic Party (CDU) lost its majority in the Lower House of the Federal Parliament to the Social Democratic Party (SPD). Helmut Kohl, chancellor of Germany throughout my entire lifetime, was replaced by Gerhard Schroeder, and of course Schroeder and his party planned to make some changes. One of the first reform bills that the SPD attempted to pass concerned dual citizenship. At that point Germany did not officially allow dual citizenship, and the SPD was planning to legalize it. Although the CDU had lost the election, it was determined to win back voters by exploiting this emotional issue. The CDU launched a campaign against dual citizenship and had its supporters sign petitions opposing the new law. And so the discussions began. The subject was debated wherever people met.

In German schools discussions are an important part of the course work, and one day my social studies class was a prime battlefield for the controversy. Strangely enough neither of the two people who always had the most to say in social studies was a native German. My friend Zita is from Hungary and I am a US citizen. However, Zita felt differently from me about the subject. She was in the process of becoming a German citizen because she wanted to play on the national basketball team; it wasn't important to her "what was on the paper." She would always feel Hungarian in her heart no matter what passport she carried. I couldn't quite understand this argument. Certainly I would always feel like an American. Both of my parents and all of my relatives are Americans. I grew up speaking English at home and we kept up with US traditions like Thanksgiving and Halloween. But at the same time there is an undeniable part of me that will always see Germany as my home country. All of my education and everything I did outside of our home was German. My knowledge of Germany, its language and culture, was much greater than that of the United States. I told my social studies class that I was not one or the other; I was both German and American. Having grown up as a part of German society, I wanted the same rights as any of my peers. My classmates had no other choice than to agree with me. Many of them had known me since kindergarten and I had always been one of them.

When I got home that day I thought about whether I truly wanted to become a German citizen. I did want to be able to vote and to decide what happened to the country, but there were also obligations that went along with this. My first recollection of one of these was in fifth grade when I was on the bus to France with my French class. It was the first exchange that I participated in. We were nearing our destination when my French teacher got on the microphone and said: "I have to tell you that it is very likely that older French people will not be very friendly to you. They remember how Hitler marched his troops into Paris down the

Champs-Elysée and through the Arc de Triomphe and they will never forget this humiliation. Many of them will hate everything German for as long as they live. I ask you to respect this." I didn't feel that she was talking to me and I was glad about not being German that day. I was glad I wasn't one of the eleven-year-olds who would have to hold their heads up high while people talked about them and their country, silently accepting the blame for what had happened two generations ago. Certainly, in such a situation one wouldn't hold one's head up with pride but rather with dignity, showing that there was nothing to argue about and that no one was trying to evade what had happened. I realized that if I were to become a German citizen I would no longer have any way to excuse myself from these confrontations. However, I did decide that I wanted to pay that price to be more a part of the country that I grew up in, to hold my own head up high when someone criticized Germany for what its people did in the Third Reich and to find the strength to be an ambassador for the new Germany.

The day that Parliament failed to pass the bill was the first time I truly felt rejected by Germany. The German people had decided for themselves that they wanted to keep "Germany for the Germans," and the CDU was happy because it had regained a portion of its lost power. The only emotion that I could define was sorrow, for I was no longer able to hold my head up high and tell the world that racism was no longer prevalent in Germany. No one can tell me that it doesn't matter "what is on the paper."

Elizabeth Holmes was born in 1981, of American parents who have lived in Germany since 1974. After receiving her primary and secondary education at local German schools, she majored in international studies at Colby College in Waterville, Maine, graduating in 2004 with honors. While at Colby she spent semesters abroad in Morocco and Bolivia and later returned to Morocco on a postgraduate research fellowship. In September 2005, she began a traineeship with UNESCO in Paris.

First Cigarette

Linda Eisele-Lockett

Putting clean clothes into the drawers of my fifteen-year old daughter, Micha, I discover an unopened package of cigarettes beneath the top layer of socks.

"Come see what I found in your sister's room," I call to her thirteen-year old brother, Mark.

He looks into the drawer. "They're not open."

"Yeah, that's something."

"Probably she's keeping them for a friend."

"A friend whose parents won't allow her to have them at home?"

"That's right."

"That's it!"

Two days later, I go for my evening bike ride through the Swiss countryside. Micha is at volleyball practice at school and due home any minute.

On my bike, I feel the exhilaration of flying as the bike accelerates downhill into green fields of corn, wheat, clover, and grass. In the slate gray, late-summer evening sky, low clouds reflect red from the earth and diffuse light from an invisible setting sun. Colors on the ground absorb intensity. A field of freshly-cut hay glows red-gold on the dark brown, rich soil. Green pastures borrow light from the strange gray sky, magically.

I pedal along the road that winds up the slope towards the village. Red, yellow, and purple flowers vibrate color in the garden beside an isolated farmhouse. On the back porch, a black cast iron lamp with four glass panes and a peaked roof, yellow bulb glowing inside like a halo, reminds me of the lamp on the post in the front yard of our Whittier, California home when I was small. "I search for connections," I tell the wind as the past rushes to meet me across ten thousand miles and forty years. Delighted, I ride along the road through a neighborhood above the school, whiz around a corner, down-shift up the last hill. The gym is dark.

Standing with a group of teenagers, Micha lowers a cigarette. Her arm disappears behind her back. The other kids lift cigarettes to their mouths, inhale, puff, lower arms in a kaleidoscope of motion. A clown's grin spreads across my face. I do not turn my head, nor call out, "Nice evening." Tears burn the corners of my eyes. She is one of *them;* not one of us. She is a *smoker.* My friend's boys, who have had encounters with the police, are smokers. My kids and their friends are not.

Entering the house, I close the front door, reach into the ceramic bowl on the shoe cupboard, grab the key ring, stick the key into the lock and turn it. When Micha comes home, if she dares, she will have to ring the doorbell. I will open the door, look at her and ask, "Do you live here? I don't think I know you," coldly, of course.

In the living room, I pace. "What am I supposed to do? How do I react?" I pick up the phone and dial my mom. Nine thousand miles away in Phoenix, Arizona, the phone rings.

"Hello?"

"Mom, I've got a situation here. I was just riding by the school and I saw Micha with a group of kids. They were smoking. What do I do when she comes home?"

"You turn it over to Hubert. Then you *just watch.*"

"You mean it's o.k. to tell him?"

"You've *got* to tell him."

"So I should unlock the front door?"

"You've *got* to unlock the front door."

"OK."

"This is what husbands are for."

"And mothers. Thanks." I hang up.

Downstairs, my husband sits in front of the television. "When I passed the school just now, I saw Micha. She was with a bunch of friends. They were smoking."

He grins. "It happens."

"So what are you going to do about it?!"

"Oh, you know, they try it out. The main thing is not to overreact."

"I found a packet of cigarettes in her sock drawer Wednesday."

"Yeah, yeah. They buy some. They try it. These kids have got to have some way to let off steam. You haven't been through the Swiss school system. You cannot imagine the pressure on them." We go upstairs to eat dinne r. I drink a glass of wine. He drinks two. Afterwards, we sit in the TV room on the sofa. I lay my head on his thigh. "So what are you thinking?" he asks.

"I'm thinking, she really blew it. We give her permission to go to Bern on Saturday nights; stay up until midnight. We shrink our trip to Spain to one week for her. We do everything for her! Well she can forget it! No more late nights in town. If she'll do this, who knows *what* she'll do! I think she was smoking pot on Wednesday. She came home from school and she was, like high. She was so happy, talking so fast, non-stop. At first I thought she was in love. She wouldn't stop talking. Then I thought she was high, but I couldn't ask her. Once I did, and she wasn't, and she was so mad at me for not trusting her. Trust. Bah! No more trust. She doesn't deserve it! And she can forget about staying for a week alone with Irene at Irene's house with no parental supervision. On Wednesday, she asked what the rules would be when they are on their own. She said Irene's parents told her she can take the midnight bus home from Bern, or if she's staying over at a friend's house, they can take the Moonliner at one or two in the morning! I didn't imagine them even leaving Irene's village, much less staying out until midnight in Bern when we don't know when, what, or where. No! That's all through. She *really* blew it this time."

"Come on. This is a small thing. Everybody tries it. So what are you going to do when she comes home?"

84

I look at him wickedly. "Who knows? Maybe I'll rise to the challenge! The trouble is, when *I* rise to the challenge, nobody knows *what's* going to happen. Maybe I'm just jealous. She gets to smoke. She gets to go out. She goes to the disco. She has friends. Maybe *I* want to go to a disco. Maybe *I* want to have some fun! Heck, when I think what I did when I was younger—Europe with a Eurail Pass, down to Spain. Meet some kids. That would be great! Maybe I want to smoke a cigarette once. Think about it. Twenty years I haven't smoked a cigarette. Why? To set a good example. She's not worth it. Well, maybe I'd like one. You know what? Let's run to the kiosk. We'll buy a pack of cigarettes. No! A carton! The menthol kind. I want the cool ones which refresh when you inhale."

"And for me, a cigar!" he laughs.

"Have you ever kissed someone who's been smoking?"

"Terrible." He hangs his head, shakes it woefully back and forth.

"That's how we'll get her. When she comes home, we'll be lying on the sofa smoking cigarettes and cigars, the whole room *full* of smoke."

"I don't want to smoke in the house. You never get rid of the smell."

"If you smoke all the time, maybe not, but not if you smoke just once? *Come on.* Let's go to a kiosk and get some."

"Have you forgotten there's no kiosk in this village?"

"Let's drive to Bern."

"I don't want to drive to Bern. I've been drinking."

"Did I ever tell you about the time I saw my mom drink a glass of wine?"

"No."

"We were in the kitchen. Mom never drank. Dad was a teetotaler. But this was after their divorce. I was home from college. When I saw her drinking that wine, I poured myself a glass and downed it right in front of her. I said, "See, I can drink, too." I wanted to shock her so she wouldn't get started. It worked, too. I never saw her take a drink after that. It's getting late. Do you think she's afraid to come home?"

"I don't know."

We hear the front door open and close. Legs sprawled up the wall, I lay where I am. Hubert and I keep talking and laughing. Micha comes down the stairs. She stands beside the sofa, arms akimbo. "Well?", she asks.

"Well what?" We burst out laughing.

"Don't you want to talk about it?"

"About what?" We looked at each other; stifle giggles.

"Have you two been drinking?" More giggles. "You have. You've been drinking. Or are you stoned? If you've been drinking, I want some, too."

"Sure! Get yourself a beer. They're in the bomb shelter."

"But don't you want to talk about the cigarette?"

"Sure. How did you like it?"

"Not great."

"Have you been smoking long?"

"That was the first time."

"No! That's unbelievable. What are the odds? You light up your *first* cigarette, and what happens? Your *Mother* rides by on her bicycle in front of all your friends wearing nerd clothes and a bicycle helmet! Now that's God. I see God in that, don't you, Hubert?" More laughter. "I found the pack of cigarettes in your sock drawer on Wednesday. Let me guess. You bought them on Tuesday."

"That's right." Her voice sounds like a guest's from the audience at a magic show. "How did you know?"

"God," I answer. "You buy a pack of cigarettes. Within twenty-four hours, for the first time in four *years*, your mom organizes your clothes for you and finds them. That's God. That's proof that there's a god, and *He's on My Side!* That's how God works, Honey."

"You guys are crazy," she says.

"Where'd you buy the pack? In Bern?"

"In the Coop."

"What?! Here in the village?! You're buying cigarettes in the village? Hey, I've got a rep to protect! How did that go, anyway?"

"Mrs. Balmer said, *'Schöne Tag, Frau* Eisele'."

"*Frau* Eisele?! She thought you were me?! She thinks *I'm* buying cigarettes?!! My God!"

"No. She knows I'm your daughter."

"Doesn't she call you *Fräulein* Eisele?"

"There's no *Fräulein* any more. I'm *Frau* everywhere. *Frau* this, *Frau* that."

"Good heavens, my daughter is *Frau* Eisele."

"Yes, yes. Didn't you notice that the pack was unopened?"

"Sure. When I showed it to Mark he said you were probably keeping it for a friend."

"That's what I was doing."

"We were right, Hubert! Mark and I were right!" I exclaim, gleefully.

"In chemistry, I accidentally knocked Hanna's pack of cigarettes into the sink. I told her I would replace them, so I bought a new pack."

"Who's Hanna?"

"She's on the volleyball team. So I brought them to practice this evening. She opened the pack when we got outside and passed them around. Everybody was smoking, so I tried one, too."

"That's good. That's *real* good." I roll my lower lip into a sausage and nod at Hubert. "Good resistance to peer group pressure. That's positive. And Irene? Was she there, too?"

"No, she left right after practice."

"Does she smoke too?"

"No. She doesn't touch alcohol, either."

"That's good," I say, thinking of the week she and Micha will live together without adult supervision.

"That's it?" she asks. "So am I grounded, or what?"

"Is she grounded?" I look at Hubert.

"Is she grounded?" He looks at me. We giggle.

"You guys are nuts," she says as she walks out of the room.

Linda Eisele-Lockett is a 56-year old American-becoming-Swiss housewife who moved to Switzerland in 1989 when her children were five and three. She met her Swiss husband in Pokhara, Nepal in 1979 on a thirteen-month solo trip around the world. She has written countless stories, a novel, and two books of poems and is currently working on a novella about Corsica and Sardinia. "First Cigarette" is her first published work. She shares her writing on her homepage at: http://swisshousewife.tripod.com/davidhager.

Life Without Borders

Liza Monroy

In my earliest memories, I'm in Guadalajara, Mexico, chattering away in Spanish with our maid, Rosa. My mother's job in the Foreign Service seems both to satisfy and encourage the wanderlust that's brought me around the world from a very young age. Wherever we lived and traveled, she set off to discover the reality of that place, not a tourist-coated approach experiencing the country as an observer, but rather participating in local culture, experiencing the life of locals—what they enjoyed, where they ate or went for an afternoon coffee. This is why we go out to Rosa's home for lunch one Sunday. She lives with us during the week and we're invited to spend some time with her family. They live in a cement house in a small town not too far outside the city. It has two stories and dirt floors, with strategically placed hand-woven throw rugs here and there. I'm doing a little jig after the car ride, so my mom brings me out back to the bathroom: a drain-like hole she helps me squat over. I wonder where the bathtub is.

Later, I play with two little boys, cousins, outside in the barnyard as goats and chickens scurry about. Rosa's mother comes out with her older brother and I watch in puzzlement as they lunge after a chicken.

"Van a matar el pollo!" one of the boys screams.

A girl of five shouldn't see her meal while it's still alive, but such is the experience of lunch at Rosa's house. Her mother waves the chicken around by the neck until it snaps off, the carcass still running aimlessly in circles. My mother takes a photo of me holding the head up, my nose crinkled in revulsion. I feel distinctly guilty for enjoying the delicious chicken tacos. Seven years of vegetarianism I attribute to this occasion; surely it's haunted my subconscious all this time.

The more profound effects of a nomadic childhood spent outside the United States are many. How each experience fits together like pieces of a random puzzle creates a richness of experience, a unique take on the world that gives an American raised abroad a look at the bigger picture, a more universal worldview. This changes the way in which we understand and relate to our country and people as a whole.

Less than a year after the chicken incident, the movers were back. Men in jumpsuits carrying boxes full of our possessions out of a house no longer our home, into a truck and eventually on to our next country.

In Rome I traded Spanish for Italian and became fond of *tramezzini* as an after-school snack. When I got to middle school, I met my friends on the Spanish Steps on weekends where we'd gossip, eat and people-watch. My friends from the American Overseas School were from Australia, Lesotho, Italy, England, Israel, the United States—and it never occurred to us to ever think or talk about this. We were just kids who all went to school together, whose parents were stationed overseas or Italians who wanted their children to have an overseas-school education. Other weekends were spent with my mother, exploring medieval towns, sampling *tagliatelle al cingiale* (wild boar) in local restaurants. We traveled the region from London to Djerba, Tunisia, where I drew the line for culinary adventurousness as my mother tried some unrecognizable globular edibles that turned out to be camel testicles.

It was much later before I became aware that my life was anything out of the ordinary. We were stationed back in Mexico, this time in Mexico City, during my high school years. My mother was the Deputy Chief of Citizen Services, helping troubled Americans who somehow made their way there. The question, "How was work today?" inevitably begot hilarious and intriguing dinner conversation. A man who claimed to be the "first pope conceived in a test tube" came to see her after traveling from Baja to Mexico City to find property "left to him by his predecessor." A famous banking family heiress, out of money and her medication, came in swearing and screaming that she had to fly to the Caribbean. Mom also recovered stolen property. A $50,000 motor-home "confiscated" by the police from a beach parking area in Baja California was found at Los Pinos, the President of Mexico's residence. It was being used to transport military personnel.

School was very different from what I'd been accustomed to—the Koreans had a Korean clique, the Mexicans socialized among one another, and same with the Americans. This segregation was part of the school's culture, which was entirely different from what I'd been used to in Italy. I realized for the first time that boundaries existed, that people could be put into categories. I found myself labeled "American," yet I'd never lived in the States. My English was unaccented and I preferred jeans and t-shirts to the designer attire the Mexican girls wore, which made me American enough in their eyes, regardless of having spent my life up until then in Guadalajara and Rome. Friends I made often had lifestyles similar to my own, and they came and went over the course of those four years—international corporations reassigned employees, diplomatic tours of duty came to an end, boarding schools presented a more disciplined high school experience.

Mexico City had very few enforced regulations. Some kids, coming from a more regimented American background, saw that alcohol wasn't taboo, young smokers were typical and illegal drugs easy to come by; they went out of control like children set free in an unsupervised candy store. Police could be bribed; sons and daughters of wealthy Mexicans (the majority of the population of my school) had drivers to take them out clubbing on weekends. Self-control and the ability to make decisions became something I learned as I grew up fast; Mexico City was a free and often wild world of adventure and potential danger.

One such instance was a strange new kidnapping technique that surfaced at one point. Outside movie theaters, booths sprang up, with banners reading "win a trip to the Bahamas" or somewhere exotic. Young people filled out slips to enter the supposed drawing, including names, phone numbers and addresses. While they were in the theater, the booth "attendants" called their parents, saying the teen had been kidnapped, to leave an easily accessible amount of cash at a certain location within an hour.

Fearful for their children's lives, parents complied without involving the police. Two hours later, the kid would come home from the movie.

The summer before my senior year, I got my first job—not scooping ice-cream, as it might have been were I in the States, but in the visa section of the US Embassy. Where I worked was aptly nicknamed the "Visa Barn." The line formed before six a.m. on the sidewalk and went all the way around the block. People were herded into the large, open holding space, sitting side-by-side on narrow benches. Some entrepreneurial applicants brought folding lawn chairs, renting them out by the hour to people who couldn't get a seat. My job was to make visas. I inputted names and printed them out of a special printer with ink used only for these visas. Then I laminated and separated them. After slipping them back into their respective passports, I rolled a big metal cart filled with hundreds of them up to a podium. I stood behind a microphone to read out the names of those fortunate enough to be receiving their visas.

"...Jose Cruz. Luz Sanchez. Manuel Menendes. Maria Hidalgo..."

Angry men and women whose names weren't called rushed over, screaming, *"Senorita! DONDE ESTA MI PASAPORTE?!"* Security would scramble to control the crowd.

In the Visa Barn I experienced firsthand the extreme differences between the Mexicans at school and the majority of the population. My classmates regularly went to college or even had homes in the States, coming and going as they pleased. These people were subjected to rigorous interviews: what was in their bank account, how strong their ties to Mexico truly were. Even a small doubt about their return to Mexico would mean their application was denied. A woman who applied for a three-month visa had put the reason for the trip as a vacation to Disneyland. When asked in the interview why she wanted to spend three months in Disneyland, she replied only: *Porque queremos visitar a Mickey.* (We want to visit Mickey.) She wasn't granted the visa and left the window with tears in her eyes, as so many did.

Mexico City was a turning point, a place I think of as a home though I've only been back to visit once since I left. It taught me independence and my visa job showed me the real value of American citizenship. I decided I would return to my homeland after high school to discover what it was like to live there and to start a life in the country I came from, a country that felt as foreign as Italy or Mexico did when I first arrived.

When I moved to the States for college, I earned a new label—an American who had grown up abroad. I'd stumbled into a category that finally made sense. The simple question "Where are you from?" had an elongated answer that began "Well, it's a bit of a long story..." By this time I was quick to adapt, but still experienced culture shock. My homeland is a foreign country to me. I've pondered this paradox often when I spend time with American friends. Conversation turns to baseball or the nuances of 80s pop culture, US history and political intricacies. The references are lost on me. People may think I just crawled out from under a rock or am deeply into more esoteric interests like philosophy or reading tea leaves. I always say that

90

I'd make more sense as a person if I had an accent. Then even strangers would understand there was an exotic foreigner hidden inside the girl-next-door American. I may be in the States now, but I don't feel as if I'm in my own country. Wherever I go, I'm a visitor passing through, a traveler, a nomadic wanderer. After college in Boston and two years in Los Angeles, I've settled (for now) in Manhattan. The city's diversity suits me, though I suspect I'll always feel as though I'm viewing the United States from an outsider's perspective, which many people in New York City do.

The hardest part about being back in the United States was relating to people who weren't interested in life abroad, who were accustomed to one way of life and had no desire to see further than what they knew. It was difficult to date people I couldn't relate to—people who were born somewhere, grew up there and still knew all their friends from high school and even before. After several failed relationships, I'm finally in a good one—with someone who went to my high school, ironically enough. He is working in New York and we came back together. He's half-Austrian, half-Mexican, and we share a similar background, which isn't a common one to come by.

I'm not certain I'll live in America for the rest of my life. I enjoy the expatriate lifestyle and hope I'll come across an opportunity to live abroad again. The perspective that living in Europe and Mexico gave me is one of infinite possibility, open to anything and surprised at nothing. I have an appreciation of other nationalities and cultures, and I owe this to having grown up abroad, to living and traveling in places from Egypt to Guatemala. Extensive travel is necessary to existence, to personal evolution. For me, that extends to living in other countries as well, gaining an understanding deeper than what is possible by spending a week somewhere. The depth of experience living and traveling abroad enriches life in ways that are unique and must be especially appreciated in the world today.

Liza Monroy, daughter of a US Foreign Service officer, grew up in Guadalajara, Rome, Washington DC and Mexico City. She received her B.A. in Writing and Literature from Emerson College in Boston and is now a freelance writer in New York City. Her work has appeared in the New York Times, The Village Voice, on Nerve.com, and in other publications. Currently, she is at work on a novel loosely based on her years in Mexico and hopes to put her love of writing and travel to work as a travel journalist. She is twenty-five years old.

Exotica

Local officials...would lay out feasts of grilled mutton, flat bread and delicious melons on beautiful hand-woven carpets, all washed down with Russian vodka and Georgian cognac, while asking what it would take for US companies to invest in their industries and what, by the way, was the origin of American representative democracy.

Michael Larsen

I looked at the nuns, not knowing what to say or how to act, hoping that by some shared look I could find somebody else who recognized what I had witnessed. But the nuns continued to hold their random, blank stares out the window.

Christopher Davenport

Looking up we could see hundreds of thousands of swiftlets as they darted in and out of the recesses of the cave. This noisy mass of birds is responsible for one of the more lucrative trades in Sarawak. The collecting of the saliva-constructed bird nests for birds' nest soup is dangerous and profitable.

Susan Ellis

This car was as far from first-class as possible. It wasn't second or even third. This car could only be described as criminal-class and there I was, wearing my London-tailored suit with my Italian-cut overcoat trying to blend in with a farmer, his dead chickens and the other old soul who seemed to have a stomach virus.

Timothy James Kelly

The ambassador, no stranger to the strangest of tales ... shook his head. "Put him on the payroll," he said, his voice absolutely deadpan, "we need a few shit-eaters around here."

Laura Williamson

Louie tops the list of my food mentors for stimulation to the mind's senses, for exotic creations so healthful and good for my body and soul, and for ambiance of the heart.

Maryann Hrichak

Steamy

Michael Larsen

The first thing that happens when you step out your front door early in the morning in Bahrain during the summer months is that your sunglasses instantly fog up. Then, during the subsequent thirty-second walk to your car you begin to sweat, in my case profusely. You feel only marginally better when the car's air conditioner kicks in, turning you from wet rag to popsicle. How we avoided pneumonia during those days was beyond me. Then again, living anywhere in the Gulf region during the summer was not—at least weather-wise—unlike our adopted "home" in Phoenix, Arizona during the same monsoon months.

Why did we bother to change one steam bath for another? The story, like those of most Americans who live abroad long, is not focused on one simple theme or set of objectives but a product of Wanderlust, a keen desire to explore and understand, and in our case as newlyweds a chance to earn a few extra bucks. During the mid- to late-1980s, life in the Gulf was particularly good, if you could stand the isolation and growing mayhem around the region. The Iran-Iraq war, then called the Tanker War, was in full flourish, and the position of our house, smack dab in the middle of the largest Shiite village outside the main city of Manama, gave some of our visiting friends cause for concern. The people in our village were great though, friendly if distant, treating us and our fellow expat neighbors with the kind of tolerance and openness that Bahrainis are famous for. There were moments of course, such as when the United States bombed Libya in April 1986 and our embassy helpfully advised all Americans to "adopt a low profile." Presumably that meant I should duck below the dashboard while driving through my village—I never did find out what they meant. Anyway, we survived.

We started a family during that time too, with my beloved heading back to *maman* in Paris for the births of our two children, and Daddy racing back just in time for "le grand moment." Shortly after each nearly effortless delivery (OK, at least for me) I made my way over to the US embassy to duly register them as natural born Americans. Will either child give us the satisfaction (if not assured retirement) of testing the proposition that Americans born overseas may in fact become President? Material for another story, no doubt (plus movie rights, use of trademark, etc). But I digress.

Hot and steamy as the Gulf was, there were pockets of relative coolness. One of the ones we thought might qualify was the early morning *dhow* to Mina Al-Khobar, across the bay in Saudi Arabia. A *dhow* is essentially a traditional wooden fishing boat, these days refitted for catching other prey, like foreign bankers seeking modest adventure. Ours had in fact been refitted not in the sense of a covered lounge, snack counter and smiling crew offering freshly-brewed Arabic coffee (the only discernible difference with Turkish coffee being that the nearest cup of the latter was to be found in Istanbul). No, refitted in the sense of a wooden outhouse dangling precariously off the stern of our little ship. A banking colleague of mine and I decided to forgo the tedium of the usual 15-minute Gulf Air flight across the water and, wearing our seersucker suits, tasselled loafers and clutching our briefcases and overnight bags climbed aboard the 6:45 am shuttle for the expected 90-minute journey.

The indifference of our fellow passengers, all locals plying trade or visiting relatives, took a bit of the excitement out of our little trip. Then again it could have been the steadily rising temperature, which by mid-day on the open deck would be particularly unpleasant. As it turned out, when our ship broke down almost half-way across, and with no back-up motor (and no oars! thankfully) we drifted along for almost two hours until the next shuttle towed us into Al-Khobar. Upon reaching our destination the twelve or so of us on that ship, now friends for life, having shared the most intimate details of our lunch boxes (a "juicy date" taking on a new meaning), bade farewell to each other, thanking the captain for saving us from an even worse fate (like having to use that outhouse) and secure in the knowledge that life does present learning opportunities … if you're not careful. *Halas.*

After a well-deserved, cool shower at the local Oberoi hotel and a Tex-Mex lunch served by real Indians (Bangalore, not Hopi) but with nary a cowboy in sight, me and my pardner moseyed down over to the airport for the 45-minute flight to Riyadh, where in this Magic Kingdom, Tomorrowland infrastructure collides with scenes from 1001 Nights, mixing and somehow matching supersized Safeways and shwarma shops, Hardees and hardly seen womanfolk. And just like in the other mouse-eared Magic Kingdom where it is darn near impossible to have a beer with your burger, those seeking stronger libations had to head elsewhere. Which made the then newly-opened King Fahd Causeway ('cos he paid for it, that's why) linking Saudi Arabia's Eastern Province with Bahrain the hottest strip of asphalt since Highway 1. That causeway, combined with a more general lack of "things to do" in an American sense, meant that we in Bahrain were a popular destination for weekend visitors, both expats and a number of our Saudi friends.

Of course, things have changed dramatically in Bahrain since the early 1990s, with the rise of fundamentalism, the threat of terrorism and the impact of such a large US military presence. The biggest change of course was that we moved. After four years of traveling across Saudi Arabia, Yemen, Oman and Qatar it was time to relocate to clammier climes, this time to London. For several years I continued to visit the Middle East, but once the Iron Curtain was raised the focus of my attention gradually shifted to the Former Soviet Union where, oddly enough, I would feel somehow "at home" watching Saudi TV, this time not in some plush hotel in Jeddah but beamed in by satellite to some (literally) flea-bitten "hotel" in places like Ashgabat, Turkmenistan. Watching the devoted circle the Holy Kaba'a seemed somehow more instructive on how local culture was evolving than footage con gratulating the Turkmenbashi on last month's statistics on tractor production. Troubling too, given how quickly modern technology can fill the void created by the collapse of one social order. On that TV were of course other channels including a few from Russia, the ever-present CNN and a fine selection of Turkish soap operas. Given this smorgasbord of ideologies, how was a hitherto closed society going to react and plan its future?

We liked to think that the Florida Bar and Restaurant in downtown Ashgabat was where hearts and minds were made over, but given an average monthly wage of less than twenty-five bucks and a bottle of Heineken costing five, it was no wonder that much of the real debate was happening elsewhere, as would be confirmed by my Turkmen hosts as they graciously toured me around the emptiness of that vast and ancient desert land. The topography, state of the roads and the number of gas stations in the country were accurately described by the Head of Consular Affairs at the US embassy in Tashkent in this comment: "Remember those first pictures from the Lunar Roving Vehicle?". Local officials, usually led by an Aksegal or "White Beard," would lay out feasts of grilled mutton, flat bread and delicious melons on beautiful hand-woven carpets, all washed down with Russian vodka and Georgian cognac, while asking what it would take for US companies to invest in their industries and what, by the way was the origin of American representative democracy. Discussing business prospects while quoting from Jefferson and joining in the singing of Turkmen love songs (not unlike cowboy–style ballads of unrequited affection), before heading off to the sauna, made for interesting call reports back to head office.

Steamy indeed.

Michael J. Larsen, a native of Los Angeles, presently resides in London with his French wife of 22 years, and two teenage children who long ago stopped bothering to ask where they were from. Previously they lived for 10 years in Switzerland (both Zurich and Geneva) and before that again in London as well as in Bahrain, Athens, New York City and Boston. Michael's 20-year career with Citibank took him on trips across the Middle East, Central Asia and the Former Soviet Union, Eastern Europe and parts of Africa, adding to cross-cultural experiences gained from growing up on-the-road across Europe and the United States. Michael, who is also fluent in French and German, received his BA in Economics from Boston University, which included one year at the Albert-Ludwig Universität in Freiburg, Germany.

A Bus Ride

Christopher Davenport

I walked unhurriedly through the narrow aisles of the cramped trade store, as a procession of cans and boxes with multicolored labels in unfamiliar Asiatic scripts paraded across the shelves before me. The air in the store was dusty and a little stale, but it was cool and it was dry, a welcome respite from the intense sunlight and suffocating humidity of late afternoon in Papua New Guinea.

I had been in the country as a Peace Corps Volunteer for almost three months, teaching English at a remote high school in the Highlands. I had not yet grown accustomed to the one-hour trip by PMV (Public Motor Vehicle), to get from the village where I lived to the nearest town, where I bought my supplies. It was an inconvenient trek to have to make every week, but there was no way around it. This was the nearest place for me to buy groceries, send mail or make the occasional telephone call. There was even a hotel in town, where I could sometimes stop for a meal and a beer.

I wouldn't have the chance today, though. Today was a "fortnight Friday," payday for everyone who was lucky enough to be employed, and those who had been paid would spend their day doling out money to hordes of relatives, friends, or anyone who could stake a reasonable claim. This was Papua New Guinea's famed "*wantok* system," in which anyone who has money is obliged by custom to share it with his *wantoks,* people from his family or tribe.

The money seldom lasted long enough to cover the needs of all of the *wantoks,* and there was rarely anything left in the end, so invariably on fortnight Fridays the atmosphere was a tense mixture of joyful festivity and pure aggression. Everyone pushed forward to press a claim while there was still money available, and the crowds were heavy and volatile. Every fortnight Friday teetered on the verge of complete anarchy, and this one was no different.

In the store, I grabbed a large sack of rice, a few cans of corned beef, some tinned mackerel, a jar of tea and a few other things that I needed. Jostled by the dense and insistent crowds, I maneuvered my way to the counter. I felt conspicuous as I paid for my items with a bundle of frayed, pastel-colored bills. I had picked up quite a bit of food, still suffering under the illusion that I might be able to buy enough to last me beyond the following week. It was awkward carrying it all, but I left the store and returned to the crowded streets, subject as always to the curious stares and pitying gazes of passersby as they watched me labor to carry my cargo to the PMV stop. By the time I arrived there, I was out of breath and my legs were burning, so I squatted to my haunches and settled my purchases in my lap, taking a few deep breaths to rest.

The smell of the immediate vicinity struck me, as it so often did, especially pronounced here, closer to the ground. The air was thick and sultry, and every scent that wandered about the place seemed caught in the suspended moisture of the oppressive humidity. There was nowhere for the musky smells to go, trapped as they were in the thick blanket of heat and swelter, so my olfactory senses were assaulted by the body odor of the pressing crowds, the droppings of free-roaming pigs, the smoke from harsh cigarettes and the sweet lime of betel nut. There was a slight breeze, which should have dissipated the emanations, but instead it only accentuated them, waving them more insistently in my face. I didn't know if the smells were affecting my mood, or if my mood made the odors seem more noxious, but either way, I felt unpleasant. I wanted to be ignored; left alone. I was aloof and standoffish. I had retreated into my head, my own world, to escape from the claustrophobic masses and disagreeable redolence of this one, and I did not want to be drawn back.

After fifteen minutes or so, a large, twenty-passenger bus approached with a dull roar, its tires squealing over the gravel and sand in the road, agitating the fragments of soil and grit and blowing them into my face. The door to the PMV opened, and the driver within simply stared ahead. I squinted through the cloud of dust and asked if he would be going near my village. In response, he nodded but did not turn his head to me. I appreciated his disinterest, so I gathered my purchases to board the bus, readjusting the food in my arms. The bag of rice, awkwardly shaped and balanced, rested against my chest and jutted so high before my face that I could barely see around it. Still, I managed to struggle aboard, and only then was I able to set my purchases down for a moment to find a seat. In doing so, I was suddenly able to see that there were about a dozen passengers on the PMV, all of them nuns. Each was dressed identically and staring straight ahead. The expression on their faces showed no notice of me.

Taken aback, I muttered, "Jesus," and one of the nuns, hearing the invocation, crossed herself absently, her gaze focused on a distant point well beyond me.

These nuns were of a different order, and wore a slightly different type of outfit from those I was accustomed to seeing in the States. Their habit was pale gray, with a matching short-sleeved shirt and ankle-length skirt. The headgear was the same, though. The shroud with the white brim made them look like bizarre, exotic birds with huge heads and wide, curved beaks. All of these women were Melanesian, Papua New Guinean natives, and like other Melanesian women I had met, they were diminutive, quiet and withdrawn, in contrast to the large and powerful features of their full faces. They were almost painfully shy. Few of them would so much as look at me, and of those who did, none would look for long. Their silent presence made the mood seem surreal, but I had found over my time in this country that I was developing a certain familiarity, and even comfort, in alternate realities.

I took the only empty seat, in the front on the passenger side. I placed my things on the floor between the driver's seat and my own and settled in to look through the window, preferring to wallow for the moment in my own tired apathy. I rested my chin on my palm and stared through the dusty, cracked windowpane, which rattled in its frame as the bus picked up speed. The road was rough and full of potholes, and the suspension on the bus was in dire need of repair, so we bounced and bumped our way through town as I sat in contemplative silence.

Then I heard a voice behind me; not loud, but smooth and steady, and all the more noticeable for that. It had a tone that was almost, but not quite, conversational, but was at the same time undeniably lyrical. I couldn't make out the words over the sound of the engine, and I assumed anyway that one of the nuns was talking to another, so I minded my own business and continued my solitary vigil. She spoke in a local language, different from that spoken around my village, one that I had never heard. There was something inherently soothing in the tone of her voice though, and without trying to interpret the words themselves, I allowed the voice to caress the back of my consciousness.

One of the other nuns began to speak as well, her voice complementing, instead of interrupting, the other, and I came to the gradual realization that it was not a conversation that was going on, since both of the women were speaking at the same time, and the rhythms and tones of their words overlapped one another and blended together. They were singing.

They finished the first phrase of the song, there was a pause, and then they started again, and this time, the rest of them joined. The song was neither joyful nor melancholy; instead it seemed to describe an ambiguous emotion unlike anything I could have recognized before coming to this country. It was quietly benign, unassuming and gentle, barely hinting at some distant darkness; not afraid of it, just recognizing it, acknowledging it. And in some strange way, their song fit my mood perfectly.

They sang on, and I now turned my head to see them. I was surprised to find that they weren't looking at each other, but instead, each stared out a window, or at her own hands. The bus lurched and bounced along the rough road, causing their shrouded heads to bob and loll in unison with each bump, keeping a disjointed time with their song. All the while, their involvement in the song itself seemed almost incidental. As if they just happened to be singing, but were really more concerned with the emerald brilliance of the rainforest passing beyond their windows, or with the seatback before them. It seemed so tenuous, as if the slightest disruption could jolt them from their contemplation.

Yet in spite of the distracted way that they were singing, and the fact that they didn't even seem to be trying, the blending of their voices was resplendent, and incredibly poignant in its simplicity. There wasn't a trace of self-consciousness in their singing, and that is a rare thing with Melanesian people, particularly the women. But this wasn't a performance to them. In fact, I felt certain that it would never have occurred to them that someone might be listening. Their singing was, to them, more of an instinct, a reflex. They were no more aware of it than they were of their own breathing, or the beating of their own hearts, and that made the sound seem as fragile as a spider's web. It was as intricate and beautiful, too. Each strand played a vital role in the wholeness of it. Take away a single voice and the strength of the unified whole would have collapsed.

I turned to face ahead, and in doing so I glanced at the driver, but if he noticed the singing, he gave no indication of it. I figured it was best to remain facing forward instead of turning to watch them. I was afraid they would stop if they realized that someone was actually listening, and last thing in the world that I wanted was for them to stop. I was mesmerized by the sound, and for that moment, I was immune to the stresses and anxieties of my life in that country. I returned my gaze absently to the obsidian shadows of the rainforest rolling past my dingy window, but I concentrated all of my mental energy on enjoying the unwavering beauty of the gently intermingling voices behind me.

I have always believed that there is a place in the realm of our comprehension where the value of words, any words, comes to nil. There are some things that simply do not have, cannot have, a designation within human diction, regardless of the intricacy of the language, or the eloquence of the speaker. Sometimes words are not enough, and in some of those instances art, or music, can succeed where words have failed. On this day, in this battered van, as I sat hugging a twenty pound bag of rice and a few cans of meat and fish, wondering where the next few days and weeks would find me, the efficacy of words failed me, replaced by the refulgent lyricism of a few seemingly indifferent nuns.

Before I knew it, the bus began to slow and I found that we were in front of the road to my school. The nuns stopped their singing, and I gathered my belongings with great reluctance and climbed down to the ground. As I paid the driver, I examined the noncommittal expression on his face, but again found nothing. He closed the door and jammed the bus back into gear, and I looked at the nuns, not knowing what to say or how to act, hoping that by some shared look I could find somebody else who recognized what I had witnessed. But the nuns continued to hold their random, blank stares out the window. And so the van pulled out, and I squinted against the dust that was once again kicked up into my face. I blinked and stared after the bus, my previous apathy overtaken by a sense of awed and speechless wonder.

Christopher Davenport was a Peace Corps Volunteer in Papua New Guinea from 1994 to 1996, and the bus ride described in this story took place a few months after he had arrived there. He now lives in Arlington, Virginia, where he is a program analyst for the US Department of Agriculture. He is also a graduate student studying creative writing at George Mason University.

Ferries, Jungles, Caves and Guano

Susan Ellis

The year-old Honda Civic rattled and vibrated as if it would split apart at any moment. Bill said something I couldn't make out.

"What?" I shouted.

"Does the car sound different to you?" he shouted back.

"You're kidding, right?" I couldn't imagine how he thought I could hear any change over the constant din.

His eyebrows knitted together and he gripped the steering wheel tighter. As he started to downshift I thought, what now? He pulled to the side of the road and stopped, a cloud of dust settling around us as he jumped out of the car.

"Shit!" he yelled and kicked the tire. "We've got a flat, we'll probably miss the ferry." I got out of the car and helped unload the cooler from the trunk so he could get at the spare. He was working fast; we had to get to the ferry between Miri and Kuala Belait before sunset or be stuck in Sarawak for the night with no place to stay and an expired visa. When we had entered the country in the morning we asked for just a one-day visa. Several people had told us it was easily a day trip to the Niah Caves from Kuala Belait, Brunei. That was the last time I would take anyone's word for how quickly you could get through the Borneo jungle even on the hard packed gravel roads.

The Niah Caves were declared a Malaysian national historic monument in 1958. The main activities taking place there were the collecting of bird and bat guano, the harvesting of bird's nests for bird's nest soup (a Chinese delicacy) and the ongoing archaeological dig.

To get to them that morning we had used the path the guano runners used to bring the sacks of guano from the cave to the river for transport. The path ran through the rainforests and was well-worn and slippery. I had been struck by the intensely verdant smell of the jungle. Here undergrowth, so thick you couldn't see more than a few feet past the path, created a wall of familiar looking plants, but familiar only because I knew them as house plants. Split-philodendron with leaves the size of dinner plates, ferns of every size, shape and shade of green to gray, orchids blooming in intense profusion, bromeliads, pothos and vines of every description. I recognized durian and rambutan trees from the edge of our yard in Brunei.

The fauna were also exotic—snakes, millipedes, butterflies in profusion. As we had approached the caves the smell of foliage was quickly replaced by the pungent, nauseating, smell of guano. The path had opened up suddenly and there before us we saw the gaping mouth of the Kuala Besar or Great Cave. Spanning nearly 800 feet across and rising to a height of 200 feet, the opening felt as if it could swallow you like some great prehistoric beast. The overpowering smell of bat and bird dung had made me cover my mouth and nose with my hands. Looking up we could see hundreds of thousands of swiftlets as they darted in and out of the recesses of the cave. This noisy mass of birds is responsible for one of the more lucrative trades in Sarawak. The collecting of the saliva-constructed bird nests for birds' nest soup is dangerous and profitable. For fifteen hundred years men have died from falls while climbing the bamboo poles to the roof of the cave in search of these nests. The soup is said to contain properties that promote longevity and sexual potency. As the nests sell for thousands of dollars a pound in today's market it is somewhat understandable why the climbers take the risk. The climbers, mostly Ibans, make offerings of tapioca wine and rice cakes to the cave spirits to ensure their safety and a bountiful harvest before beginning their climbs. The array of bamboo poles dangling from the ceiling reminded me of the pipes of a huge church organ, adding to the spiritual feeling of the cave.

On our return journey in the afternoon, as we were changing the tire, monkeys and hornbills watched us from the trees, squawking and cackling from time to time as if telling their neighbors to come watch the two "white-faces" struggle with their car. I handed Bill the tire iron and lug nuts as he needed them and watched the sweat spread across the back of his shirt as he lowered the car off the jack. So close to the equator the sun is merciless, and we were on a white gravel road that reflected the heat back up into our faces.

With the tire changed we hopped back into the car and sped off down the road trying not to think about what would happen if we lost another tire. The open windows provided some relief from the heat, which we affectionately called four-forty air-conditioning (four open windows at forty miles an hour), but sweat still ran in rivulets down my back.

A few miles further on we started noticing people, a few at a time, standing along the side of the road. This seemed strange since on the trip down we hadn't seen a soul. The people became more numerous, were obviously interested in us and stared long and hard as we passed. I looked at Bill with a question and he just shrugged his shoulders. Conversation was still impossible even as we slowed down. Up ahead I could see the steel beams of the suspension bridge we'd noticed earlier as being oddly out of place. Now the crowd was thick and someone in an army uniform was waving at us to stop. Then I saw the red ribbon tied across the bridge. My heart sank. We had remarked to each other earlier that the bridge looked awfully new and that you could see the remnants of the old bridge downstream. We had unknowingly picked the day of the bridge dedication and opening to make our trip.

This would be a huge challenge. My vocabulary in Malay was pretty well limited to housekeeping and shopping terms that I'd learned from our amah, and Bill's was limited to "bring two beers please," "that's good," and "where's the toilet?"

I walked up to the young army officer and said, *"Selamat datang, tolong saya pergi,"* or something along the lines of "Good day, please I go," and I gestured with my hand in the direction of the bridge. He looked at me as if I were crazy and simply said *"Tidak!"* or "NO!" So I apologized for not speaking very much Malay and asked to speak to his boss.

He led me closer to the bridge and said something to another officer while I gestured to Bill to move the car a little closer. The second officer came up to me and asked what I wanted and I repeated, *"Selamat datang* (insert big smile), *tolong saya pergi."* He shook his head and said *"Tidak,* no possible." I pleaded with a few *"tolongs"* and started acting a bit panicked. I showed him my passport with the one-day visa and gestured wildly at the bridge. He seemed impressed by the visa and called over yet another man who I learned shortly after was the deputy mayor.

As luck would have it he spoke excellent English so I pleaded with him to let us pass and explained that my infant son was in Brunei and I needed to get back before the last ferry from Miri departed. Then I showed him the visa and explained that I would be in his country illegally if I couldn't pass. He shook his head and said he was sorry but he couldn't move the ribbon.

I told him I understood but that I had a small car and if he would just lift the ribbon for us we could drive under and be gone before the officials arrived to cut it. I was getting a little hysterical and he was getting a little uncomfortable. He called another man over and they discussed our situation at length, which made the crowd more and more curious. I glanced back at Bill and he was giving me the "what's going on" look. I walked to the car and said, "I think it's time you got out." The deputy mayor was watching and I could see his expression change as Bill unfolded his 6' 4" frame and leaned on the car. I really hate using intimidation but when all else fails, it pays to have a little muscle on hand.

The deputy mayor called me over and said that they had decided to let us pass but we must go quickly and not stop. Before he could change his mind we got back into the car and started toward the ribbon where the two men were holding it over their heads. This triggered speculation in the crowd and they started to move toward our car waving and cheering as if we were important officials who'd come to dedicate their bridge. Once on the other side of the bridge Bill floored the accelerator and we never looked back. We'd lost another ten or fifteen minutes at the bridge and were almost certain we wouldn't make the ferry before dark.

Shortly afterwards we saw a Mercedes that we recognized as belonging to an acquaintance named Tan Boon Heng. Tan Boon Heng not only handled the catering for the local Shell oil company but he also owned several grocery markets in town and was a very important man in Kuala Belait. We figured he was heading back to Kuala Belait and Bill got on his tail and followed as closely as he could. If they would hold the last ferry for anyone they would hold it for Tan Boon. Here the road changed from the hard-packed gravel to sand, which mounded up in places from time to time causing innumerable potholes. I thanked God silently for seatbelts and shock absorbers and was extremely impressed by Bill's ability to stay with the souped-up Mercedes.

The sun was going down quickly and up ahead we could see the ferry station. The last ferry was just leaving the dock when they spotted Tan Boon's car. The attendants frantically waved the ferry back to the dock. They opened the gate and Tan Boon pulled onto the ferry with us a foot off his bumper. The attendant tried to stop us but I jumped out of the car and called to Tan Boon to please tell them to let us on. He recognized us and told the attendants to make room for us, which was not difficult since the ferry wasn't full anyway.

Once the ferry pulled away from the dock Bill and I breathed easily for the first time in several hours. We thanked Tan Boon, who seemed pleased with himself for helping us, and chatted with him for the duration of the ferry ride. He told us he had to get back in time for a high-stakes poker game at Nolan Gilbeaux's house. Nolan was the area manager for Reading & Bates Drilling Company and Bill's boss. Saving us from being stranded in Miri would give him fodder for lots of jokes that evening around the poker table. In less than twenty-four hours everyone in Kuala Belait would know about our adventure.

Susan Ellis *currently divides her time between Aberdeen, Scotland and Houston, Texas. Her first love is poetry but lately she has been working on her memoir. She has had several poems and short stories published in various literary magazines. Scotland is her ninth country of residence and it is that multicultural experience which is expressed in her work.*

Trapped on a Train

Timothy James Kelley

I was on a train to Shanghai from a city whose name I never knew, and the dead rooster hanging above my head dripped blood on my suit.

The day had been a disaster and I had insisted to the horrific Chinese agent, my travel companion, that I take the first train back to modernity, my sanctuary in the world's tallest hotel. I had been late to every appointment, each one entirely fruitless. What made things worse was that the ineffectual nature of each two-hour meeting was apparent within the first five minutes. I ate lunch three times and dinner twice and now, as my train trundled its way through another nameless Chinese city, I recalled each meal as the man next to me vomited every twenty minutes. After the fourth emission, he still occasionally gasped and produced just enough bile to trickle from his mouth the way the blood dripped from the birds hanging overhead. I was the fox among the chickens, and in China fox was a delicacy. I could feel the knives sharpening around me as I struggled to remain as inconspicuous as possible.

After the second dinner, it was apparent that my agent never intended to return that evening. His plan was to take a plane in the morning which, given his track record, meant that I would clearly miss my flight out of Shanghai to Hong Kong the next afternoon. When I presented this dilemma to him, he would merely smile his yellowed smile, and stroke my shoulder with nicotine stained fingers.

So, before dessert arrived, I decided to adjust my docile, man-of-all-cultures approach. I shifted into American caricature and demanded, with all the subtlety of the marines invading Iraq, that we explore train options and we do so now. Aghast at my horrible manners, the agent grumpily drove to the station and disappeared into a teashop after instructing his 14-year-old assistant to do what I had asked. When she returned with tickets in hand, I smiled. The marines had landed and the beach had been captured. I just didn't realize it was the wrong one.

It was 2:00 in the morning. The train was to leave the station at 10:00. Instead, I sat, waiting, with hundreds of others at the station until 12:00. Suddenly, and without announcement, the entire group squeezed itself through two small doors with all the gentle precision of a carefully choreographed ballet. I thought of the Yellow River and watched it pour onto the train. I managed to find a conductor and showed him my tickets. He stood silently by my side, the both of us a small eddy in the river of humanity. He was clearly confused but pulled me through the crowd and placed me in the last car. There were only a few seats and most of the other folks were sitting on bales of fresh manure. This car was as far from first-class as possible. It wasn't second or even third. This car could only be described as criminal-class and there I was, wearing my London-tailored suit with my Italian-cut overcoat trying to blend in with a farmer, his dead chickens and the other old soul who seemed to have a stomach virus.

For two hours I sat as quietly as possible vowing to return to this amazing country if not for any other reason than to kill the agent. I had no doubt that he had returned to our dinner, cackling about the rude American he had placed on a train that seemed to stop every ten minutes. I stayed awake, examining each station and its indecipherable signage because I had no idea how long the trip was, or which stop was Shanghai. My only hope was to see my hotel towering above the Shanghai skyline. I couldn't risk sleeping. Besides, there were two men across the way that appeared hostile.

Then things got even worse.

The conductor arrived and without hesitation moved right in my direction, gesticulating wildly. I could not comprehend his intentions but he did manage to attract the rest of the car; everyone was chirping enthusiastically until the cacophony awoke one of the chickens. Apparently, it had only been stunned earlier on. The bird began to wail and the farmer next to me desperately whacked away at the poor bird, beating it into submission once again. The voices around me screeched and yelled until silence once again reigned.

A policeman was standing next to us now and he beckoned for me to stand.

I did as he asked and he frisked me, pulling out my passport, attracting yet another wave of speculation and interest amongst my fellow criminals. The fox had been identified, and for all of those in the car, it was confirmed. I was rich. I was American after all.

The policeman signaled for me to follow him and my heart sank with each step. The conductor stepped in behind as we walked through car after car, three men in uniform, my Western suit as conspicuous as the colorful costumes of my escort. Eventually we ran out of cars and I found myself in a first class compartment. The policeman sat me down, smiled and handed me my passport. The conductor then asked for money—the internationally accepted way—by rubbing his two fingers together. I handed him some, thinking it an appropriate tip, and he walked away only to return with another ticket and some change. He also had a small woman with him who spoke French and through her I realized that the conductor had upgraded my ticket from criminal-class to first for the paltry sum of $2.

He had also saved my life. The woman explained that the criminals at the end of the train had been preparing for an assault that only the real marines could have repelled, and as my train pulled into Shanghai at 5:00 in the morning, the welcome sight of the world's tallest hotel heralding our approach, I sat back in my seat and dwelled on life's ironies. For someone who had attempted to blend, it was my cultural difference that preserved me. That and the kind conductor who did not forget my plight.

I plan to return again to China someday. The marines and I need to pay a visit to that agent.

Timothy James Kelley has lived in Switzerland for six years and is currently the Headmaster of the Leysin American School. Prior to his travels here in Europe, he served as the Artistic Director to the Spiral Stage in Boston, Massachusetts and worked with the Noble and Greenough School as the Director of Performing Arts. In addition to directing over 80 different theatrical productions, Mr. Kelley has been a teacher of history, English and film theory.

This Side of Paradise

Laura Williamson

"Whatever you do, don't use the local fertilizer."

It is a truth universally acknowledged that a Foreign Service family in possession of a new assignment must be in want of a guide. However little known the feelings or views of such a family may be on their first evening entering the country, this truth is so well fixed in the minds of the surrounding families that the new arrivals are considered the rightful recipient of some aspect or other of their wisdom.

The preceding is, of course, a rewording of the opening lines of Jane Austen's *Pride and Prejudice,* written in 1813. Nothing much has changed in human nature for a very long time, and chief among the primal instincts are the seeking of pleasure and the avoidance of pain, or at least the avoidance of embarrassment. These wholly understandable impulses underlie the tips and "what you should know" advice that inevitably circulate within expatriate communities worldwide and particularly in areas loosely defined as the Third World. That the advice may be imperfect, or even truly flawed, is merely circumstantial; it is, in the main, well intended.

Arriving in Tehran, Iran in 1973 the US Embassy's newly appointed cultural attaché and his wife were not total beginners; not prone, therefore, to immediately embracing resident expatriate dicta. Prior postings had included Japan, Cambodia, Singapore and Vietnam, each at a point of significant local and regional political change, internal unrest, even war. Iran held the promise, certainly initially, of relative stability; and with a history pre-dating Biblical times, there would be much to discover and enjoy. Persia was mosques and minarets, ancient poetry and the pleasure of ruins. Tradition even held that Cyrus the Great had built an enclosed garden in his capital at Pasargadae that so rivaled the gardens of Babylon that it was referred to as *Pardeiza,* or Paradise.

Which is, in part, how the notion of a rose garden first surfaced.

They moved into a house in Darrous, a residential suburb in the foothills of the Alborz Mountains favored by middle- and upper-middle-class Iranians: professors, rising government staffers, businessmen, engineers. The foreign community had found their way there as well: Russian and French diplomats, German construction contractors, American defense contractors. Rising above the hustle of Tehran, the air was cooler, the surroundings quieter. The houses tended to be walled and gated, more private than neighborly. The streets, winding as they rose up the hills, were lined with narrow *jube* ditches which channeled the rain and melting snow. In the dark, you had to watch your footing.

New houses, old streets, older customs: through the hills of Darrous in the early morning came donkeys and camels bearing fruit, vegetables, kitchen pots, handyman's tools and garden fertilizer, their presence announced with saddle-bells which would gently sound as trader and beast walked upward into the suburb. Over time you would recognize the distinctive sound of a particular vendor, saving you the trouble of a trip to the market or store.

The house was in reasonably good repair but faced a garden without charm, an enclosed area in the traditional Persian style. Ali, the gardener hired by the previous resident, set about persuading the attaché and his wife not only to continue his employment, but to allow him to "make a paradise." He spoke little English, but through an odd vocabulary of Italian and German and the linguistic services of the attaché's secretary, who translated the rest of the Farsi, he held forth. Roses, he said, Persian musk and damask roses, fabled throughout the Middle East, their fragrance at the height of blooming season so prevalent that they scented the air for miles around the province of Fars, the finest of the rose-growing regions and the home of Cyrus's paradise. Ali, it became obvious, hailed from Fars. The prior resident, he said, did not understand.

So it came to pass that the attaché's wife and Ali, the gardener from Fars, embarked upon a plan to recreate Paradise in the enclosed garden. On mentioning this to his colleagues, however, the attaché was cautioned: "Whatever you do, don't use the local fertilizer. It is dried camel dung, stinks when wet, and attracts flies." "Have you used it?" asked the attaché. "No, but nobody in his right mind would."

Ali had purchased two large sacks. The attaché's wife, recognizing the object of an admonition that might have some merit, tried to explain that she did not want it used in the garden. That it was dreadful, bad. Ali was beside himself. "This is need for Paradise!" he maintained. When hand gestures and her limited Farsi resulted in an impasse, the attaché's wife telephoned the embassy and once again asked for the secretary's help. In a blizzard of translation worthy of a UN simultaneous interpreter, the secretary explained Ali's position, without his customary hyperbole: no camel dung, no scented roses.

Hanging up the telephone in the kitchen, the two returned to the garden, the attaché's wife unconvinced, the gardener unwavering. He walked over to the burlap sacks, tore the ties off one, reached in and grabbed a handful. "*Not* bad!" he said, "Is *gut!*, is *buon!* Is need for Paradise! You see?" He took a mouthful—and ate it.

The US ambassador at the time was a man known for his economy of words and let's-get-on-with-it style, an approach that quickly became characteristic of his senior staff meetings at the embassy in Iran. He was also interested in even anecdotal experiences that could, in informal ways, shed light on local customs or ways of thinking that might prove useful at an unknown time down the road. So while meetings were handled with efficiency, they were never concluded without his signature request for "some color."

The story of Ali and the roses was thus duly recounted. The ambassador, no stranger to the strangest of tales, veteran of countless depositions and of endless testimony before Congressional committees, shook his head. "Put him on the pay-roll," he said, his voice absolutely deadpan, "we need a few shit-eaters around here."

110

It was by far, he said, one of the most memorable stories of his career.

Postscript: Ali was hired away by an Iranian family and was replaced by Hussein, who proved to be an acceptable but less passionate and poetic gardener than his predecessor. Roses had been added, of course, and lilies and even a grape vine along one wall. The trees were pruned and the grass clipped. The resulting garden attracted all manner of birds and was pleasant but fell, admittedly, well short of paradise. Camel dung remained the fertilizer of choice; odorless and beneficial, it never attracted a single fly during the attaché's entire four-year sojourn in Persia.

Laura Williamson was born in Washington, D.C. and grew up in the US Foreign Service, living in seven foreign cities and Washington, D.C. over a twenty-year period. She holds a Master's Degree from Georgetown University, and has enjoyed a long career in investment banking and asset management for major US and non-US clients in East Asia, Southeast Asia, Latin America and the Middle East. Ms. Williamson's prior experience included three years with the consular section at the US Embassy in Tehran, Iran.

Ka Lui

Maryann Hrichak

When I left the ice and snow of a cold Washington, D.C. January several winters ago, I had little idea I would fall in love with the tropics. After many long hours on a Northwest Airlines flight, we landed, nearly at midnight, at the Manila Airport, smack in the middle of what I thought was the "year of living dangerously." Two days later, Philippine Airlines whisked me away to the lush island of Palawan in the South China Sea, where my love affair with the tropics took root.

Still reeling with transpacific jet lag, I arrived in Puerto Princesa, Palawan's capital city, just in time for a mid-day meal. Louie, one of the Palawan natives, who was actually from the island of Masbate, greeted me with a bundle of fresh, sweet, jasmine-smelling flowers and gently announced that lunch was waiting for me in the *kubo* (house-like structure) of the Badjao Garden. Lunch? Waiting for me? I felt like a queen. Was such a glorious welcome intended for me? Yes, indeed.

I don't remember what we ate for lunch that day, although I'm sure it was some combination of fish and rice, calamansi juice (citrus) with tuyo (Philippine soy sauce), mangos and papayas, all of which soon became my steady diet. Whatever lunch was that day became the inspirational *raison d'etre du jour,* which introduced me to Louie's world and his numerous passions for the preparation, display and consumption of wonderful island delights.

Louie and I quickly became friends and partners in inventive cooking. Sure, I had cooked before (didn't we all learn how to survive in college?), but cooking with Louie was so much more of a wild adventure. Early in the day we would go to the market. I listened as he bantered with his *sukis* (regular vendors) for the best prices. I'd watch as various colors and flavors of rice sifted through his fingers. I laughed as he prodded and poked the day's fresh catch of fish. "Going to market" now had an energetic, revitalized feeling. Fun and adventurous, what I learned just being by Louie's side could never have been learned through any book.

Louie never used recipes. "Circumstantial cooking, Maryanna," he would often tell me, with tales of how he learned to cook "on land, in the mountains, on the high seas." Food combinations and cooking intuitively oozed through Louie's pores. A pinch of this here, a handful of something else there. The end result was always a delicious taste treat. I marveled at Louie's abilities and his finesse over an open fire. Simple ingredients bonded our souls.

Then, in the heat of the sultry tropics, the wild seed of Kalui planted a foundation. Kalui, whose Tagalog version means "Ka Louie" for "Brother Louie," now rests as an elaborate nipa hut restaurant of sorts next to Island Divers just off Rizal Avenue, Puerto Princesa's main street. All you have to do is make reservations. There is no menu. As *chef extraordinaire,* Louie goes to the market and prepares whatever the-

112

day's fresh catch presents itself to be. If Louie's delicious aromas and tastes don't bring you back, Kalui's ambience certainly will. Stone pathways lined by native plants and flowers and sturdy bamboo flooring beckon you inside. Don't forget to remove your shoes before entering. Off in the corner of this nipa creation, you'll find a collection of native Palawan baskets, originally used for grain storage. One entire wall of Kalui is lined with publications to read while you wait for dinner or books to borrow for a short time until you return for another meal. Perfect ambience—a starlit sky on a warm tropical night, a belly soon-to-be full of the day's fresh catch with complimentary herbs and spices, and the fragrance of fresh sampaguita flowers. For several months, I was fortunate to be with a chef who fed my body and an artist who fed my soul.

Louie tops the list of my food mentors for stimulation to the mind's senses, for exotic creations so healthful and good for my body and soul, and for ambiance of the heart. The freshness and vitality Louie brings to any meal have filled me with endless tropical treasures. I now cook as an ode to joy and as an ode to Louie, whose passionate inspirations in a tropical kitchen planted the seeds for countless gastronomical explorations, a truly wonderful experience like no other.

Maryann Hrichak wrote this story in March 1998 about her initial experience going to work in the Philippines. Maryann currently lives in San Francisco, California and has fond memories of the nearly five years she spent living and working in the Philippines.

Living History

"Señor Conklin," she said, "The switchboard operating room is filling up with soldiers with machine guns; what should I do?"

Roger Conklin

I had read about the miners' visit to quell student protests in June of 1990 and the ensuing violence. Now they were returning.

Beth Henson Tudan

I was in the presence of pure, shared human grief.

Sue Burke

Others were just grateful to be alive, particularly those who were hurt and had only the clothes on their backs. It seems that the closer people came to death, the more elated they were to be alive and the less they were concerned with their possessions or where they would sleep.

William Cox

The engines had stopped. The ship was still. Over the loudspeaker, came the order, "To the lifeboats! Keep calm."

Mavis Guinard

In the Middle of a Military Coup

Roger Conklin

The date was October 3, 1968. I was executive vice-president and deputy general manager of Compañía Peruana de Teléfonos S. A., the Peruvian telephone company majority-owned by the American company, ITT. At 2:30 in the morning, while I was sound asleep at our Lima home with my wife Nancy and our four small children, the phone rang. It was the night chief operator at the long-distance switchboards. In those days direct dialing had not yet started in Peru, so all long-distance calls had to be completed by an operator. *"Señor* Conklin," she said, "The switchboard operating room is filling up with soldiers with machine guns; what should I do? It looks like a *golpe de estado* (a coup)." I recommended she listen intently to the instructions of the officer-in-charge, and follow them. The objective clearly was to suspend telephone communications between Lima, the rest of the country and the outside world as the first step, prior to deposing the then-president.

She thanked me and hung up. I immediately dialed the US Embassy and asked the Marine guard on night duty at the Embassy switchboard if he could provide me with the unlisted home telephone number of John Wesley White, the US ambassador to Peru, identifying myself and indicating that there were some "happenings" going on that I was sure would be of interest to Mr. White. The Marine replied that he was not permitted to give out that information, but he did give me the telephone number of the Duty Officer who I called and awoke from a sound sleep. He became very wide awake when I told him the purpose of my call. He took my telephone number, thanked me and hung up.

Within a minute or so my phone rang and it was the Embassy Security Officer, who asked me to repeat everything. This I did. He asked that if I should receive any more calls, to please find out everything possible. I told him I doubted there would be any more calls, but certainly would do my best if called again. The Embassy had no clue of what was going to happen that night. He said he was driving immediately to the Embassy and would call me as soon as he arrived there. I checked my radio and all stations were off the air, except 24-hour *Radio Reloj,* a news and time station which was broadcasting only the time every 30 seconds. There was no news.

About 45 minutes later I received another call from the Security Officer who had arrived at the Embassy. He asked if I had received any other calls. There had been none. I asked him what he had seen on his way to the Embassy. He had seen three tanks—one in front of the Presidential Palace, another in front of *Radio Nacional,* the government radio station, and a third at another location which I do not recall. Calm reigned supreme in the streets.

The call from the night chief operator at 2:30 came about 15 minutes before Army troops entered the Presidential Palace and aroused President Fernando Belaunde Terry from his sleep. Army guards at the Palace did not resist the arriving troops. President Belaunde was taken to an army base where he was held until about 7:30 a.m. He was then transferred to Lima's Jorge Chavez International Airport and

117

placed on board a commercial 707 jetliner of *Aerolineas Peruanas,* which had been reserved a few days earlier by the Army for a charter flight leaving that day from Lima to Buenos Aires, Argentina. He was sent into exile.

It was a bloodless coup. At 6:30 am, three radio stations came on the air simultaneously broadcasting a proclamation signed by the *Junta Militar de Gobierno* (Military Junta) announcing that there had been a "change of government" and the Armed Forces were now in charge. Life returned to nearly normal after a couple of days of minor confusion. General Juan Velasco Alvarado, formerly the commanding general of the Joint Chiefs of Staff of the Army, Navy and Air Force, was the new president. It happened that I knew the General personally, having served as the interpreter in a meeting between him and a visiting vice-president of ITT from New York some six months earlier.

Press reporters from around the world began arriving in Lima to report on what had happened. Two days after the coup, together with a fellow worker having lunch in a downtown Lima restaurant, we overheard the conversation of some foreign reporters at a nearby table. One of them asked, "Who broke the news of the coup?" One of the others responded, "Nobody seems to know for sure, but I heard a rumor that it was someone in the telephone company." I just listened, not saying a word.

Three days later on October 6, the military president Juan Velasco Alvarado went on TV at noon to announce that the military forces of Peru were, at that very moment, seizing at gunpoint and with bayonets drawn the *Brea y Pariñas* petroleum installations of International Petroleum Company, a subsidiary of the American-owned Exxon. Instinctively we knew that the telephone company would likely be next, and we later learned that indeed this had been the plan. But because of the adverse world reaction to the coup and the takeover of International Petroleum, the generals changed their plans and, after 16 months of negotiations, paid cash and purchased the telephone company.

Four years after arriving in Lima, a city we loved very much and where we made many Peruvian friends, we moved to Rio de Janeiro to start my next assignment with ITT. We obtained a visa for Carmen, our Peruvian maid and took her with us so our children would not forget their Spanish as they became immersed in Portuguese. Thirty-four years later, they maintain their native fluency in English, Spanish and Portuguese and use these languages daily in their professions.

Roger Conklin was born in Michigan. He and his wife Nancy and their four children lived and worked 11 years in South America. He was executive vice-president and deputy manager of ITT-owned Compañía Peruana de Teléfonos in the 1960s, until it was nationalized by the Peruvian Government. He later served in executive positions in Brazil with ITT, Continental Telephone Corporation and Brazilian-owned Telcom S.A. Returning to the United States in 1977, he was then a vice-president of sales with Nortel Networks at their Florida headquarters for the Caribbean and Latin America, during which time he traveled extensively throughout that area until retiring in 1993. He continues as a self-employed consultant in Latin American telecommunications marketing. The Conklins live in Miami.

An American in "Little Paris"

Beth Henson Tudan

The Dream

When I was five years old, I decided I wanted to join the Peace Corps. Since the Peace Corps ws not accepting kindergarteners, I determined to find a way to serve overseas. Thus, I studied French, received my undergraduate degrees in History and English, and went to graduate school to earn an MBA at the University of Tennessee

In the fall of 1989 the collapse of the Berlin Wall was followed by revolutions all over Eastern Europe. I became interested in going to Eastern Europe to work in economic development. I applied for a Fulbright in Romania to study the changes to the free market economy, teach marketing, and consult with budding Romanian entrepreneurs. Romania was also getting less attention than the big three of the time: Poland, Hungary and Czechoslovakia. Thus, the possibilities there would be more open than in other East European countries. I learned of my acceptance in May 1991

The Journey to Bucharest as the Adventure Begins

In September 1991, after a summer in Geneva, I boarded the train for Bucharest.Civil War had erupted over the summer in Yugoslavia, resulting in a longer route via Hungary. I soon passed through the mountains of Transylvania, quaint villages, and fields of sunflowers

After thirteen hours, The Dacia Express arrived at Bucharest's main station, *Gara de Nord*. The station was dusty, dirty and decrepit, showing years of neglect under communism. Bedraggled children begged to help with the bags. My taxi driver, an engineer, speaking English, explained he was earning extra money for his family. He showed me around the city, creating a favorable impression. He even gave me change (a miracle as I would quickly learn).

A group of Fulbrighters was staying at the Hotel Lido for the first few days. The hotel, filled with antique furnishings, beautiful wood paneling, and crystal chandeliers, exuded old world charm. That night we attended a reception honoring the new Fulbright Scholars at the villa of Mark Asquino, Cultural Affairs Officer of the United States Information Agency. His home was in an old part of Bucharest that former Romanian president Nicolae Ceaușescu had not destroyed. The area is one of the few historic areas remaining, to show why Bucharest had been nicknamed, "*The Little Paris*."

In 1977, an earthquake measuring 7.5 on the Richter scale rocked Bucharest, killing more than 1500. Ceaușescu's government used it as an excuse to tighten control over the country. The communist officials began condemning old sections of Bucharest, tearing down entire historic neighborhoods. They tore down centuries-old streets and villages, giving the occupants just hours to collect their belongings and move. They built a wide boulevard lined with empty storefronts and white stone apartment buildings.

119

Ceauşescu was perhaps the only person inspired by North Korean architecture.Following a visit to North Korea, he ordered the destruction of one-fifth of the historic core of Bucharest. He began building the second largest building in the world, second only to the Pentagon, his *Casa Poporului* (House of the People) that he would never allow the people to enter. He ordered The House of the People filled with expensive items. One Oriental rug was the size of an American football field and reportedly took 400 men to lift.

The day following the reception as I walked around Piaţa Universităţii (University Square), a fellow Fulbrighter found me, warning that the miners were coming. I had read about the miners' visit to quell student protests in June of 1990 and the ensuing violence. Now they were returning. He told me that the U.S. Consulate had ordered our group to go back to our hotel, lock the doors and stay inside. The Consulate warned us to look neither western, nor intellectual.

We returned to the hotel and gathered with other Fulbrighters in an upstairs lobby. After an hour, we ventured to University Square. Many Romanian students were milling about, talking, gesturing. There were also many elderly people – intellectual looking elderly people. Professors, perhaps?

As we observed the Bucharest citizens, we began hearing a booming sound. Boom, boom, boom. Cannons? Grenades? Everyone in the square stood still. Boom, boom, boom. The sound was getting louder and louder. Then we saw them: the miners, wearing lighted hats. They were marching from *Gara de Nord* and chanting. As the miners approached the crowd, the students and elderly intellectuals began chanting, too. Then, suddenly, the students, the elderly and the miners joined arm in arm … and began dancing the Hora, laughing and chanting together.

What were they saying? "*Jos Iliescu, Jos Iliescu*." What does that mean, we Americans asked? "Down with Iliescu," they explained. The current Romanian president, Ion Iliescu, a second line communist, had brought in the miners in 1990 to put down student protests. Now the miners were disillusioned with Iliescu because promised pay increases and bonuses had not materialized. They had come to get their pay.

The miners stayed for four days. They marched from morning to midnight, sleeping in hotel lobbies. They fought with police. Miners marched up Boulevard Magheru, directly under our balcony. We saw the police marching, too, holding up plastic shields and wearing riot gear. We heard sporadic gunfire. We coughed and cried from the wafting tear gas.

After the first night, I managed to call my parents in Memphis. Mother said they woke up to the news on NPR, "Miners are rioting in Bucharest, Romania." I assured her that all was well. The adventure had just begun.

Introducing the Free Market Economy to Former Communists
When the miners returned to the earth, I began work at the Academy of Economic Studies in Bucharest. I began teaching marketing classes and writing case studies. As I worked with Romanian colleagues, some were friendly to me as an American while

others were not. Eventually, I learned that many of the older, and unfriendly, professors had changed the titles of their courses, but not the content.

The younger professors and the students, however, welcomed an American into their fold. They wanted to know everything about the United States – economics, politics, music, pop culture, and later about how the Rodney King episode could cause LA to burn.

I began consulting at the Small Business Development Center at Polytechnic University in Bucharest. Entrepreneurs came to seek our help in developing business plans and marketing strategies. Helping business owners craft target marketing strategies was straightforward, as for many, their only goal was to reach "rich people." Since there were few of those in Romania at the time, we worked to find who else might want their services or products. I helped others brainstorm inexpensive marketing strategies. They had heard of neither fliers nor coupons. As I hail from generations of entrepreneurs and concentrated in entrepreneurship during my MBA program, giving advice on start-ups was easy.

Romanian Markets and Living Conditions

When I arrived in September 1991, the Romanian open-air markets were full of locally grown fresh fruits and vegetables. By January, they were almost empty. One day I arrived to find only celery root. Since I had no idea what to do with it, I went home empty-handed.

The grocery stores shelves were equally bleak. The canned goods were rusty with labels askew. The bread stores were either empty or had long lines. After the earthquake of 1977, Ceauşescu decided to pay off Romania's national debt. At the expense of the standard of living of the Romanian citizens, Romania began paying. The standard of living fell through the end of the 70s and throughout the 80s. One friend recalled, "During the 70s, my mother sent me to see if the bread was fresh. In the 80s, she sent me to see if there was any bread at all."

By Christmas of 1991, though, there was a display in a private store by the University Square that had three oranges decorated with Christmas tinsel. It was so shocking to see this outward display of marketing that I took a photo of it.

In early December, a huge snowstorm swept through Romania, blanketing Bucharest with three feet of snow. The radiators in my apartment remained cool, as had been typical in many apartments in communist times, and I could see my breath inside. Even Romanian visitors would not stay long for a visit, complaining it was too cold. The telephone stopped working (frozen, perhaps?) and would remain broken for months.

I lived in a Stalinist-style gray apartment building. During the winter, there was no gas for cooking in the apartment during the day. Other apartment inhabitants had drilled larger holes in their gas stoves so that they could keep their burners on to heat their apartments. I found that I could cook at 3 am as my neighbors would be asleep and had turned off the gas during the night.

I was lucky in that I had hot water in the morning from 7 to 8. The apartments higher up in the building did not have hot water because the water pressure could not reach them.

Bucharest Begins to Brighten

After a winter break in Switzerland, I returned to Romania in January 1992. I was surprised to see how much brighter everything looked. What was the difference? Coca-Cola had arrived. The company's logo was everywhere – on storefronts, on umbrellas at cafes and restaurants, on kiosks. The red and white emblem brightened up Bucharest. Romanians were thrilled to have the American beverage. To many of them, it symbolized freedom and modernity. They did, however, complain about the outrageous price of 15 cents a bottle.

With the coming of Coca-Cola, some Americans worried about the "corporatization" of Eastern Europe. Romanians felt differently. They felt as if they were finally joining the West. Coca-Cola introduced a new standard to Romania. The bottles were clean and the labels were put on evenly and were replaced whe n worn. The drink quality was consistent.

Throughout 1992, more private stores began opening. Not many Romanians could afford to buy much in them, though, as they were being hammered with inflation. A Romanian friend was saving to buy a TV. He said, "The more I save, the more prices run away from me." Other Romanians complained that they had had more than enough money during communism, but there was nothing to buy. Now, however, there were goods available, but there was not enough money. During 1991, inflation had reached 50% and the GDP shrank 20%. Privatization would put a strain on ordinary Romanians for the next few years.

Learning Romanian For the Sake of a Chocolate Chip Cookie

One day before joining a Romanian family for dinner, I decided to make the quintessential American dessert, chocolate chip cookies. I bought chocolate chips at the tiny commissary at the US Embassy, and then set out to buy eggs in the open-air market. It was close to Easter and the markets were full of eggs. Thus, I asked,

"*Aveți trei oi?*" ("Do you have three eggs?")

"*Nu, n-am,*" ("No, I don't have any") I was repeatedly told. And yet, they had them sitting there. It was impolite to point, so I kept going to different vendors, wondering why they didn't want to sell me their eggs.

Finally, I came to a man, dressed in a long, woolen cloak. "*Aveți trei oi?*" I asked.

"*Ba da,*" ("Of course,") he answered.

"*Cit costă una?*" ("How much is one?") I asked.

"*Doisprezece mii de lei*" ("Twelve thousand lei, the Romanian currency") he answered. That was the equivalent of about sixty dollars. Now, as an American, I didn't mind paying a little more than the average Ion, but 600,000 times the going rate seemed a bit high.

"*Doisprezece mii de lei pentru un ou?*" ("12,000 lei for one egg?"), I asked. He began laughing and called out to the other vendors in the market. They all laughed until their sides shook. Finally, one calmed down enough to explain that an *ou* is singular for an egg, but that the plural is *ouă*, not *oi*. It turns out that *oi* is sheep. Now, sixty dollars for a sheep is probably not a bad price.

Learning Romanian was fairly easy. Knowing French helped. Romanian media add subtitles rather than dubbing movies and television. Thus, I was able to hear English or French while reading Romanian. I learned the language more quickly as a result.

When I met Costi, who would later become my husband, we spoke French together. Then he surprised me by beginning to speak English well. At one point, he said, "I ain't gonna do that." I asked, "Where did you learn that?" "From the Blues," he replied. Being a native of Memphis, Blues country, I was smitten.

Romanian Attitudes Towards Americans

Romanians, except for a few communists, loved Americans. Upon learning my nationality, they would personally thank me for ending the Cold War and freeing their nation. They also praised Bush and Reagan – something I had rarely heard during my travels in Western Europe. Some women insisted I marry their sons. Some stroked my cheek, stared into my eyes and kissed my hands, saying they had never seen an American before.

Something, though, that I heard again and again was "Yalta." Romanians were convinced that Franklin Delano Roosevelt and Winston Churchill had sold them out at the Yalta Conference in February 1945. Why, they wanted to know, had Roosevelt deserted them when they had been Allies during World War II? I learned to point out that FDR had been ill during the conference and died less than eight weeks later. I explained to closer friends that Romania had indeed switched sides during the war, having originally sided with Nazi Germany.

A colleague at the Academy of Economic Studies, Mura Elena Crăiuțu, told me that her grandfather had waited for the United States to come to rescue Romania. Because he had been the mayor of a village before World War II, the communist government was suspicious of him. He had lost his home and his brother to the invading Soviet Army. His family became refugees twice during the War, escaping the second time in a horse-drawn carriage with few household belongings and heirlooms. He, his wife, and young son traveled hundreds of miles through war-torn Romania before finally settling down again. He and his wife became teachers in another village, Prisaca Dornei. Each night, for decades thereafter, he would hide under his covers and listen to Voice of America (VOA), waiting for news of the arrival of the Americans. He died in 1985, four years before the Romanian Revolution would bring hope to millions of Romanians. He might be surprised to learn that his three great-grandsons are now both Romanian and American citizens as I married his grandson, Costi Tudan.

More To Buy; Less to Buy it With

I requested and received an extension for a second year, as did more than half of the other Fulbrighters. Applying for an extension was unusual, but we were fascinated by the country and by our experiences there. A lack of heat or hot water and long gas and bread lines were not going to keep us away.

In 1993, more private stores opened. The communist-era stores began to have less and less on their shelves while the private stores had more and more. Inflation spiked to 256% percent, but the GDP was beginning to stabilize. As private bread stores opened, the lines were shorter at the state bread stores as Romanians were delighted to purchase fresh, warm bread.

A Middle Eastern company opened a fast food restaurant called Spring Time in *Piaţa Victoriei* (Victoria Square). Romanians flocked to it even though it cost three days' average wage to eat there.

Many people shopped in the new stores, but few were buying the more expensive goods. When my fiancé Costi went for his tuxedo fitting before our wedding, the tailor shook his head, asking how young people could afford to get married and wondering how they could be optimistic about the future or afford to have children.

Romania Today

Costi and I were married at Suceviţa Monastery in July of 1993. Since moving to the States with Costi in August of that year, we have often returned to Romania and are impressed with the progress. By 2003, the lei had stabilized against foreign currency, inflation was down to 15 percent, and unemployment had fallen to seven percent. The economy is predicted to grow 5.4 percent in 2005. Romania joined NATO in 2004 and hopes to join the European Union in 2007.

The younger, educated people have done well. Our friends have started successful businesses in architecture and construction, while others work in international banking or for multinational conglomerates.

Elderly people have had a harder time as inflation has eaten away the value of their pensions. The lucky ones have children who help support them. But people of Costi's parents' and grandparents' generations complain with feeling about the reversal of roles and how theirs are Romania's "lost generations."

Our sons Paul Cassian, Alexander, and Thomas, spend time each summer with their grandparents in Prisaca Dornei. They hear the stories of the hardships of war and communism and the hope that their great-grandfather felt as he listened to VOA. And if they ask, they can listen to the very same radio that their great-grandfather, Cassian Tudan, used as he listened while hiding from the communists. They are the future generation of Romania and America.

__Beth Henson Tudan,__ a native of Memphis, Tennessee, was a Fulbright Scholar studying the changes to the free market economy in Romania from 1991 to 1993. She currently lives with her Romanian-American husband, Costi, and three sons, Paul, Alexander, and Thomas, in the state of Rheinland-Pfalz, Germany.

Madrid is Weeping

Sue Burke

"It was like September 11th," an American friend told me. In 2001, she had just moved to New Orleans before the attack on New York, and in 2004 she had just moved to Madrid before the attack on March 11 that killed 192 people and injured 1,900 on morning rush-hour commuter trains. She didn't yet know her neighbors when a wave of emotions washed over them all.

I had been in Madrid on September 11, when the bustling city grew quiet and stunned. March 11 was like that and much more. I live a half-kilometer from the Atocha train station where most of the victims died. My husband and I heard the bombs: long, scraping rumbles. Then sirens wailed continuously until late afternoon.

People wept on the streets and friends greeted each other with relieved handshakes. A call went out for blood for the injured; another friend, a tall, blond farm boy from America's Midwest, joined the line to donate, reading an English-language novel during the five-hour wait, obviously foreign, and said he had never felt more welcome and at home.

The morning after, radio announcers were saying *"saludos"* instead of *"buenos días"*—"greetings" instead of "good day"—because it wasn't going to be a good day. Spanish flags draped with black crepe were hanging from balconies, which surprised me because the flag had long been identified with the Franco dictatorship, but suddenly that didn't matter anymore.

I saw my neighbor, a pediatrician, as he was leaving for work. Children as well as adults had been injured in the bombings, and every doctor was working double shifts. He looked sad and already exhausted.

I couldn't give blood, but I could go to the protest that night with my husband right after our Spanish class. I hoped that the protest would be Madrid's largest-ever, more than a million people. A lot of friends went too, both Spaniards and expats, but we never saw them because, despite the cold pouring rain, more than two million people filled the streets chanting, "It's not raining, Madrid is weeping."

The next 48 hours saw a political earthquake. The hardest part for me and many American friends was explaining it to the folks back home. The election threw out a pro-Bush prime minister. Was there anti-Americanism? Yes, some of it ugly, but never directed at us personally, perhaps because, having lived under a dictatorship, Spaniards could separate citizens and their government.

The dead and injured included many foreigners on their way to work from a poor neighborhood, and some were illegal immigrants, but Madrid wept the same. A shrine for the victims sprang up at Atocha train station, with bouquets, messages and mementos in many languages, but most of all candles, hundreds of candles. A few signs carried political messages, but competing messages were respected, and when a candle went out, someone would relight it.

A week after the attack, I joined those contemplating the memorial with somber faces and lowered voices, and without expecting it, I began to cry. A breeze, warmed by candles and scented by flowers, brushed my face. I was in the presence of pure, shared human grief.

I'll admit I am still jumpy a year later since Spain is still under terrorist threat, but terrorism had threatened the city before March 11, and we already knew how not to change our lives out of fear. But there is a change that has endured despite relentless attempts by Spanish politicians of all parties to turn the attack, its victims and terrorism into a political football. As someone wrote at the Atocha shrine, "We were all riding on that train. We won't forget."

Sue Burke *and her husband have lived in Madrid, Spain, since December 1999. For many years, they dreamed of living overseas to learn another culture and language, and when they got a chance to go to Madrid, though they had never visited it, they packed and moved, and it turned out to be a good idea. Sue has worked as a writer, both in journalism and fiction, for thirty years. More of her writing is available at www.sue.burke.name. She and her husband still take public transportation without hesitation.*

The Waves That Changed People's Lives

William Cox

Tender rays of sunlight began to flood our hotel room at the beautiful Patong Merlin Hotel—a resort hotel located both close to the city center and right on Patong Beach, a bustling tourism center in Thailand. It was the day after Christmas, December 26, 2004, and my wife Natasha and I were just beginning to open our eyes at the beginning of a day that would change many people's lives.

At roughly 8:25 a.m. we were still in bed but wakened by a gentle rocking of the bed. The rocking gained a little force and I got up, noticing that our balcony was moving back and forth in relation to the tall palm tree which stood right out in front of the hotel room. I thought, "Wow, a small earthquake, my first ever." Nat hardly acknowledged in a weak voice "...an earthquake..." There were three slight shakings, the second being the strongest. Then it stopped.

I returned to bed for 20 minutes, enjoying the paradise-like situation we were in: perfect weather every day, palm trees, extremely nice people, amazing food and great night life whenever we wanted it. The previous night we had just been out to one of Patong's best seafood restaurants, The Savoy, in celebration of Christmas. Nat had ordered four huge prawns, each weighing about 200 grams. Every day I had gone running on the beach and worked out in the gym. The breakfast buffet was always sumptuous. We felt good—really good. Often I had gone jogging before Nat got up—in the morning on the beach without shoes or shirt. What a feeling!

And the night life—hundreds of bars and several discos all within walking distance. And what an atmosphere. The Thais always greeted us like special guests.

But this was all to change within minutes and without warning. It was 9:50 and time to head for breakfast. We had long forgotten the small earthquake as we closed our room door, clutching the key 5401. Our room was in Building 5, located within safe distance of the beach and roads; quiet and with a view over the pristine pool and impeccably kept greenery. Everything was always so perfect, so peaceful and cheerful.

We normally took the stairs, pointing to the overweight guests in the hotel who took the elevators. As we descended the steps to the breakfast there was a loud bang. Some people thought it was a terrorist act. People ran to the backside of the hotel overlooking the road behind the hotel. Nothing there. When we reached the breakfast room, the emergency lighting was on but everything else was normal. People were helping themselves to the buffet, as usual.

We were directed to our table, also as usual. Then we noticed people getting up and running out of the restaurant, all to the area to the right. I thought that perhaps a platform which the hotel personnel used for putting up New Year's decorations had fallen over and people were rushing to help. At the same moment a mass of water full of sewage and debris swamped the entire facility. The bright blue of the pool changed to a smelly brown. Wooden sun chairs floated around. I thought, "There goes our morning at the pool," not realizing at all what had happened. Although alone in the breakfast room, which was elevated, Nat and I proceeded to the buffet to start our breakfast. We thought it was a small flooding because the water was neither deep nor fast-moving.

The breakfast restaurant also had full view of the road and parking area on the other (rear) side of the hotel. What we saw there was more intimidating: masses of brown water shot out onto the road coming from the side alleys right and left of the hotel, flooding the road and parking lot within seconds. The water was over 1-2 meters deep on the road already, carrying huge, 100-200 kilo flower pots and the remnants of blue wooden beach chairs from the beach (about 100 meters away). People just watched, stunned. Was this something serious or not, and WHAT was it?

We didn't hear any major noise, crashing sounds or screaming. The 100-meter long resort hotel facility was full of dense vegetation, three pools, two elevated bar platforms and restaurants. It kept the noise out of the main area of the hotel. It had kept the water away from the main building, which housed the restaurant, lounge, main reception and bar.

The water fairly quickly receded within the hotel facility. Some people ran towards the hotel areas near the beach. We still didn't know why, or what they were going after.

What we didn't know yet was that Patong beach had been hit by the first tsunami, the smaller one. It had already taken many lives. The ten thousand beach chairs lined up along the beach were not yet filled, but a lot of children and families were already on the beach—typical for Sunday morning. The waterline had suddenly gone down, a very strange thing. Then the wave had emerged and caught anyone on the beach or walking on the front road or in the endless shops, and hurled them against the cement wall, cars, trees, whatever was in the water's way. The wave hit the beach with a speed of over 60 miles per hour. It destroyed the waterfront, the front areas of our hotel, all cars, buses, shops. It instantly killed virtually all people in the small supermarket next to our hotel, for example, where we always bought mineral water and fruits to snack on in the evenings. Luckily we had bought water there the evening before. Otherwise I would likely have been there.

The scene inside the supermarket must have been a nightmare. The supermarket was located slightly underground, directly facing the beach. The electricity had gone out and the water poured in to the ceiling within seconds, pinning people under the large racks holding merchandise. There was no way out. Death was inevitable. Next to one of the entrances to the market was our hairdresser's shop, where I had had my hair cut a few days before and last year. If our hairdresser was in the shop, her chances of survival were minimal.

But all this wasn't yet clear to us at this point. Back to the restaurant: For our part, we quit eating and decided to look for the highest accessible parts of the hotel. The reception was suddenly abandoned. We couldn't get to our passports, tickets and documents, which were in a safe deposit box behind the reception. Getting a new Russian passport for my wife would be hell. I could forget about my business trips in early January, I thought.

Just as things began to quiet down, the big wave hit Patong: thirty feet high or more, faster and much more powerful than the first. We were on the third floor on the way to our room, not knowing where else to go or what to do. People scrambled up the stairs in the hotel, searching for the highest place in the four-story hotel. They yelled: "Go up, go, go…" From the third floor we looked out on the back alleyway, where water now was roaring by and rising by the second. Now we were scared. This was powerful. The inner facility of the hotel was now flooded as well. We felt as if we were on an island or a ship that might soon be submerged.

In the front of the hotel facility and along the entire waterfront, the toll on human life and facilities was high. Mountains of debris cut off the front part of the hotel from the main areas in back. All rooms in Buildings 1 and 2 of our hotel up to the second floor had been torn apart, flooded. Taxis, jeeps and even a bus were in the front areas of the hotel garden, their horns stuck and blowing. The concrete walkways along the beach were simply neutralized, 100-kilo blocks lying every-where except in their proper places. The road in back of the hotel was totally flood-ed. People in the hotel packed their essentials and were going in all directions, some climbing onto the dangerous roof of the hotel.

We climbed the stairs to a platform on top of our building. Others were there with countless water bottles, as though they expected to spend a long time there. It was hot, for the first time unpleasantly hot. The roaring of water on all sides of the hotel was the predominant sound. In the background were those unnerving car horns, stuck as cars were in heaps. Looking out back, we could see that the water had gone much farther inland, down the side streets, carrying structural elements of buildings, wooden planks, bushes, large flower pots, t-shirts and endless items from the shops along the waterfront.

Normalcy and paradise had ended in Patong. People ran in all directions. There was no way out of the hotel. And we didn't know how big the next wave would be: 30 or 50 meters? A 30-meter wave would finish us off, no doubt. The situation had a strange Titanic feeling. People were scared, including the two of us.

Nat and I decided to try to find a higher place than the platform on top of Building 5. Building 6 had the highest tower, but when we got there, it was locked. Down to the main reception. A woman held her dead child. Another young woman lay on the floor on towels. Hotel guests were giving her first aid. She didn't move. The entire hotel staff had disappeared. There was no electricity, brown water sur-rounded us.

Later we learned that the second wave had washed people all the way from the beach into our pools. Supposedly the dead child was one of these people. Even so, at this time we didn't know the extent of destruction further forward, toward the beach. We went to a higher floor, trying to continue, but the hotel buildings were only partially connected. We only got about half-way. The walkways through the facility were totally blocked with even more debris. Concrete walls had been destroyed. We met an American who had been coming to Thailand for over 20 years. He said that between the first and second waves he had helped save a woman from out of the massage room. Another woman from Germany lost her two kids, both presumed dead. He warned that the biggest wave was on its way and would hit us at 13:00, in about 20-30 minutes.

From our vantage point, we could see the destruction everywhere. Cars and debris lay on the open lot on the other side of the hotel. Small restaurants were destroyed. Suddenly people again starting screaming and yelling. Another wave? But we saw nothing.

What to do now? We were confused. We decided to return to our room. Every place seemed abandoned. We saw people leaving on the Merlin staff bus, hanging on its back platform. It was packed. Leaving the hotel seemed too dangerous. We decided to stay. The building structure of our hotel was solid concrete.

The hotel halls were a sad sight. Normally they were perfectly kept and clean. Now they were empty; dirty towels and linen lay on the floors. People stormed the main hotel bar, stealing beverages. We later heard that others had broken into the hotel boutiques and stolen goods as others just watched. From perfect control to chaos in hours.

Back in our room and without a clear game plan, I stood on our hotel room balcony waiting for something to happen. Something good or bad. One thing seemed clear to us: There were only three earthquake jolts, so there could only be three waves. The third wave had seemed minor, just like the last jolt. We didn't believe in a new megawave. One o'clock passed. No more waves. Now what?

Just then a Thai without a hotel uniform yelled at me from down below: "Come down fast. You must leave the hotel." We did, taking almost nothing except our room and safe deposit keys. We hardly had any cash. But we did have my credit and ATM cards because we had been out the evening before. The bus was parked in the middle of the rear parking lot, which was covered with dirt, sand, mud and debris, but where the water had subsided. It was an open bus normally used for personnel, with 3 benches the length of the rear cabin. It was half full and people were nervous. We were too. Being in the bus was not a safe feeling. People were in their bathing clothes, without possessions. One man took his time, insisting on taking his large suitcase, occupying space and not considering anyone but himself. He was slow and people yelled at him to hurry up. The bus filled slowly. It was like a lifeboat—small and unsafe.

No one told us where we were being taken. But the hotel already had a clear plan: evacuate everyone left over to a nearby hill overlooking Patong. Supposedly the authorities were convinced that the biggest wave was yet to come.

The ride lasted only about ten minutes and we were the last ones to arrive. Roughly 1,000 tourists were already there. People climbed higher on the hill, waiting to see something spectacular. The sea in Patong bay was as quiet as ever, turquoise colored. From a distance it again looked like paradise. We went to buy water. The bottles cost a small fortune, using up a chunk of our last cash.

We asked around. What next? "We'll wait here until 14:30 and then return to the hotel," said one bus driver. We waited for three hours. Peoples' feelings were obviously mixed: gratitude, shock, disorientation. Others were again eating, buying snacks offered along the road by mobile vendors.

Rumors were not in short supply: the waves that hit us had been 3 meters, 10 meters; there were 200 dead, 300 dead; the earthquake epicenter was in Malaysia, it was just off our coast, a huge wave was still on its way...It would hit at 14.30, 15.00...

We recognized people from our hotel in the crowd of people dispersed along the road and in the steep hills rising up from the road. Other hotels were also bussing their guests, dropping them off here and going back for more, for example, from the nearby Meridien. Tourists complained about the unclear organization, always quick to make suggestions on how it could be done better. We couldn't see anything to complain about.

After several hours our hotel bus got an OK to start bringing the tourists to the Phuket Merlin Hotel, the only one of four Merlin hotels that had survived. It was located in Phuket City. Our own strategy was simple: be on the first bus so if there were rooms, we would get one. The drive there took us past beaches and partially flooded areas. The streets along the beach were covered with sand, branches and wooden objects but damage was less than in Patong. These areas were protected by a water breaker located about 300 feet in front of the beaches.

Arriving at the Phuket Merlin Hotel caused mixed feelings. Phuket was a typical Asian city: dense with a lot of traffic, hot and loud. One shop was lined up next to the other. It was a far cry from the relaxed beach atmosphere of Patong. We had been in Phuket for a day the week before and could not wait to get back to Patong and our Merlin hotel overlooking its paradise-like gardens.

The atmosphere in the Phuket Merlin where the bus of "refugees" arrived was amazingly calm—business as usual. We were quietly and politely guided into the coffee shop were a complementary buffet lunch was served. The hotel's strategy was also clear: hungry tourists are irate tourists so feed them first.

After lunch, hundreds of tourists began arriving at the Phuket Merlin as buses unloaded them. Some had suitcases, most did not and many were only in bathing clothes. The lobby was packed with people, overwhelming for the Phuket Merlin reception which could do little. We were asked to fill out a form and hope and wait for a place to stay.

And we were lucky! By about 8 p.m. we were taken to Phuket city's best hotel, the Phuket Royal and put in a room with two closed-mouth young Australian men. We went next door to have a drink with a group of friendly Israelis who offered us a drink in their room. They had just arrived from Bangkok when the waves had hit.

The Australians left the room voluntarily and found places to stay in the hotel's gym, preferring this over sharing a rather compact-sized double bed.

What had happened was obviously international news and once settled in our room, we went in search of an internet café to get word to my dad in Germany and Natasha's parents in Russia that we were OK. Phone lines were hopelessly overloaded and it was impossible to get a line out. After a 45-minute walk, we found an internet place and sent emails to friends of our parents. None of our parents had let themselves be convinced of the virtues of internet connections and preferred living without them.

Our only hope was that our messages would reach them before the news. The certainly dramatized news reporting would set them into a state of shock. And given that Phuket was six hours ahead of Germany and four hours ahead of Russia, the chances of our emails reaching them before the news were not good.

Our room was only for one night. After that everyone had to reshuffle and spend most of the day waiting in hotel lobbies for their next room assignments. After breakfast, a hotel minibus took us back to our destroyed hotel, the Patong Merlin, to pick up our things.

Since the waves had hit, we had not been able to venture forward into the areas of the hotel facing the beach. Leaving our bags in the lobby, we walked through the hotel facility towards the beach, passing three pools full of debris, piles of cement blocks, beach chairs and uprooted bushes. The closer we got to the beach, the worse the destruction. Here the water had reached the second-floor rooms. The water had stripped the first-floor rooms of everything that was not concrete. Then we saw a yellow taxi on its side and four other jeeps and cars piled up in the corners of what had been the front reception area. The massive wooden roof was still in tact. Its pillars were several feet thick. Everything else had just been washed away. The bus that normally ran between Patong and Phuket lay on its side inside the front hotel bar, the bar having been completely destroyed. All other structures and barriers were gone.

The beach area was full of people watching rescue operations by the authorities, who had been working all night. The beach itself, normally covered with ten thousand wooden beach chairs, boats, beach umbrellas and excursion craft, was washed out. Most sand was in the hotels, on the roads or had been washed out by the receding water masses. A mid-sized boat lay on its side lodged between the palm trees. A restaurant barge, which had been moored on the other side of the bay and was known for its expensive food and romantic ambience, had been torn from its moorings and now was on the beach instead. Debris and engines of ships lay strewn between the largely intact palm trees. The concrete walkway along the beach, which had just been completed, was largely destroyed, its 100-kilo supporting blocks having been ripped out of the ground and thrown across the wall separating the street from the beach.

We took no photos. We wanted to remember things how they had been just a day before. We felt that it was unethical to photograph the destruction of peoples' lives, death and chaos, unless you were a journalist reporting on the tragedy.

Returning through the hotel, we saw that the hotel's temple (every house in Thailand has an ornate temple made of wood and painted colorfully) had survived and the hotel staff had placed it on top of a pile of rubble. But our gym had not survived. It was a glass room at ground level. The machines, including one full of weights and weighing hundreds of kilos, had been catapulted through the inch-thick glass walls before coming to a halt elsewhere. We could see from the dirt rings on the wall that the water had reached the ceiling.

We went back to the Phuket Merlin hotel downtown by bus, still trying to digest what we had seen. The lobby was still full of hotel guests and bags. Most did not know where to go or what would happen next. Rumors abounded as did stories of what people had experienced, like the woman who climbed a palm tree in seconds until she reached the top but couldn't climb back down and waited for a long time before she was rescued. Others were less credible, such as an older German man who boasted of how he fought the water and won. Less entertaining was the sight of our next night's roommate, an elderly man from France, who spent his days searching the hospitals for his wife.

Others were just grateful to be alive, particularly those who were hurt and had only the clothes on their backs. It seems that the closer people came to death, the more elated they were to be alive and the less they were concerned with their possessions or where they would sleep.

There was little point in spending our days in dusty Phuket city waiting for our hotel room for the coming night, so we accepted the offer to fly out to Frankfurt after the second day. The two German tour operators were completely un-bureaucratic. Anyone wanting to fly to Frankfurt with them could, with or without a passport, with or without a ticket.

The flight arrangements to Frankfurt reflected this concern and compassion in every detail. The airline had organized doctors and psychologists to be on board to help the physically or psychologically hurt. We all filled out forms on board with our names and data. The airline would send this data ahead so that friends and relatives would know when we would be arriving. Service on board was especially caring.

Arriving in cold and dark Frankfurt at 6.30 a.m. a day before New Year's eve caused more mixed feelings. Our vacation was perhaps the best ever, but was cut short. We were grateful to be in perfect shape but wondered about the others who weren't. On our train ride home, we already began thinking of our next Christmas vacation, which would be in Patong, of course.

William Cox was born in Germany into a US military family, growing up in Germany, Italy and the Netherlands. Although an American, Bill spent little time in the United States. He lived there as an undergraduate student when he studied at Boston and Georgetown Universities. Later he completed his Ph.D. at the London School of Economics. Bill runs a corporate governance rating and research agency in Madrid.

Sailing from War to Peace

Mavis Guinard

When I was six, my father was transferred to run Gillette's branch in Paris. With no qualms, he put me straight into a French *lycée*. An American businessman abroad since the twenties, he believed in languages, the more the better. It took me a few weeks to understand what the teacher wanted but like any child suddenly immersed in a strange environment, I struggled to adapt. I turned into a French schoolgirl, complete with heavy satchel, beret, navy blazer, kilt and beige socks drawn up to bare knees scabby from falls on the concrete playground. Once I became bilingual, I tried to teach my British mother to pronounce *"grenouille"* correctly. Though she adored frogs' legs, she never got beyond "grrr-noo-y." Aside from such efforts, we only spoke English. At school, I recited Racine by heart; at home, I'd cuddle up to read *Winnie-the-Pooh* or *Little Women*.

After September 1939, that cozy routine changed. War, at first, was exciting. We were glued to the news. We queued for gas masks, carrying them everywhere in a metal case hung smartly over one shoulder. Every Thursday at noon, air raid sirens were tested. Shop windows were crisscrossed with strips of brown tape. The imaginative florist on our corner cut out a virtual garden of flowers. Posters boasted: *Nous vaincrons parce que nous sommes les plus forts* (We'll win because we are the strongest) and warned against lurking spies: *Les murs ont des oreilles* (Walls have ears). After Sunday school at the American Cathedral, I'd join the volunteers who rolled bandages, knitted khaki balaclavas, hummed the popular, *We're Gonna Hang our Washing on the Siegfried Line*. Suddenly, war became boring. Nothing happened. A phony war, the grownups called it. Still, Paris schools emptied, children were evacuated. I was packed off to friends in a seaside village in Normandy.

Back home for my birthday. May 10, 1940. At dawn, sirens rushed us down to the cellar. My spaniel whimpered. I cupped my hands to protect his poor ears from the shattering noises of anti-aircraft barrage. After the all clear, the concierge found out that a bomb had hit a Citroën factory a few blocks away. On the radio, we heard that Nazi tanks had invaded the Lowlands. I was sent back to the safety of the coast. By night, the sky lit up as German planes bombed Le Havre. By day, Belgian and Dutch cars, topped with mattresses, poured southwards. The local scout leader had us wear our uniforms and help in a refugee canteen. We peeled vegetables, laid tables, cut bread, dished out soup, ran around to find billets for tired families. I was enjoying a heady feeling of being useful when Mother came to fetch me. Dad wanted us to return to the States, just the two of us.

Of that heart-breaking decision, I only remember ongoing argument. Dad insisted, Mother resisted. She'd stayed in London all through the Great War. One day, she stopped pulling things in and out of suitcases and took me to see *Fantasia*. In the lobby, she ran into an old acquaintance, a be-medaled and be-whiskered French colonel and asked his advice. While I curtsied politely, he kissed her hand and told her not to worry. *"Chère petite Madame, we will stop them at the Marne, comme toujours."*

At dinner, Dad received that piece of news with a glare, adding: "I finally have your passages. You're leaving." The very next day, he bundled us off with a driver in a blue Gillette van. Through the rear window, I saw him beside our cook and my dog, getting smaller and smaller.

Dad felt he had to stay behind to look after the company and the staff. Besides, as an US air force veteran of the last war, Air Minister Pierre Cot had asked him to broadcast a plea to America for warplanes. In crowded Bordeaux where we found only a billiard table to sleep, Mother made a last attempt to stay. When she tried to turn in our tickets, the American Express agent refused: "You must be crazy, ma'am!" As we sailed out, I recognized him, a lone figure at the end of the dock, waving to his wife and little boy.

Our 24,000-ton liner had been sent by President Roosevelt to bring back some of the 40,000 Americans stranded in Europe by the blitzkrieg—mostly women and children but also diplomats, nuns, missionaries, teachers, students and a few businessmen. Its sides were painted with American flags and the name, SS Washington, in huge letters. Promised safe conduct from the nations at war, under this brave paint, floodlit at night, the refugee ship sailed without a convoy.

The third day out, we awoke to clanging bells, feet racing down the passageways. Someone flung open our cabin door yelling: "To the boat stations. Hurry ... hurry!" The lady in the cot next to mine pulled her mink coat over a chiffon nightie and wafted out. The lady in the upper bunk begged for help. We had to heave her down and knot the loosened strings of the stiff pink corset she wore. "Otherwise, I cannot walk." My mother then grabbed my hand and tugged me along. A pint-sized expert on Atlantic crossings, I protested: "Stop running! ... We've done boat drill ... After we sailed ... It's for those who came on at Lisbon yesterday ..."

I was wrong. At the boat station, stewards handed us life jackets. One quieted me. "Hush, lass, it's a submarine." The engines had stopped. The ship was still. Over the loudspeaker, came the order. "To the lifeboats! Keep calm." Seamen swung boats out on the davits, ready to lower, then helped us clamber in. Though we were later praised for orderly behavior, some pushed and others shoved. I saw one sailor punch a portly man aside: "Naw, not you, Mister. Captain says women and kiddies first." Huddled on the benches, we waited. No one said a word.

Suddenly, the engines throbbed, the whole ship shuddered, swung round and began to zigzag. At full speed. The suspended lifeboats swung out. They tilted and I could now see the ocean, way below, ultramarine, before the boats crashed back against the sides. Could they shatter? Could we spill out? As Dad kissed me goodbye, he'd whispered: "Look after your mother, babe." I began to worry. She couldn't swim. If we ended up in the water, could I manage to tow her?

After a half hour, the pace slowed down. Captain Manning's voice came over calm and clear. "You were put in the lifeboats because we were stopped by a submarine. We have been allowed to proceed. You may leave the boats." The crew handed us out, the ship's photographer snapped pictures. We did not learn the full story until it was posted on the daily bulletin.

At 5:16 a.m., officers on duty had seen signals from a submarine: *Stop ship. Ease to.* As Captain Manning reached the bridge, came a command: *Torpedo ship. Ten Minutes. Leave ship.* The flashes ceased. While we were being hustled into the lifeboats, Captain Manning had the signal officer blinker a nonstop tattoo: *American ship - Washington - American ship - American ship.* Later he said he'd hoped to gain time until the liner became more visible in the lifting fog. When the ten minutes were up, barely a quarter of the 937 passengers were in the lifeboats. Then came the message: *Thought you were another ship. Please go on. Go on.* It was then Captain Manning attempted the zigzag dash into the rising sun in order to blind the sub's periscope. Though a bellboy sighted a second submarine only an hour later and quietly informed the Captain, there were no further alarms. But why was the Washington stopped and why were we allowed to go on? A mystery.

Some figured that sinking a ship full of Americans might have been a plot to entangle an unprepared, isolationist America into war. Many older passengers kept repeating: *Remember the Lusitania!* That Cunard Liner had been torpedoed in 1915 by a German sub off the coast of Ireland with a loss of 1200 passengers. Among them were 124 Americans and the tragic incident was believed to have influenced American opinion to join the Allies. In *Berlin Diary,* correspondent William Shirer—who had unsuccessfully tried to repatriate his wife and child on the SS Washington—found it suspicious that the German government had warned the American chargé d'affaires only a few days earlier that the British secret service intended to torpedo the refugee liner. He added, "I'm convinced that Berlin itself gave orders to sink that ship in order to poison Anglo-American relations."

Asked for comment, Sir Peter Sitters, Naval Attaché to the British Embassy in Paris at the time, recently e-mailed: "Of course the idea that the Royal Navy would have done something as silly as that is ludicrous. But either of two other explanations makes sense. It would have been lunacy for the Germans to sink such a ship and, although Hitler might not have perceived this, any sensible U-boat commander— and they were a pretty good lot—would have done so. The other explanation, equally plausible, is that the U-boat commander simply thought it improper. At that stage of the war, this was quite likely. Laws of the sea have always been respected."

The day after the incident, the German Admiralty did admit it had been one of their U-boats and apologized, alleging they had not been told officially of the SS Washington's intended course—a bureaucratic slipup blamed on the US Embassy in Berlin.

On board, passengers signed a letter congratulating Captain Manning for his cool courage but some passengers petitioned to return to New York with no further stop. The resolute captain—himself a survivor of rescues at sea, typhoons and air

136

crashes—ignored them. Following his orders from the State Department, he proceeded to Galway to evacuate 855 more Americans heeding Ambassador Joe Kennedy's warning: "This might be the last American vessel until the end of the war." As neutrals, Americans were not allowed to travel in belligerent ships.

In Ireland, a parade of pink and blue carry-cots came aboard and 1500 gallons of fresh milk were loaded onto what became a floating nursery. We were now 1787 passengers. Seventy-seven slept on cots in the Palm Court, others doubled up in the cabins, crammed into the post office, the library, the gym, the empty swimming pool and the Grand Salon.

The event of the day was the terse news bulletin posted at the time stewards rolled around the cart of bouillon and water crackers: - Paris was declared an open city and the Germans marched in - They had crossed the Loire - Churchill vowed to fight on but the French government had fled to Bordeaux - Reports said France's roads were clogged by a panicky exodus of civilians and soldiers trying to escape by car, horsecart, bike or on foot, repeatedly strafed. Fellow passengers from Denmark, Antwerp, Brussels, Louvain nodded, they'd known similar experiences.

Where was Dad? When he escaped occupied France a year later, he told how he drove his Delage south as long as gas lasted, sharing a few chocolate bars with our cook. On board, our cockney dining steward tried to cheer us by ladling out caviar from a crystal bowl. "Chef says enjoy it, ma'am. No more passengers, no more luxury stuff. Kitchen has odds on we'll be a troop transport next."

The Statue of Liberty appeared out of the dawn mist of June 21. Around the harbor, fireboats spouted hoses of water in welcome, hooting tugs brought alongside a flurry of photographers and reporters, press cards tucked in the hat bands of their fedoras. In New York, we shared the front page with the news of France's surrender.

On the pier under the letter G, as on every home leave, Uncle Frank was waiting, arms open wide. His first words were: "You're lucky!" Mother nodded, teary-eyed; he smiled. "Yep! Really lucky. I've got tickets for the ball game."

We'd sailed out of war into an unconcerned and isolationist America. The submarine incident was a scary, quickly forgotten footnote. An American kid again, I went to that ball game in white bobby socks, became a high school cheerleader, lined up with my favorite cousin to scream for Frank Sinatra. The little French girl within me had lots to learn.

I never curtsied again.

Mavis Guinard went from a French lycée in Paris to American high schools in New York and Buenos Aires before graduating from Mount Holyoke. Her first job was on the Buenos Aires Herald, a snap course from obits to international conferences. Her French husband's transfer to Switzerland cut off that career. She became a housewife overseeing three daughters' homework. This, with trips to discover Switzerland, provided a mine of offbeat information way beyond chocolate and cuckoo clocks. She used it to freelance for the International Herald Tribune.

Who am I?

What has happened to me? Perhaps the best way to answer this question is to compare my sense of self with a house.

Alice Visser-Furay

We were once separated by an ocean, by traditions, by language. But the strength of family heritage overcame all obstacles and drew us together.

Kim Schrantz-Berquist

After all these years of being on the outside looking in, perhaps now I finally made it to the inner circle.

Patricia Guild-Ganora

The word expatriate conjures up a romantic image. As everyone knows, expatriates sit at sidewalk cafes in Paris, sipping wine with their friends and discussing life, art and ideas.

Hildegard Esper Enesco

Our mother taught my sister and me small town American moral, spiritual and community values, as well as admiration and respect towards the US flag, national hymn and other symbols.

David Lobo VI

It's her identity. There's no way of getting around it. She can't simply wake up one morning and not be American any longer. A change of passport, a change of citizenship on paper, cannot change who you are.

Robin Herrnfeld

The Musings of an Expatriate

Alice Visser-Furay

All good people agree
And all good people say
All nice people, like us, are We
And everyone else is They
But if you cross over the sea,
Instead of over the way
You may end by *(think of it!)* looking on We
As only a sort of They!

(*"We and They,"* by Rudyard Kipling)

Am I "We" or am I "They"? Am I American or am I European? The obvious answer is that I have an American passport, I spent my entire childhood in the United States, and my parents and siblings are all American—therefore I am an American. And yet I have spent most of my adult years in Europe; my husband, children, and best friends are European; I dress, eat, and often think like a European; even my accent has an Irish/European twinge to it. Fourteen years in four European countries can't help but have shaped my identity in a myriad of ways. The end result of my life experience is that the question "Where do I come from?" presents no problems for me—I come from the United States of America. But the question "Where do I belong?" has become infinitely more complex for me to answer.

What exactly does it mean to belong? A dictionary definition of the word *belong* is *"to be a part of; to be related to or connected with."* A place can create this sense of being a part of something—wide open prairies, a city skyline, medieval cobblestone streets, a familiar neighborhood, or a well-loved house might bring peace of mind because you feel at home there. After being away you come back to this place and feel relief—in this environment you can be your best self. You belong.

Even more important are the groups of people that give you that sense of connection. Family, friends, occupation, religion, race, regional or national culture—any group in which you perceive others accept you, appreciate you, hold the same values as you, and recognize you as one of their own—is significant. The recognition you get allows you to be comfortable with yourself, which is in turn a confirmation of your identity. You feel at home with the group. You belong.

Life offers us continuous little lessons on what it means to belong—and how it feels to be "left out." Remember that sense of camaraderie with the neighborhood kids as you ran through the sprinklers during the sticky, hot summers? Remember that feeling of loneliness in second grade when you realized that you weren't invited to a classmate's birthday party? Gradually we learn that we belong to some groups, but not to others.

And yet perhaps the most important group identity of all—nationality—generally remains untested. Many people are patriotic in the dictionary definition sense of "love of country," but most of these people are unaware of the extent to which they are connected to their national culture. Why is national culture such a fundamentally important group identity? As Raymonde Carroll *(Cultural Misunderstandings,* University of Chicago Press, 1988, page 3) explains, "My culture is the logic by which I give order to my world, and I have been learning this logic, little by little, since the moment I was born." Culture is how we relate to friends and family, the values we have, how we organize our lives, and what we feel is important. Our culture teaches us how to interact with strangers, what it means to be a friend, what is "good" and "bad" behavior, how to make people laugh. These lessons give us the foundation from which we all develop individually. The end result is that by the time we reach adulthood, our overall sense of self is intimately connected to our national culture. We belong to our culture in the most essential way, even if we are not aware of it.

Enter Rudyard Kipling: "But if you cross over the sea..." Those of us who have lived abroad have a much deeper insight into the ways we belong to the national culture that has shaped us. Why? Because we have experienced that feeling of being "left out" of a foreign culture. When I first moved to the Netherlands, I was painfully aware of the fact that I didn't belong. Not only did I lack the basic language skills to buy a stamp, I also seemed to do the "wrong" thing at every possible opportunity—from walking on bicycle paths to mistaking Dutch directness for criticism to making weak coffee. For months I had a desperate feeling of being isolated and alone—that second grade "left out" feeling exponentially multiplied.

That was fourteen years ago. Since then, I've learned to make strong coffee. I also adjusted to life in the Netherlands well enough to marry a Dutchman, and then I successfully lived in three other European countries—Sweden, Ireland, and Germany. I started my career, I learned languages, I made friends, I had children. That "left out" feeling dissipated as my connections to Europe and Europeans developed.

In the process, the "logic by which I give order to the world" has changed. Significantly, my attitude towards society, government, and public policy has become, well, European. This "adoption" of European values happened over the course of many years; it started with the gradual realization that while there are numerous differences in culture, language, and lifestyle between the European countries, Europe's shared history has created common underlying societal values, particularly in Western Europe. Many of these values are manifested in the way Europeans approach public policy: the death penalty is an anathema; guns are strictly controlled; excessive patriotism is seen to be dangerous (history has had some hard lessons for Europe on this subject); personal faith is kept out of politics; maternity leave is guaranteed and paid; health care is a fundamental right; four to six-week vacation privileges are the norm; and a strong welfare state—with the resultant high taxes—is taken for granted. At some point, I can't say when because

142

it happened so slowly, I stopped looking at these European societal values as an outsider and adopted them myself. As these values became *my* values, my connection to Europeans deepened dramatically.

For me, it is not just common values that make me feel at home in Europe. The continent as a place feels like home to me too. For Europe's history has given it a recognizable architectural identity. Narrow and winding cobblestone streets, Romanesque and Gothic churches, Renaissance style city halls—basically a sense of history behind each building—all contribute to a unified sense of place. As I wander through the cobble-stoned streets of the *Altstadt* (Old Town) here in Düsseldorf, and look at the buildings and people around me, I feel content. I know I belong in Europe.

The strange thing is that when I visit the United States, I sometimes feel as if I'm in a foreign country. I feel overwhelmed by the sights and sounds surrounding me. The massive stores, the service with a smile attitude, the above ground telephone poles, the billboard advertisements on the highway, the fast food restaurants on every corner, and the fact that I can do my grocery shopping at 3 a.m. can all be dizzily confusing for me. More fundamentally, I am uncomfortable with the cultural values that allow so many people to remain uninsured; I don't like that "vote-for-me-because-I-have-faith-in-God" dimension of American politics; I find it sad that society doesn't recognize that extended, paid maternity leave and long vacations can make more productive workers.

And so I wonder—do I still belong in America? Or do I belong in Europe? What has happened to me? Perhaps the best way to answer this question is to compare my sense of self with a house. Twenty-four years of experiences in the United States helped me to build a cozy and wonderfully familiar house. Then one day a huge truck came and moved my house, foundation and all, to Europe. At first my house seemed terribly out of place; but as I began to experience life-transforming events in a European context—marriage, career, friendships, motherhood—the major renovations began. Walls were knocked down, a second story was added, extra bathrooms were put in, a new kitchen was built. Five thousand days of experience in Europe, five thousand days of interaction with Europeans, five thousand days of living in European society, meant that even the day-to-day minor renovations—a coat of paint here, rearranged furniture there—brought significant remodeling. The end result is that my house looks strikingly different than it did when I was twenty-four years old.

The crucial question is, have I sacrificed my cozy American house for a hodgepodge do-it-yourself European house because I didn't want to feel "left out"? Have I given up my American identity so that I could feel I belong in Europe? My situation is too complex to answer this question in a simple way. I do know that I haven't moved to another house, I've simply changed around the house I already had. I believe that the reason that my house now looks so different is due more to the life transforming experiences I have had in Europe and not simply to a desire to fit in. For example, I first became a mother in Sweden. Every first-time parent is insecure, and it was Swedish midwives, Swedish friends, and Swedish books that "taught" me what to do. Indeed much of what feels "instinctive" to me as a mother is based on the Swedish approach to parenting. I have racked up a multitude of such formative experiences that have molded my identity and changed my sense of belonging in a way that I never could have predicted.

Furthermore, I don't think my house is as dramatically different as it may seem on first glance. For the essence of any house is the foundation and the structural beams. And for me, these things are very American and remain firmly in place. Strangely enough, it was the tragedy of September 11, 2001 that made me understand this. I watched events unfold from my Irish home, and collapsed on the floor in tears as I saw the second tower crumble down. I realized with a deepening sense of shock that *my* country was being attacked. With profound insecurity I wondered what would happen next, when people could hate America enough to slaughter innocent people like that. I felt connected to the country of my origins in a way that almost stunned me, as my odyssey into my European identity was well underway.

Equally important, I was overwhelmed by the level of support for America in Ireland and throughout Europe—it began with the dinner my neighbor brought me that horrible evening, continued with mile-long lines at the American Embassy to sign the Book of Condolences, and culminated in the Day of Remembrance when every shop, business, and pub in Ireland was closed in mourning for the people who had lost their lives. On September 11, there was no "We" or "They." As a writer in a large German newspaper said, with a twist on the words that John Kennedy used some 40 years before, "Ich bin ein Amerikaner"—"I am an American. Let us scream out that sentence across the Universe. We are all Americans."

And so my gut reaction on September 11, plus the wave of gratitude and relief I felt as I saw the European support of America, reinforced both my intrinsic American identity and the legitimacy of my newer European identity. The value differences between the Americans and the Europeans pale in comparison to what we have in common. I realized that my European hodgepodge house sits very well on that American foundation.

This realization caused me to explore my American identity in a new way. What are the fundamental characteristics that define Americans? Like other Americans abroad, I am able to see the United States from afar, and this gives me a unique perspective on what it means to be an American. It is with pride that I describe what I believe are some of the key features of the American culture—the foundation and structural beams which give my house its structure.

The first thing I love about Americans is their friendliness, warmth and genuine interest in talking to people they meet. Some Europeans feel that Americans don't care about the rest of the world because their geography and language skills are poor; that is not precisely true—the size of the United States means that Americans don't get the opportunity to meet people from other countries in the same way that Europeans do, and therefore don't need to know geography, speak languages, or understand different cultures as people from smaller countries need to. When Americans do get the opportunity to talk to strangers from home or abroad, they usually open their minds, their homes and their hearts. Again, some Europeans think this friendliness is superficial, because in Europe it would take a long time for people to "bare their soul" with each other in the way that Americans do fairly quickly. But Americans are traditionally used to moving a lot more often than Europeans, and they have simply learned to make friends quickly.

These friendships help newcomers feel welcome in a strange place, help them know they are liked, and help them understand that they are accepted. If you go back to my description of what it means to "belong," it follows that it is easier for many people to feel as if they belong in the United States because they feel welcome. Perhaps this is the reason why so many immigrants are passionate in their love for their new country, the United States. And perhaps if I were to move back, it is this dimension of the American character that would help me to adjust to a life quite different from what I have become accustomed to.

The generosity and compassion of Americans is another characteristic which appeals to me. Yes, Europe has a stronger social welfare network than the United States, but how many Europeans open up their check books at the end of the month to give to various charitable causes? How many Europeans volunteer their free time (of which they have much more because of the number of paid holidays they get) to help those who are less well off? I was particularly proud of the compassionate way Americans pulled together and helped one another after the September 11 attack.

A third feature of the American way of life that I respect is the strong work ethic and emphasis on individual responsibility. "Be all you can be," say the Americans, and they believe that as long as there is a relatively level playing ground, it is completely up to the individual to be a success—or a failure—in life. The American cultural heroes are often individuals who have "made it," usually from "rags to riches" despite all they had going against them. Americans traditionally believe that willpower and willingness to work hard are enough to overcome difficulties; or, as my father always says, "When the going gets tough, the tough get going." Intellectually I completely accept and respect the European way of looking at things—that for many individuals a level playing field is not enough and that some people need extra government support in a variety of ways. I'm glad that this support exists in Europe and I am willing to pay high taxes to ensure it remains in place. But *for myself*, I think I retain that American instinct which tells me if I want something I have to work hard for it, and not depend on anyone else (as long as I get at least 5–6 weeks of paid holiday and a year's paid maternity leave, anyway. I have been somewhat spoiled here in Europe!)

Fourth, some dimensions of American pragmatism appeal to me. Americans like clear communication and *USA Today*-type statistics that simplify complex problems, instead of abstract theories without explicit answers. They are action-oriented and eager to solve problems. Furthermore, Americans tend to see issues in "black and white," whereas the Europeans tend see the world in shades of gray. To a large extent I agree with the Europeans on the existence of a "gray world," and I would like American foreign policy to reflect this complexity. And yet, American pragmatism is built on a fundamental premise: if something works, use it, if it doesn't work, fix it. It is this "fix it when it is broken" attitude that may lead to problems because situations are oversimplified, but it also brings hope for the future. Americans may not be able to "fix" the Middle East or bring peace to the many troubled areas, but they do have some control over their own image in the world. When Americans realize how "broken" their image in the world is, I am confident they will do what they can to repair it. Americans are proud, but they are even more practical.

Finally, I am also attached to America as a place. How awe-inspiring the landscape of the United States can be! Stunning natural wonders like the Grand Canyon and the Colorado Rocky Mountains, flat and fruitful prairies, lush valleys, meandering and powerful rivers, and vast space that make you feel as if you own the world—all are a part of America, and in a way, part of what has shaped the American dream. Yes, I feel at home as I walk on Europe's cobble-stoned streets amidst buildings that are centuries old. But I also feel at home when I see the beauty that is America.

And so this brings me back to the question of where I belong. Am I "We" or am I "They"? I am not an emigrant, and under no circumstances can I foresee myself giving up my American passport. My American identity will always provide me with a foundation and structural beams, no matter where in the world I end up. But I'm also much more than a visitor in Europe—the renovations to my house have been substantial, and to be honest, I love my European hodgepodge house. What is the end result? I have decided that cultural identity is not a take it or leave it proposition; nor does my sense that I belong in Europe exclude the possibility of an equally valid sense of belonging in America. The fact is, every December when I am in the United States for Christmas, there is a moment when I take a deep breath and say to myself, "This is home." The fact is, every January when I return to Germany, there is a moment when I take a deep breath and say to myself, "This is home." Perhaps the whole question of "We" and "They" is irrelevant to long-term expatriates like myself. Instead, I'm both. Now that is something all good people can agree on.

Think of it, Rudyard Kipling.

Alice Visser-Furay was born and raised in St. Louis, Missouri. She has lived in Europe for the last fourteen years—first in the Netherlands, followed by Sweden, then Ireland and Germany and very recently England. She is married to a Dutch citizen and has five young children born in three different countries. Alice has taught history at several international schools and eventually hopes to pursue a career in freelance writing.

One Genealogy, One Family

Kim Schrantz-Berquist

Butterflies turned in my stomach as I made my way through the busy Luxembourg mall. Colors vivid, yet sounds muffled; shoppers stood distant, although surrounding me on all sides. The air was thick with everydayness. Only I was at this place, at this moment, for the reason of a lifetime.

I spotted an elderly gray-haired gentleman. Seventy or so, tall in stature, stoic, somber, square-jawed. He had eyes that smiled cautiously, a brow that betrayed he'd seen too much during his many years and a stance that balanced it all with the dignified formality of the older generation. He looked exactly like me, my father before me, my brother, my grandmother.

"Alphonse?" I asked.

"Kim?" he replied.

I extended my hand—a handshake or three kisses. Our cultural differences holding us back in just the first seconds. In typical American style, I pushed past the invisible European barrier, extending my other hand as well, clenching him in a heart-felt hug.

At first he stood back, then leaned into it, warmed by my open display of affection. He even grinned in the way that Europeans do when they're humoring Americans for their larger-than-life traits.

We broke our embrace and returned to formality. I reminded myself that I didn't actually know this man. Nor did I know his father, mother, grandfather or grandmother. But I knew my grandmother, "Marie," as he referred to her, and that her mother and his grandmother were sisters.

Now more like work colleagues than family, we walked into Oberweis, a well-known and mouth-watering *patisserie* in Luxembourg City, and took our seat. My favorite patisserie had turned out to be his favorite as well for its sumptuous cakes.

Strict European dining rules replaced the awkward greeting formalities as I held back to genteelly tuck into a chocolate delicacy called a *Pot Symphonie,* and he, a rhubarb tart.

Discreetly and somewhat guardedly, he pulled out a folder. "Old family photos. Would you like to see them? They're a gift if you're interested."

"Of course!" I replied.

Suddenly, the stiff formality evaporated, and eagerness took its place. Family.

Alphonse carefully lifted out the ancient black and white dog-eared photos. A stern-faced woman and a little girl that I recognized immediately stared back at me. "Young Marie with my grandmother," he explained. "Marie was raised by my grandmother right down the street from here at our old house in Neudorf." He turned to the next picture, a wedding photo. "Your great-grandmother Marguerite and Nicholas, her husband, on a cruise to Cologne." And the next. "The three sisters as grown women," he explained. "Marie, she's there in the middle. That's how I remember her from when she visited, and how we looked forward to her news from America. And her sisters Anne and Susanne on either side. Susanne's husband died in '45 at Mauthausen."

Faces on paper. It was hard for me to take in all these people who were a part of my ancestry. But slowly, the unknown faces were becoming known.

When Alphonse's basic English would tire, we would switch to French. When my basic French would tire, we would return to English. Stilted, but enthusiastically, we swapped stories using his knowledge of four languages and my translation abilities. He even whispered to me about an abortion scandal by a doctor in Trier in which my great-grandmother had died. That's how young Marie had come to live with his grandmother. The new wife didn't like the children. He explained the good as well as the bad, whether out of jealousy because of the hardship it placed on his family, or just for fact, I couldn't determine through the stoic facade of an older generation. Either way, I quickly understood that the life my family had endured in those days was difficult. No silver spoon fed their mouths, no easy life had been granted to them. But their bond as a family more than made them wealthy. What surely caused his family extra effort, was gratefully my family's gain.

At our goodbye, I embraced Alphonse again. This time it was expected, and he returned the hug comfortably and whole-heartedly.

I drove home reveling in all that I had learned about my ancestors, and naturally my thoughts drifted to the one unusual event that had led up to our meeting—Mr. Ensch.

Two years before, I had been transferred to Luxembourg by work. At the time, I'd never even thought of my workplace as a Luxembourgish bank. It was an international clearing house. My ear wasn't yet attuned to the occasional Luxembourgish spoken in some of the cubicles.

I got a week's notification. Before I knew it, I was sharing an apartment with another employee on a busy thoroughfare called the *Côte d'Eich,* which leads directly up a hill into the heart of Luxembourg City.

At the time, all the sights, sounds and smells were foreign to me—the old-style affluence, the leafiness, the cliffs, the languages of French, German *and* Luxembourgish, the continental indifference, and of course the expectation that one should fit in *immediately.* I was barely coping with the "go to work – socialize – then go home" rhythm, and looking forward to the day when my new surroundings would fit me like a home-away-from-home.

In my blur one day, I phoned my parents. "I'm in Luxembourg," I told them.

"Luxembourg? Your grandmother's from Luxembourg," my father replied, spitting out the sentence before he even said hello.

"Huh? You always told me she was from France." I shrugged my shoulders. I didn't get it.

Dad heaved a sigh down the telephone line. "Years ago, I used to say she was from Luxembourg, but no one in America had ever heard of the country. It's smaller than Rhode Island, and way over in Europe. They kept giving me puzzled looks, so I switched to saying she was from France. It was just easier."

Okay. Question asked. Question answered. In my haze of having just moved, I'm not even sure that I completely processed what he'd said. The phone call was merely a courtesy. Its purpose was to quickly update the folks. It would take several more weeks before I'd be settled enough for lengthy meaningful conversation with them or anyone.

The next day, I knew I had to chip away at some "settling down" tasks. One of the first was to obtain a *Carte de Sejour.* I didn't know what those words meant, but I knew I needed one to stay in Luxembourg. So off I went. That's when chance struck a full blow.

At the Residents Office, there was a long queue. I waited. Finally it was my turn. "I'm here to work," I told the man behind one of the many desks. I handed him my contract of employment, explained that I was a dual-citizen, and then gave him my American and British passports.

He filled out his paperwork, and occasionally asked me questions in well-spoken English. He told me my *carte* would be available in a couple week's time, and pointed to the desk where I could pick it up.

I thanked him and got up to leave. "My grandmother's Luxembourgish," I muttered, perhaps not even facing him.

"There's a man upstairs on the second floor who makes family trees for Americans with Luxembourgish heritage if you're interested. His name is Mr. Ensch."

I walked out and started descending the stairs. I glanced at my watch. I'd taken the morning off, and didn't need to be back at the bank for another hour. I turned around and headed up the stairs instead.

At the top of that flight was Mr. Ensch's office. It was so easy. I knocked and he was there. I went in. His office was atypically unrefurbished. The space was dominated by an oversized desk heaped with papers.

I explained why I came to see him, and handed him a fairly blurry piece of paper. It was still in my purse from the day before. Mom had faxed it to me after our conversation. It was one of those "heirlooms" of my family history that was handed down from generation to generation, or in my case, faxed to me by mom's rickety fax machine. Names, towns, and dates were scribbled all over it in old script-like handwriting. Clearly meaningful enough to warrant passing around the family, but all certainly quite illegible to my eyes.

Mr. Ensch took it, examined it, and made a short, simple reply. "I'll have a tree for you in two days."

The meeting finished as quickly as it had started. He was a very matter-of-fact sort of man who made his point in few words. I didn't know what to expect. I didn't even know why he was doing this for me. I would later find out that he was a well-respected genealogist who specialized in Luxembourgish-American heritage, and he had even written a well-known book on the subject.

The rest is history. In fact, literally my family's history.

I walked into his office two days later. And indeed, he had a full family tree sketched out for me in pencil with copied certificates to support it.

"You live within fifty meters of where your great-grandfather is buried. Here's the number of his plot if you ever want to walk up the hill and visit his gravesite."

I hadn't even known that there was a cemetery tucked into the hillside near my home. How odd that I should return three generations later to almost the exact spot where my great-grandfather was buried. Two world wars had passed, Luxembourg had gained its own freedom, countless Luxembourgish natives had emigrated to America to search for a new life in the new world including my grandmother. But certainly few Americans of Luxembourgish heritage had traveled in the other direction, *to* Luxembourg to reside. And here I was, by chance, living within a stones-throw of my great-grandfather's grave. I was even lucky that it was still there. As I later found out, most graves in Europe are only leased, not permanent.

I leaned forward in my seat, captivated.

"Your family was from Hoscheid, up north, in the hills of Luxembourg, near *Esch-sur-Sûre*, one of our famous beauty spots. I can trace your great-grandfather's lineage back to 1821, and even a few names back to the 1700s. His father and grandfather, and all his family before him would have lived in Hoscheid, at that time, a tiny hamlet of fifty people. As farmers, they would have worked the land every day, and they certainly wouldn't have moved from the village, and seldom even left it at all. Especially in the hills of the north, Luxembourgers lived a very isolated life at that time. Roads between towns would have been mere paths and difficult to cross, especially in winter. People certainly didn't travel back then with the ease they do now."

Visions of rural life flashed before me. I realized that I knew the actual spot my ancestors came from. Not just one of my ancestors, but an entire lineage. I knew one line of my *true* origins going back centuries and centuries and centuries.

"Your great-grandfather was a railroad worker," Mr. Ensch continued. "Although he grew up in Hoscheid, the age of transportation had started and he was a part of it, so he moved every few years. That's what brought the family to Luxembourg City. Beggen, the town was called. Your grandmother was born in Beggen. It was part of an area called Eich at the time, but is now part of Luxembourg City. All this is written in the Eich Register," he said and handed me a copy of the exact page.

"Eich? *Côte d'Eich!*" I started chirping. "I live on the *Côte d'Eich*. It's the name of the street where I live."

"Yes. Your grandmother was born in a house on that same street or just off of it, only a few kilometers from your apartment."

"Less than a couple miles."

"Yes, in English terms. I purposely didn't make a copy of your grandmother's birth certificate. I thought you might like to find it yourself. Our National Archives are located in the town center on a ridge called the *Corniche*. All the documents of that period are written in Old German, but the staff speak English and can help you."

"I know your cousin too, Alphonse," Mr. Ensch said. "He's in my genealogy society. He has a *vignoble*... a vineyard. He grows grapes for Luxembourgish wine. Our wine is well-known throughout Europe, you know. Here's his phone number."

Then our meeting concluded. The whole conversation probably took no more than half an hour. In that short time, Mr. Ensch had told me about hundreds of years of my family history, and about countless generations of my ancestors.

150

Mr. Ensch—a fascinating and mysterious man. One day he walked into my life and became a key, yet humble player in one of the most meaningful events of my existence. Then the next day, he walked out, having awarded me and my family the gift of genealogy forever. I'm indebted to him for more than he knows. Or maybe he does know, and that's why he does it.

Excited, I immediately typed up my family tree, printed it on elegant paper and mailed it to all my relatives back home. I was proud, and they were proud. And I'd walked up that hill and found the cemetery, and my great-grandfather's grave, and paid my respects.

That very next weekend too, I went to the National Archives and searched for and found my grandmother's birth certificate. I'll always remember that Saturday morning, sitting in a centuries-old building, trawling through microfiches, totally immersed in my own world. The monumental event (at least to me) that filled that Saturday, captivated me fully. Certainly those around me had no idea of the enormity of that moment for me, and the language blocked me from sharing my excitement. So there I was, sitting in absolute silence, reading a language I couldn't read, struggling to find a name, a clue, something I could recognize. Anything, in fact. And then I found her name, barely decipherable in sweeping Old German handwriting. It was her birth certificate. And I beamed!

I also contacted my cousin, Alphonse. I set up a meeting during one of my parents' rare visits. We were all eager to meet him. Then the day before the meeting, he cancelled. His mother had died suddenly. We felt badly for him. He could barely utter a word over the telephone. But at the same time, we were understandably disheartened. My parents were returning to America the next day, and wouldn't get the chance to meet Alphonse after all.

I too was personally disheartened. After the chance discovery of my Luxembourgish heritage, was it going to turn out that my relatives weren't particularly friendly? After all, my grandmother had only left me a handkerchief when she died. And while she was still alive, I always felt that she was distant with me. Even my father was distant by nature. Maybe the line of my family that I didn't know well wanted to stay that way? Or maybe it was just a cultural difference.

At that moment in my life, that's where I left it.

Then a couple years passed, and something made me think of Alphonse. I phoned him again. This time, it was surprisingly easy to organize a meeting. And that's how we met at the patisserie, Oberweis, only a few days after that short simple phone call.

A few months after our first meeting, he even took me to the house in Neudorf where my grandmother grew up. A house from 1900 that stood still in time since about the 1950s—rectangular ceramic room heaters, doilies on end tables, a television lit by tubes. A house that he is still proud to have in his family, the aging aunt that owns it in an old-folk's home. Alphonse visits her faithfully every week, but inferred that she's too weak to recognize visitors.

During our unhurried stroll through the house, Alphonse lapsed in and out of his memories of the by-gone era. "Your grandmother, little Marie, would have slept in this room," he said as we walked up some stairs made for the tiny feet of decades gone-by and into a bedroom. "My grandmother took Marie and her two sisters into her charge and her home right after their mother died. That means your grandmother grew up as one of seven siblings: the four children from my direct family including my father, and the three children from Marie's family. They all grew up right in this very house, although the boys were gone all day at work. They even slept in this very room: four girls here, three boys in the room next door."

"If my grandmother was brought up by your grandmother, you and I are more closely related than our family tree lineage," I said. That fact had finally just become clear to me.

I scanned the room. It was tiny for four, even though the house itself was spacious. I tried to imagine four young girls sleeping within its walls, especially my grandmother, two to a bed, rough wool blankets, horse hair mattresses. Cramped and basic by our standards, but surely three abandoned young girls would have been thankful to have a home. A family. All these details I'd never known about my grandmother. There was a deep, even tragic side to this distant woman after all. No wonder she was such a private person.

I glanced at the gray cracked walls and the rough oil paintings which adorned them, the once-ornate ceiling now yellowed, and the coarse hard-wooden floors, surely the originals from 1900, over which generations of my family had walked. I certainly treasured Alphonse's tour.

Some day the aunt will pass away, and the house will be sold, one of many traded every day on the sought-after housing market of Luxembourg. No one will sleep in that room ever again and think of my grandmother or any of the seven children, or of the struggles and joys, or of the sacrifices that were made for kin, or of the enormous dedication they had as a family.

Now, thanks to the stories that my cousin has relived for me, I'll remember the history first-hand. I took photos, and even movies of Alphonse and the house. And less than an hour after my visit, I used the modern technology of a broadband link to send the photos of my cousin and my grandmother's house, lost in time, almost lost in meaning, to my relatives in the United States.

New world—old world. We were once separated by an ocean, by traditions, by language. But the strength of family heritage overcame all obstacles and drew us together. Families.

Our family. Now we are once more united. Thank you Mr. Ensch, Alphonse, all my family.

Kim Schrantz-Berquist *is a native of Buffalo, New York. She has had a 15-year career in technical writing, and owns her own European-based business. She has also raised a family in Europe, and published three fiction novels. As an American-English dual citizen, she has lived in Buffalo, New York; Manchester, England; London; Luxembourg and Brussels.*

Italian Treasures

Patricia Guild-Ganora

Spring 1997—Milan, Italy

"There's no way I'll live there," I say to Francesco. We are standing outside an apartment building in Milan, checking out the building and neighborhood the evening before we were to actually see the flat. The building is probably the nicest looking one on the street. It was clearly built before World War II with nice stone balconies on the lower levels, even if the stone has turned a dingy gray from time and pollution. The neighborhood itself isn't bad either. It is near where I am currently sharing an apartment with a girlfriend. At least I know it is safe. It is also convenient—only 15 minutes or so to the center by tram with easy highway access for me to get to work. Francesco's office is a 10-minute walk away. I am desperate to find a place as I can only stay in the other apartment with Cecilia for another month. Honestly, it is the street the building is on that I hate. *Via Monte Ceneri* (Ash Mountain Road) and it seems about as dirty as the name implies. It is one of the rings around the city and a very busy thoroughfare. At this particular point a second level was added to improve traffic flow, allowing express traffic to bypass several intersections. The local traffic passes by on the street level. Parking is at a premium throughout Milan and the area underneath the bridge—not to mention the sidewalks of many nearby side streets—are crammed with parked cars. The traffic, noise and pollution seem totally unacceptable. Even so, we keep the appointment for the following day. I need a place to live and do not have too many options.

Signora Bianchi meets us in front of the building at 6:00 p.m. Without much information we enter the door off the street—a smaller door cut out of an extremely large door. We walk up the few steps taking us to the landing of the ground floor apartments and pause merely a moment before starting to climb. Up and up we go. Signora Bianchi pauses a moment after three or four flights and I thought we had arrived. I soon discover it was just to catch her breath, and we continue on until we arrive at the very top of the building. We are on the sixth floor above ground and the busy street out front seems not to exist. The apartment faces the back of the building and no street noise can be heard. The apartment is extremely modest, a mere two rooms, entryway and bath. The kitchen houses a large round wooden table, four metal folding chairs, an old gas oven/stove, metal pantry and cupboards along with a half-size refrigerator. The narrow bathroom is just big enough to house the essentials: toilet, bidet, shower and sink. In the main room of the apartment sits a twin bed, nightstand, and a rather large glass-top table functioning as a desk with a daybed/sofa along the opposite wall. A large closet occupies another wall of the room. Everything is old and in desperate need of a good cleaning. The sparsely furnished rooms give the impression that the flat is larger than it actually is.

153

It seems hard to believe that I left behind a beautiful studio apartment in Chicago's trendy River North neighborhood with a 24–hour doorman, swimming pool and gym, and that now I am considering this dingy apartment a find. But there is something welcoming about this little apartment. The sloping ceilings, the small windows looking out over the neighborhood houses, many with small gardens, even some with trees and grass or roof terraces. I can actually hear birds chirping and the church bells sounding the hour. It is a cheap apartment—not easy to find in Milan and I am not on an all-expenses-paid expat contract. Finances are tight and price is critical. I'll take it. My expat adventure is truly beginning and will start with a major spring-cleaning project.

Something about having my own place has always been important for me. Even though I have been living in Italy for nearly five months, moving into the apartment on *Monte Ceneri Avenue* seems my moment of arrival. I am no longer just bunking in with someone or using the spare bedroom. I now have my own flat and that gives a sense of permanency to my stay in Italy that prior to that moment had not existed. To an outside observer it must look as if I am moving backwards. True, the apartment is not what I imagined before embarking on this experience. But I am pursuing a new life and love and gaining a new perspective. It is a thrilling and frightening time of my life. Do I really know what I am doing? How much do I really know about Francesco, the man for whom I left family, friends, a good job and everything familiar?

Summer 1997—Milan, Italy

It is hot on the top floor without air-conditioning. Thank goodness there is a ceiling fan. Still it is a hot and sticky summer evening in Milan, and while normally I hate the artificial feeling of air-conditioning tonight I miss it.

"Come on, *tesoro*," says Francesco. "*Facciamo una passaggiata*" (Let's take a walk). *Tesoro is* used in Italian as often as "sweetheart" or "dear" is used in English. Still, in this early phase of learning Italian I am literally translating everything. *Tesoro* means treasure and I struggle not to be overwhelmed that I could actually be someone's treasure. Perhaps I am reading too much into a simple word. I shake my head. Anything must be cooler than this top floor apartment. "Let's get out of here," I reply. We feel a reduction in the temperature just going down to the ground floor. The exterior walls of the building must be at least a foot thick. I wonder if the heat will ever penetrate them. "Can't we just sit here?" I wonder to myself.

We open the door to the street and are attacked by a blast of hot air mixed in with a heavy dose of pollution. I still hate via Monte Ceneri. "Where should we go?" I ask. Francesco shrugs and just starts walking. We walk to the first side street and turn right. I understand immediately that we are heading for the neighborhood we view from the apartment. We meander down the long city block that takes us to Piazza Pre-Alpi. We are in a lower-middle class neighborhood of Milan. Many of the buildings facing the piazza are also pre-World War II. Not exceptional, but certainly more interesting facades than many more recent constructions. This is not the elegant or trendy environment I left behind in Chicago or that I imagined I would live in before moving to Italy. The piazza is full of life at 9:00 p.m. this summer evening. Seniors occupy the small area with benches near the fountain and under large trees. The men smoke and talk about politics or soccer, some in their sleeveless undershirts desperately trying to find relief from the heat. The parents with young children are gathered around the small jungle gym complete with rickety bridge and slide. The teens are off in a corner, chatting and obsessed with their cellular phones—either sending/receiving text messages or playing games. We spot a *gelateria* (ice cream shop) facing one side of the piazza. Perfect! Just what we need on a hot summer's evening. Francesco and I get our usual chocolate and coffee gelato. One taste and we both agree that this is the best ice cream we've ever had. What a find and just a block away from that street I hate so much.

We finish our ice cream and continue our walk. Francesco alternates between holding my hand and putting his arm around me. I can't remember when the last time was that I just went for a walk in America. Always on the go, I never just walked for the sake of walking—there had to be a purpose or destination in mind. Tonight we have no particular destination. *Facciamo una passeggiata* (we are taking a walk); the walk is our purpose. We simply explore the neighborhood and talk, catching up on events at work and making plans for the future. Every so often Francesco stops walking to emphasize a point or look into my eyes to see if I understand. Francesco speaks to me almost exclusively in Italian now. Even though he is fluent in English we've decided full immersion will accelerate my language acquisition. It is exhausting to talk in one language and think in another. I am still translating in my head. It's getting late and finally cooling off some. We head back to the apartment.

I am just beginning to understand and appreciate the *passeggiata*. It's a simple activity. Anyone can do it anywhere in the world. Yet, when I talk with other American expats living in Milan we all agree; there is an art to the Italian *passeggiata*—walking without a particular destination in mind. I'm also enthralled with the importance of the piazza in Italian culture—the neighborhood gathering point for young and old. I am still on the outside looking in and for now that is OK. As I sit here with the man for whom I left home and with whom I think I want to spend the rest of my life I wonder: Will I ever make it to the inside? Is that what I really want? There are so many things I have to learn as I re-start my life in another country. The language up until now has been my focus, and while that has its difficulties, I am beginning to realize that it is probably the easiest of the tasks ahead of me.

Christmas 2003—Domodossola, Italy

It's the annual Christmas party. After several years, it has now become a tradition among our group of friends in Domodossola, Italy. Francesco, a native of Domodossola and my main link to this group of people, and I, the American expat, enjoy hosting this event. I've always liked giving parties and, well, we have the good fortune of having an apartment, while small by American standards, which has an ample entryway and living room—suitable for a large crowd. The two-meter dining table occupies nearly half of the room. We've moved the bench from the kitchen and all the straight-back and folding chairs we own around it. The couches and a coffee table in the sitting area will handle the overflow of whoever can't get a spot at the table. Traditional Christmas carols (English/American) filter through the hum of voices chatting and catching up.

In all there are typically 20–25 in attendance, including a few kids. Each year there are more children as couples marry and start families. My son Federico is four and the oldest of the children present. He loves the pandemonium of a house full of people. His brother, Alessio, is just under two and not terribly happy about all the commotion. It seems hard to believe how my life has changed since those days in the sixth floor apartment on *Via Monte Ceneri*. Now Francesco and I are married, I've become fluent in Italian, the mother of two beautiful boys, and am creating my own traditions for my family that attempt to balance both the American and Italian influences.

The menu is my version of an American potluck supper. I provide light snacks, beverages and a pasta dish. All the guests are requested to bring something to share. I've long since renounced trying to systematically assign dishes to the various participants that would insure a balanced menu. This year we have lots of *panettone*—an Italian fruitcake that is traditionally shared among family and friends for the holidays. No matter. We eat whatever arrives and while the menu may be heavy on desserts one year and side dishes the next, there is always plenty of good food and good times.

Moreno, currently single, compliments my cooking. "Anyone who can make *orecchiette* as good as this may be able to convince me to marry again." A rush of gratitude fills me. Over the years, being the only American in this group, I have often worked myself into frenzy about the cooking. Even I must admit that my culinary skills have come a long way from those single days back in Chicago when my roommate and I very seriously studied the jello package instructions.

Chiara follows me into the kitchen offering to help as I prepare a second batch of the *oriecchette con cima di rapa* (pasta with broccoli rabe). "It's true," Chiara says. "The pasta is great. You've really adapted to life here in Italy in so many ways. Way beyond cooking pasta. By now it's like you've become Italian." My response is noncommittal. After all these years of being on the outside looking in, perhaps now I have finally made it to the inner circle. I am one of them, not just a bystander or worse still, that "American" who doesn't know how to cook the pasta properly. Yet, being American has been such a crucial part of my identity, especially all these years as an expat. Am I really ready to give that up?

Am I now more Italian than American? And what exactly is it that makes one "more Italian" or "more American"? Perhaps I've developed some kind of strange chameleon-like split personality: American when back "home" or around other Americans and Italian when in Italy or among Italians? It is true that these days with

156

so much of the world against the US foreign policy one does not flaunt being American when abroad. However, I think that to be true to myself I must realize that one cannot fully renounce one or the other. I grew up in America and there are so many of its values that I treasure: hard work, perseverance, and equality for all. Italy has opened my eyes and heart to additional treasures: the simple pleasures of taking a walk or sharing a gelato, the history and culture that is so accessible to all regardless of income and the sense of community you find in the piazza. I don't have all the answers but I find myself hoping, pleading, and praying that it is possible to be both, while I am thankful for the treasures my expat experience has helped me discover.

Patricia Guild-Ganora has lived overseas for eight years. She left family, friends and job when she moved to Italy to pursue a relationship with an Italian man, who became her husband. She currently lives with her husband and two children in Domodossola, Italy.

My Life as an Expatriate

Hildegard Esper Enesco

The word expatriate conjures up a romantic image. As everyone knows, expatriates sit at sidewalk cafes in Paris, sipping wine with their friends and discussing life, art and ideas. They write novels in Lisbon, they paint in Tahiti, beach comb in the Caribbean, or practice yoga in Tibet. In short, they live life more fully and intensely than if they had stayed home in Pittsburgh for the nine-to-five drudgery in an office.

As an American living in Montreal, it had never occurred to me that I too, was an expatriate. I followed my daily teaching routine year in and year out, never writing a novel, defying society or kicking over the traces. Enlightenment came one day in the most unlikely manner. There in my mail was a brochure from the IRS entitled "Tax Tips for Expatriates." I couldn't believe my eyes! I was an expatriate! A free spirit! An adventurer! A new door had opened. A vast unexplored world lay at my feet. But for a moment I was assailed by doubts. Could I really be a top-notch expatriate in Montreal?

After all, we expatriates have certain requirements: exotic surroundings, quaint local customs, the stimulation of living in another culture, and a heightened sense of reality to stimulate our artistic creativity. Could Montreal fill these basic needs? I began to review Montreal's qualifications as a site for expatriate activity.

First of all, we expatriates require sidewalk cafes. Yes, that criterion is met. There certainly are enough sidewalk cafes in Montreal. They line Prince Arthur Street, Crescent Streets and Place Jacques Cartier. In fact, there is a cafe on practically every corner. Score 10 points for cafes.

Next, we expatriates like to live in countries with picturesque local customs unknown in the United States. That fits, too. No one in the United States ever queues up for the bus or eats poutine. When greeting friends, the typical Montreal custom is to kiss on both cheeks. This procedure is highly alarming to one's friends from the Midwest. Score 10 points for quaint local customs.

We expatriates like to widen our cultural horizons by learning a new language and exploring the rich heritage of another culture. Montreal is a functionally bilingual city. I never would have learned French if I had lived in Kansas City. Score 20 points for culture.

We expatriates don't even mind political instability. The cost of living is lower in unsettled countries. Once in the expatriate mode, we can easily move on if we have to. Besides, instability keeps us on the alert and involved with life. Complacency cannot creep in and dull our perceptions. Montreal's referendum anxiety and the threat of Quebec separation fill this need perfectly.

I had read that expatriates undergo a strange transmutation after spending some years abroad. On returning to their home country, they perceive life differently from their compatriots. They are like outside observers or anthropologists observing a foreign tribe.

Actually, this has happened to me, too. I was in the United States recently on the Fourth of July. There were sparklers, firecrackers, fireworks, horns blowing, bands marching, barbecues, cookouts, huge gatherings in the parks and in the streets. How strange! We don't do that on Canada Day; we show much more restraint.

A trip to the United States during the Gulf War was even more startling. There were yellow ribbons to show support for the troops everywhere: on people's doors, fence posts, mailboxes, cars and trucks. Crowds pressed around TV sets in malls and public buildings to keep up with the news. There were American flags everywhere. How curious! I have never seen such a sustained outpouring of emotion in Canada.

Even a trip to Plattsburgh, New York induces culture shock. Once you cross the border, things change. There are no more potholes in the highway; it must be a secret of Yankee technology. It is a shock to see signs in English; it must be legal to post English signs in New York State. At the shopping mall the clerks are effusive and full of pep: "Can I help you, dear?" "What are you looking for, honey?"

The fact is that I have become more and more Canadian over the years. I am proud of Canada's tolerance, its health care system and its peacekeepers. I recently became a Canadian citizen, and it shows. I now say "zed" instead of "zee." I spell "colour" and "honour" with a "u." I celebrate Victoria Day, St. Jean Baptiste Day and Canada Day. In the morning I watch "Canada AM" instead of "Good Morning America." I question American cultural imperialism. I fit right in, but I shouldn't forget that I am an expatriate.

Now that I have two passports, I have doubled my potential as an expatriate. I could leave both of my home countries and head for Mexico or Tunisia. With this in mind, I shall have to start taking my expatriate status and responsibilities more seriously. Creativity is essential for living the expatriate life to the full. Could I write poetry? Could I paint? Could I write a novel? People do write novels in Montreal. Think of the famous Canadian writers Hugh MacLennan and Mordecai Richler. My friend Olga is writing a novel. I wonder if I could write one?

In fact, I have already begun. I have laid up a good supply of paper and pencils, and purchased a slim leather attaché case. I have acquired a rakish French beret and a sweatshirt emblazoned with the Quebec fleur de lys. I have just picked out my favorite table at the Cafe des Artistes. After all, I am an expatriate, a free spirit! I am Prometheus unbound!

Hildegard Esper Enesco was born and grew up in Seattle, Washington. After majoring in biology at Reed College, Portland, Oregon, she continued her studies in Zoology at Columbia University in New York. She received her M.A in 1959 and her Ph.D. in 1962. Postdoctoral studies at McGill University brought her to Montreal, Canada where she has lived since 1962. She taught at Concordia University in Montreal, where she became full professor and served as Chairman of the Concordia Biology Department. Her Canadian husband and she both retired in 1995, and enjoy writing, literature, art and travel. They winter in Delray Beach, Florida

American After All

David Lobo VI

I was born in Venezuela 67 years ago, where I live today.

My father, David P. Lobo V, was Venezuelan. He had studied electro-mechanical engineering at Lehigh University in Bethlehem, Pennsylvania, were he met and married my mother, both 19 years old. My mother, Isabella Kugler, was the eldest daughter of six children in an immigrant family from Germany and Hungary. Her father was from Germany and hardly spoke the English language.

So here comes along David P. Lobo V, from a country they never heard of, and takes Isabella back to Venezuela in 1930.

Our mother taught my sister and me small-town American moral, spiritual and community values, as well as admiration and respect towards the US flag, national hymn and other symbols. We were indeed considered US citizens by birth when our parents registered us at the nearest US Embassy. We attended a year of grammar school at Freemansburg, Pennsylvania in 1946–47.

Surprisingly my US citizenship, acquired at birth through my mother, was taken away from me under the 1940 Nationality Act because I naively voted in the Venezuelan presidential elections in my early 20s.

Paradoxically, instead of the logical reaction, this new situation increased my love for America and its values. I ended up being Senior Resident and Fellow at the Boston Children's Hospital, Harvard Medical School, and a Peace Corps physician, as a *foreigner.* I worked and lived in the United States from 1967 to 1971 and then again from 1979 to 1981. I even took a sabbatical to help out with four children so that my wife could pursue post-graduate studies at MIT in civil engineering. We owned a house and our love, expectations and respect for Wellesley, Boston, New England and the United States always grew. But we remained foreigners on limited visas and finally had to return to Venezuela when the visas expired.

In the winter of 2001 someone at the US Embassy here in Venezuela spontaneously advised me on the US Supreme Court 1967 ruling *Afroyim v. Rusk,* which overturned the section of the Nationality Act mandating automatic loss of citizenship for voting in a foreign election. And BINGO two weeks later I had my brand new US passport, and it is considered at the age of 67 that I had never lost my US citizenship throughout the previous five decades. According to the Supreme Court ruling, my citizenship had been *unconstitutionally* taken away from me. The basic point of the Supreme Court's ruling in *Afroyim v. Rusk* was that the 14.th Amendment to the US Constitution—while originally intended mainly to guarantee citizenship to freed Negro slaves and their descendents—had effectively elevated citizenship to the status of a constitutionally protected right. Hence, Congress had no right to pass a law which had the effect of depriving an American of his citizenship without his consent.

Now I heartily plan to change the image that the United States has here and to diffuse the American Way!

David Kugler Lobo VI was born in 1937 in Caracas, Venezuela, of an American mother and a Venezuelan father. He studied medicine in Venezuela at the same university where his grandfather, David Lobo IV, had been President and Rector. He pursued his career in pediatrics at Boston's Children's Hospital, Harvard Medical School, and subsequently was Fellow-In-Medicine in the same hospital. He lives in Venezuela where he is a pediatrician, director and chief physician at the Children's Orthopedic Hospital and a physician and medical director of the Peace Corps. He has founded a volunteer association for hospitals, working in shanty towns, as well as Centro Medico Docente La Trinidad for teaching and Instituto Medico La Floresta.

Living Between Worlds

Robin Herrnfeld

Do I have a story to tell? Maybe.

A story of an American in Germany. A story of a life lived between worlds, of belonging, it seems, neither here nor there. The up-rootedness of it all. The ambivalence.

I sit in my apartment in Berlin, all the melancholy of a grey and rainy March day filling the room, listening to Max Bruch's concerto for violin and orchestra no. 1 in G minor. The music is melancholy, too, but beautifully so. The beauty and the melancholy, I think, are like the ambivalence of these years spent in a culture not my own.

I wonder where the story starts. I close my eyes and think back some twenty-five, thirty years.

There's a girl named Robin, grown up in a small Californian mountain town. Sheltered, shy and naïve. Just graduated from high school. Loath to leave "her mountains," but curious, at the same time, about the world outside. Braving the step and then never being able to really answer the question she is most asked over the years: Why did she leave sunny southern California and move to dreary and rainy Germany? Why did she?

Her family, it seems to her, is not your typical American family. They have foreign exchange students live in their home; the parents think that one of their daughters will have to be an exchange student, too, and "go abroad," "broaden her horizons." Robin is the only one of the four older daughters who seems to be interested.

She has read lots of books about quaint old England and thinks it must be ever so much nicer there than in California. So when it comes time to apply to an exchange organization for the year abroad, England is where she wants to go. The exchange organization, though, is basically only accepting applications for Germany, because that is where it has the most host families.

Robin has been to Germany before, with her parents, and liked the greenness and the castles on the Rhine they saw. All right, then, she thinks, Germany. Then there is, of course, the added benefit of being able to learn a foreign language if she goes there. A rational argument. So when she graduates from high school, she flies off to live with a family in Germany for a year and spend a year at a German high school.

Besides being naïve, Robin is impressionable, and falls in love with Germany and things German. She adapts to the culture and likes learning the language. When she returns to California and goes to college, the obvious thing to do seems to become a German major. Her parents might have preferred for her to get a degree

162

in business, but at least learning German, thinks her father, is a skill that will help her find a job later on.

Her third year in college, Robin is back in Germany on the Junior Year Abroad program. Again, she would have liked to go to England and study medieval history (her second major), but, then, there is the language thing, and the argument about the better employment opportunities (thinks her father, who, after all, is paying for all this), so it's better to concentrate on German.

Her university career ends back in the States with a couple of quarters as a graduate student, earning her tuition by teaching German. (How right her father was!) Then an employment opportunity in Germany presents itself: the German chapter of that high school exchange organization is looking for a home-stay coordinator. Robin applies for the job. It helps that she, in the meanwhile, has a German boyfriend who happens to be a volunteer working for the German chapter. She likes her graduate studies and teaching at the University, but she likes the German boyfriend, too. So when she gets the job, it's "Auf Wiedersehen, America!"

December, 1978. Robin leaves LAX for Hamburg.

She leaves behind:

- her parents, who probably are proud to have a daughter going off to work in Germany, but are also a little skeptical of the wisdom of this step and more than a little alarmed at her going off to a foreign country, not only to work, but to live with this young German man whom they've met only briefly, and who seems to be nice and intelligent, but then you never know...

- four sisters, who are probably all too involved in their own lives to really care about what Robin is doing, but who basically think that it sounds like a very adventurous undertaking;

- some friends who feel she is betraying not only them but also her country, who, although they hold with the line from a popular play of the early seventies that "the worst Americans are those who love everything about America," are still patriotic enough to feel that anyone who would leave America is behaving in an extremely disloyal manner;

- a friend with a Jewish boyfriend who isn't interested in remaining friendly with anyone who would willingly and happily go to live in Germany, which is, the friend seems to think, still full of Nazis;

- an admirer or two whose prides are possibly injured by the fact that she seems to prefer "cultivated European men" to their more laid-back Californian types.

Arriving in Hamburg, in the midst of the decade's worst snow storm, she finds:

- the "cultivated European man" she'll marry some years later;

- an apartment in a graceful old villa inhabited by people whose studies are lined floor-to-ceiling with books and who listen to classical music all day long;

- the new experience of having a nine-to-five job in an office in a large city;

- the Opera! Beethoven's "Fidelio" (what an amazing experience- she has never been to an opera before);
- art museums;
- good coffee, better wine;
- a whole new world of the arts, of history, of culture.

She also finds: anti-Americanism. Not quite as bad now, in the early 1980s, as it was back in 1973-74 during the high school exchange, when Allende was overthrown in Chile and the more leftist-oriented German students saw the evil CIA in any and every American they encountered. Not to mention Vietnam. Now there is the NATO decision to station American nuclear missiles in Europe, the German peace movement is at its height and along with it another wave of anti-Americanism. Later, there is the ridicule to be suffered when a Hollywood actor is elected President of the United States, (she hardly dares mention that the former Governor of California once shook her hand!). Still later there is the embarrassment of being American under President George W.

Robin is sensitive; it hurts when people equate her with "the Americans" and seem to hold her personally accountable for all the evil for which "America" seems to stand. Her initial (unconscious) reaction is to try to compensate by total assimilation into the German culture. ("Let them think I am German, so they won't bother me with this anti-American stuff.") But at the same time, it hurts to hear the verbal abuse, to hear Germans referring to Americans as "Amis," which always sounds derogatory to her (although it is probably not meant that way). And it hurts her feelings when they make fun of American accents, of the way Americans pronounce their "R"s-long, broad, drawn-out. After about twenty years she finally gets thoroughly sick and tired of hearing people blame America for all the horrible things happening around the globe while at the same time they most willingly import the very worst of American culture-the TV soaps, the violent action movies, the fast-food.

And there are the various day-to-day problems coming from living as a foreigner in Germany. At the beginning, of course, the bureaucratic hurdles involving registration and job permits:

"You have to have a work permit in order to get a residence permit," they tell her at the registry office.

"But you must have a residence permit before you can get a work permit," they say when she goes to the employment office.

Mind-boggling. It takes time to understand the finer logic of the system.

And then the problem with the passport. Having to use your passport as identification so that everyone immediately knows you're a foreigner. Having to go through the longer immigration lines for non-European citizens at the European airports, though this is not a serious problem. A more unfortunate problem is not being allowed to vote in Germany. She lives in Germany and works in Germany, pays social security and taxes in Germany, but she may not vote in the local elections. Let alone the federal elections.

"Aren't you a German citizen?" people ask.

"But you're married to a German. Doesn't that make you a German citizen?"

"Don't you want to take on German citizenship?"

Obviously it would have its advantages, she thinks. She would be entitled to a German passport, could get an "*Ausweis*," the identity card the Germans use, would be eligible to vote and would have a better chance on the job market.

"No," she realizes. "I'm American."

It's her identity. There's no way of getting around it. She can't simply wake up one morning and not be American any longer. A change of passport, a change of citizenship on paper, cannot change who you are.

In spite of all this, though, Robin is totally immersed in Germany for a long time. The years fly by. She's busy with her job, with her husband, with more German literature studies at the University. At home, at the work place, at the University, she is surrounded by Germans, speaks nothing but German. Her German was already good when she came, but after awhile it is so good that some people don't even realize that she is not German. The gaps between her trips home to California grow longer until finally she is shocked to find that she hasn't been back for four years!

When she finally goes home, people laugh at her German accent, and she can hear the mistakes she makes speaking English. It is as though she has started to forget her own language! But when she returns to Germany, she has already forgotten a lot of German words and her American accent is back.

Her husband gives her a funny look when they're in America.

"You laugh a lot more when you speak English," he says.

"Do I?" she wonders. Mentality must have much to do with the language, she thinks. Speaking German means thinking German, and thinking German means taking on, somehow, a German mentality. And Germans, she finds, (without wanting to fall into the stereotype trap) are thoughtful, highly theoretical, serious and inclined to lengthy discussions, thorough in whatever they do. This can be frustrating sometimes, given her preference for good old American learning-by-doing and finding practical solutions. So maybe it's not surprising that she doesn't laugh as much in Germany.

The identity problem is not just a question of citizenship or passport, she finds. It's much more complicated than that. It's more the language, the mentality, the cultural affinity that makes up identity. Sometimes it all makes her feel somewhat schizophrenic.

"Which language is really mine?" she asks herself. "Which personality is really me-the American one, or the German? And which would I rather be, where would I rather be?"

When in Germany, she thinks how nice it would be to be in America. When she's in America, she remembers all the good things about Germany. She doesn't know which is better. If one is better than the other.

Living in Germany means living with its history. The Third Reich, the

Holocaust, are ever present. Robin watches endless rows of documentaries on TV, hears endless discussions, endless political uproars caused by politicians who again and again make stupid remarks about Nazis and Hitler and anti-Semitism. On a more personal level, she listens to the never-ending stories told by the war-damaged parents-in-law: the Prussian refugee father-in-law, the mother-in-law who was sent off to the countryside as a child to be out of the way of the bombs. The guilt they can't help having for what their generation and their parents' generation did. The things they seem to feel they have to say in their self-defense so that the American daughter-in-law will understand and not think they were Nazis.

And then 1989. The wall falls. Germany is reunited. Chancellor Kohl speaks of "blooming landscapes" and the general euphoria is great, but behind it lurk dark shadows. The economy in the East is at level zero; people in the West aren't all that enthused about having to help pay for rebuilding the East. Unemployment is high and right-wing violence is on the rise, and not only in the East.

The stories Robin reads in the newspapers about Neo-Nazi attacks on foreigners are disturbing. In 1992 and 1993 there are attacks in Mölln (a lovely small town she has pleasant memories of) and Solingen. Turkish homes are set on fire by Neo-Nazis; children and their mothers die. Horrible pictures. *"Ausländerfeindlichkeit."*

The wife of the German Foreign minister decides to take a public stand against xenophobia and founds a volunteer organization that supports victims of anti-foreigner attacks. She is looking for someone to help out in the office. Robin volunteers to do the job and works for Aktion CURA for ten years. The work makes her think she sees what many people and politicians do not want to see-that racism is still latent in a large part of the population-and not just in Germany, but in all of Europe, in the United States, in the whole world.

Some of the cases she works on could shatter her faith in humanity in general and in the Germans in particular (though she knows rationally that it is not right to feel this way). A black man is beaten and thrown into a lake. Another thrown off a moving train. An Italian worker is beaten into a coma with a baseball bat.

She has read enough, has watched enough news on TV, to know about the terrible things people will do to each other in the name of religion, race or love of the fatherland. But dealing with these victims, it becomes a first-hand experience. Especially when the Neo-Nazis attack a British Jamaican and leave him with a broken neck, paralyzed from the neck down, wheelchair bound and totally dependent on other people to feed him, to wash him, to scratch his nose or shoo the flies away.

Aktion CURA pays for his ambulance-flight home to England and raises money for a van that can accommodate his wheelchair. Robin translates all his correspondence with Germany and helps him communicate when he returns to Germany to lead a march against racism. She visits him, listens to him. Hears about what it means to be black, to be disabled. The discrimination, the humiliations, the frustra¬tions he has lived with. The misery. The injustices, the legacies of slavery, the crimes carried out by Europeans in the name of liberty and freedom. The

166

Americans going into Iraq.

It's a long way from the mountains of California to this apartment in Berlin. The music, beautiful and melancholy. The ambivalence. America, Anti-America. Good, evil. Love, hate. Black, white. They may be far apart, they may lie close together, but the borders between the different worlds are often blurry.

At the end of the story I want to know: What would her life have been like if she had stayed home? Would she see the borders more clearly?

I'll never know the answer.

Robin (Vandenberg) Herrnfeld, born in 1955 in Fullerton, California, grew up in the San Bernardino Mountains, where her parents were both teachers at the local high school. After graduating with a B.A. in German Languages and Literature and Medieval Studies from the University of California, she worked as a Program Officer for the German Youth for Understanding Committee, an international youth exchange organization in Hamburg, Germany, and also completed an M.A. in German Literature at the University of Hamburg. Currently she works for the German-Russian Forum, a non-governmental organization dealing with German-Russian relations, and lives with her German husband in Berlin.

The Lessons of Culture Shock

As new eyes bring new insight, old truths, once shaken, demand a deeper restoration.

David Snyder

A small child shouted "yovo!" and I laughed, remembering how annoyed I used to get hearing children scream "foreigner" at me dozens of times each day.

Lynn Heinisch

Two years ago we were graced by an extended encounter with a person who in the States would be an outcast or reside on the fringe of our society.

Jerome Kilmer

Aloneness. Guilt. Caring. That's the Africa I know. Oh, yes, I forgot something. Laughter.

Tracey Buckenmeyer

I am free, at least for the afternoon, from my bubble. But most of the time I'm not thinking about freedom. I'm thinking of cages.

Katrina Sue Lehman

Lessons from a Naked Man

David Snyder

It was a naked man in Penn Station who welcomed me home. Waiting for the train to Baltimore, I watched as he climbed the stairs into the terminal, as if a naked man was the last thing even he himself expected to see, and disappeared into the rush of the station. I cast a sideways glance at the faces of those around me. No one seemed to notice.

Seconds later a shout arose from inside the terminal, growing louder and more urgent as the naked man returned, sandwiched now between two broad-shouldered policemen. As he was dragged past, the man twisted purposefully to direct his tirade at the commuters gathered around me.

"Work all of your lives in an office building, for what?" he screamed. "You are all insane! Can you hear me? You are all insane!"

His cries bounced off of the green tiled walls, then died amidst the rush of the station. As he was led from the hall, commuters filled the space behind him. The middle-aged woman standing beside me grunted and turned back to her newspaper.

One week before I had been in Sudan, watching as Africa's largest country bled out its Western populace in a fit of genocide. The months before that had begun to blend into broken bits of sensory collage—a woman dying of AIDS in Malawi, a man who had threatened me in Haiti, a monsoon rain in Guatemala. I added the naked man to my litany and boarded the train to Baltimore.

After six years in Africa, such are the markers by which you begin to measure your life. Having spent much of that time working in disaster zones around the world, those markers assume an odd and irregular pattern, like the gravestones of soldiers buried as they fell on some distant battlefield. It is a life where places, not days, become the measure of time, and so it remains for many of us who live outside the familiar patterns of life in the United States.

It occurred to me that I had crossed some Rubicon as I was packing my suitcase in a rented apartment in Macedonia. It was July 1999, and for three months I had been burning myself out amidst a million refugees from the Yugoslavian province of Kosovo. Only two years into the work of relief and development, it was my first big emergency—my introduction to the unbounded world of the professional humanitarian. Some in the field will tell you such work is addictive—the pace and tempo of disaster. But the job is not for everyone. Many burn out quickly and ease back into the comfortable pace of long-term development. Others return home, develop their photos and tuck the experience into their memory.

But some stay, chasing headlines from one passport page to the next until only the monumental can hold their attention. For many of them—and there are many out there—the gap between past and present grows wider each year, until the key to home is worn so smooth by distance that it never quite opens the door again.

Eventually, they cannot go back. Packing my bag that night in Macedonia, I told myself I would not be one of them.

As I write this now, I am sitting at my desk in a leafy suburb of Johannesburg, South Africa. I have to ground myself in this place and time because casting a net over the years that have elapsed since that night in Macedonia seems nearly impossible. On my resume I will list that I have traveled in Uganda and Timor, Angola and Sierra Leone. I will explain to some future employer perhaps that I have worked with Afghan refugees in Pakistan, volcano victims in Congo, and tsunami survivors in Sri Lanka. I will try to find employable ways to explain that I have met amazing people and seen amazing things.

But that may not be enough. If my future boss is like other Americans I have met in these intervening years he will sit uneasily, having asked of my life overseas, his eyes setting slightly at the answers I struggle to proffer. He will study my face for a moment as if the subtitles flashing through the air between us do not match the movie he has paid to see. Sensing the disconnection I will fall back on brevity, condensing my experiences into sweeping understatement, reducing my life to bland overview. Suddenly, there will be no place for most of what has become important to me. That gap I feared will widen.

To know how different America can look—to understand that gap—you must see it first from afar. It is at once a remarkable and uneasy experience, like reading the diary, decades later, you kept as a troubled youth. As new eyes bring new insight, old truths, once shaken, demand a deeper restoration. That process can be wondrous or fearsome, dark or transcendent—both the risk of the journey and the reward of the traveler. But the price paid for either can be steep, an exchange of the common currency for decorous and wonderful bills you cannot tender.

Physically, of course, you are far removed overseas from everyone who once defined you. To remain connected, you must schedule the events by which your family marks its history—a cousin's wedding, the birth of a child, a high school graduation. You are forced by distance to choose the memories in which you will participate, those pages of the family album on which you will appear, and sacrifice the others to long distance calls over broken lines at early hours of the morning.

But you are removed in other ways less tangible, less immediately evident. From 8,000 miles away you lose touch with what, since you left, has become the fodder of day-to-day conversation. You come home reading from a different book, the easy sequence with which you once turned the pages lost.

You notice it subtly at first, offering pieces of your year to friends who shake their heads, smile, and turn the conversation gently back to more familiar ground—college friends, moves and purchases, baby news. Over time, you find yourself searching for segues into the lives you once shared, your experiences at times an awkward suffix to the communal banter of your friends.

Each time you come home you must ease into your past. In the first days back you study the photos on your mother's wall, buy fast food burgers and stand on the porch to scan a sky full of northern stars. You call friends and flip through the

172

endless choices of radio stations. You watch *Jeopardy* and have pizza delivered.

But you must also ease back into America itself, divine from its unfamiliar pace the changes that have taken place in your absence. Having lived now for six years overseas, I find myself less able to reconcile the life that I left with the life that I am living. It is not a fatal flaw, I hope, not something that proper time home will not be able to restore. But the disconnect is real, if ineffable—a tectonic shift, deep and imperceptible, that finds you casting lines across the cracks that have formed at your wandering feet, asking more questions and finding fewer answers.

Coming home, there are constants on which you depend—the smell of spring, the wave of an elderly neighbor—and baselines against which you test your memories, like side-street directions and the phone numbers of friends. Part of the pleasure of travel lies in the fulfillment of reconnection. In that sense, home is always home, real and tangible. But in the larger sense you can struggle to wrap your head around the concepts of home, concepts heightened like senses by your time away and worn by the new perspective you bring to bear: America as vital and vibrant, as history and as touchstone; America as unquenchable energy.

Coming home from a life abroad reminds you that there are tolls we pay for that energy, tolls I think we do not as Americans allow ourselves to tally. Increasingly it seems, tomorrow has become the object of today, and possession the measure of our lives. Home on leave I catch myself wondering through my window at the lives of the workday commuters around me, at the ordered pace with which we sacrifice our time to the enigma of happiness. If there is one thing that strikes you coming home from Africa it is the relentless predictability of the life our wealth affords us in the United States, at the way routine becomes more comfortable than change. Sometimes, suffocated by it, I find my mind wandering to places unbounded, searching for a single marker by which to measure the day, one thing to set today apart from yesterday. That a week can pass without one is perhaps the greatest fear I have of moving home.

Weighted with that feeling, I stepped off the train from New York and inched into the Baltimore station. Dragging my suitcase up the stairs I entered the yellow glow of the terminal. It was after nine p.m., and the station sagged from the toll that day had taken. A woman in a beige skirt suit sat thumbing through a glossy women's magazine, waiting on a late train home. A station attendant pushed a dirty mop head into the corners of the terminal, its echoes hollow in the open space.

I moved towards the door and emerged onto Charles Street. The air was damp and city cold. Shrouded in the red haze of their exhaust, two yellow cabs crawled up to the curb where a businessman in a grey suit stood waiting. I had seen him board the train in Wilmington an hour earlier. He had taken a seat a few rows up from me, folded his jacket into the overhead rack, and disappeared into some paperwork spread carefully on the small fold out tray of the seat back.

I stood watching as he opened the door, eased his briefcase in ahead of him, and sank into the back seat of the taxi. As the cab crept away from the curb I stepped into the space behind it and glanced at the back of the car, where I could see him slumped in the rear window, his head silhouetted by the green glow of the fare ticking off the final minutes of his journey home. I stood there for a long moment struggling with all the newness of home—with the cold night air, with the year behind me, and with the nagging thought that maybe the naked man had it right after all.

David Snyder is a writer and photographer for an American non-governmental organization based in Baltimore, and he has been living in Africa since 1999. He travels often with his work—35 countries in the last 6 years—and so has drawn on that to share his insights.

Once a Yovo

Lynn Heinisch

When I went back to Allada, we killed 11 chickens. Five years had passed since I left the town where I spent one of the best years of my life. It seemed a good excuse for a party.

I stayed again with Maman and Papa Ahodi, who hosted me my first weeks in Benin. Taking a bucket bath in their outhouse reminded me of my early impressions. I recalled learning to use the small plastic bowl to scoop out water and dump it over me as I squatted naked on the concrete floor. The smell from the toilet hole just three feet away. Going in at night, seeing the cockroaches, dreading to pick up the metal cover, banging on it with the toilet paper in a futile attempt to scare them off.

Oh, but that cold water felt good running down my hair and my back. I learned fast to carry a handkerchief everywhere so I could wipe my face of the relentless grime that came from dirt mixed with sweat. The closest I ever got to feeling clean was in those few minutes drying off after a bucket bath. The moment I stepped into the yard in my flip-flops, the red dirt found me and the battle started all over.

And I loved it. The sense of being alive, and raw, and real. Feeling fear and anger and joy and delight and confusion. Stripping away the ability to go numbly through the motions of life, buffered by comfort and routine.

Preparing for my trip back, I realized I was nervous because it had been such a good experience. It seemed better to leave it as a pleasant memory. My hard-earned French had faded away from disuse. I was older and more worn. I no longer felt like the eager, enthusiastic volunteer whom they had embraced. They still had my heart, but I was afraid I would disappoint them.

Casmier met me at the Cotonou airport and we hailed *zemijohns* to the taxi stand. The motorcycles pulled up and we climbed on. Slinging my bag and purse across my chest, I straightened my spine and remembered how I had learned not to hold the driver, but to brace myself with one hand behind me on the metal frame. It was false security, with no helmet and traffic that seemed void of any rules. We joined the fray and I felt all over again the sense of freedom. I loved zipping around the city, part of the dust and chaos.

I remembered being overwhelmed by the otherworldliness of it. No amount of reading, not years of studying Africa, nothing had prepared me for girls and boys walking by with trays on their heads, selling food, clothes, kitchen appliances, soap, candy. The gorgeous multi-colored fabric and grace of the women in their *pagne* skirts and head wraps. Wood furniture for sale on the side of the street, metal workers welding, vegetable stands, tropical flowers. A blur of images raced by and I started to remember. The post office. The mosque. The roundabout where the taxis picked up passengers. It felt familiar, but as if I was catching flashes of last night's dream. A place I had known, but never really knew. I claimed it on one level, but always as an outsider, lacking the intuitive awareness and nuanced understanding of a local. I had my bearings, but a very loose grip.

Casmier and I climbed into the taxi for Allada. I had the front center gap between bucket seats, propped up on a pillow. Out of habit, I angled my legs to the right so the driver could reach the gearshift. Four more people squeezed into the back and we were off. We weaved among cars equally loaded down, trunks overflowing with baskets and bags. Like all the drivers, our chauffeur made generous use of his horn, though it was hard to imagine it would make any difference, given our speed.

Seeing Casmier reminded me of the kindness he had shown me that year. How he helped me clean my house to prepare for my family's visit, invited me to his village, cooked local foods for me, taught me to navigate social norms and customs. I remembered going to the American embassy to find out the requirements for people to come visit me. How badly I wanted to repay their hospitality. And what felt like a slap when the woman explained that US policy assumes people are trying to emigrate. They must overcome that presumption, she said, in order to get a tourist visa. I remembered the shame and disappointment of telling this to people who had been so good to me, most of whom would never qualify for a visa.

About 45 minutes out of Cotonou, I recognized the school on the right and Casmier's voice started to fade into the back of my head. My mind shifted gears and years. There was the incline up to Allada, there was the sign for the *Las Palmas buvette*. Soon, we would pass the hospital on the right and the wood shop where Ambroise worked.

My fears were displaced by a surge of joy and amazement. We started down the dirt road to the Ahodis. There was the library I helped set up. We crossed the tracks of the train station, where the market happened every four days. A steady stream of people walked on the roadside, many of them students in their khakis, carrying rolled-up paper notebooks. A small child shouted "*yovo!*" and I laughed, remembering how annoyed I used to get hearing children scream "foreigner" at me dozens of times each day.

We arrived at the wooden gate, painted with the signs for Alpha and Omega. I knocked. Knocked again. "*Ko ko ko!*" I called out. It opened and there was Papa. He grabbed me and then pushed me away to get a better look. "*Sika!*" he said, calling me by the name they had given me—Gold, first child.

We found Maman in the school behind the house. The school they started with one boy the year I was there. It now had six classrooms, 120 children. Everywhere that week I was struck by growth—four internet centers in a town where there had been none, mobile phones, paved roads.

"Do you remember the first time I came?" I asked them. "I couldn't speak any French and I just sat here." Maman had tried to break the ice by playing a cassette of "*Yakkity Yak*." I remembered when my nephew was born and the message came via someone who rode up from Cotonou, where they had gotten the phone call. The

176

Ahodis served me pineapple juice and rum. I grabbed Papa and hugged him. He was stiff as a board and I realized that wasn't done.

Overcome with wanting to see everyone, I headed into town with Casmier. We went looking for Célestin, the 13-year-old son of the caretaker at the house where I had lived. I had paid for Célestin's schooling that year. I had a soft spot for the skinny boy with the bursting grin. The boy who spent hours in my house studying. The sharpshooter with the sling shot. The boy who cooked for his brother and father, his mother having left the family for another husband, a better provider. He would set the cast-iron pot on three rocks over a fire and stir the ground corn and water into the grits-like dish "*pâte.*" The boy who was a devout Celestial Christian, the church of the white robes and all-night worship services, because God had spared him from a deadly voodoo curse. The hero who came to my rescue when I found a mouse in my house, and who giggled at my fear.

He wasn't home, but his father was there, sitting on the curb. Same toothless grin. Me speaking in French, him in Fon, talking at and past each other, just like before. I gave him the key chain I had brought. Merci, he said. Then he pointed to my bag and pantomimed his hand to his mouth. Didn't I bring him anything to eat? My old conflict—the routine requests. I never mastered the good-humored deflection for which they called. I remembered my discomfort at knowing—and them knowing—how much more money I had. Struggling with how, and if, and why, to give. Feeling resentment at the asks. Feeling guilt at the resentment. Too late, I learned from Casmier the trick of "next time."

Célestin wasn't at church either, so we went to the buvette for a beer. After dark, a figure stepped into the doorway and called "Lynn!" I replied "*C'est qui?*" "Célestin!" We grabbed each other, jumping around in a circle. He was skinny as ever, but at least three inches taller than me, same beautiful toothy smile and bubbling laugh. I was afraid to ask, was he still in school? "*Oui!*" Unbelievable. Turned out, he was actually 23 years old, but had stuck to his story of being younger and was now in the eighth grade, paying his way doing masonry.

There at the buvette, the party was hatched. The three of us reminisced and planned until late, and they walked me home. Walking along a dirt road in the dark of night was always one of my favorite things in Allada. Roadside stands with women selling food, lit by kerosene cans. Crickets chirping. And the biggest sky ever, sprinkled with stars.

The next day after lunch, Papa placed a straw mat in the shade of the garden, and we met to discuss the party. On the agenda: drinks, pâte rouge, mouton and music. Followed by a list of invitees: Ahodis, Djihintos, Koucoïs, Zinsous, Casmier, Ambroise, Célestin and friends, Lynn.

We quickly ruled out the goat as too expensive ($30), and settled on chicken. I wanted pâte rouge, the gourmet version of the grits dish, mixed with tomatoes, garlic, onions and chili peppers. We budgeted for 72 bottles of sodas and beer, a serious miscalculation.

Papa and Maman asked me to teach their students an English song the next

177

morning, and we planned to start work immediately after. The students performed *"If You're Happy and You Know It, Clap Your Hands"* with gusto, though a first-time listener would have had a hard time deciphering the lyrics. We clapped, stomped our feet, shook our heads, and danced with reckless abandon. During the next two days, as we worked, strains of *"If you're happy"* floated from the classrooms.

Célestin arrived an hour late with a basin of ground corn on his head. We took it to the kitchen and headed to market. The road was busier than usual, with buyers and sellers en route. Suddenly, someone called out to us. Tucked in the shade of the shops was Casmier, pointing out his cache of hidden chickens. In low tones, as if explaining a spy operation, he explained that he had bought them one at a time from vendors going to market. If he had asked for 11 chickens at once, a seller would have raised the price. He was going to the Ahodis to drop the birds and rig up lights.

At the market, Célestin and I were joined by his friend Giroux. In the football-sized field, we wound through stalls and between vendors carrying bananas, oranges, dried fish, chilies, okra, charcoal, wooden sticks used as toothbrushes, plastic sacs of water, peanuts, purses, spices, dried plants for voodoo, tennis shoes, T-shirts. The loud negotiations in Fon had seemed at first like arguing, but I came to realize was a manner of speaking—animated, engaged, passionate. The sound of sucking teeth as people signaled "come here." Scorching sun and smell of dirt and sweat. Acquaintances greeting *"enfongonjiya!"* Young people clasping hands that slid into snaps. At the tomatoes, Célestin slipped into action: "Maman," he beseeched respectfully, "the price is too high." And the bargaining began.

The intensity exhausted me and I remembered that nothing was easy in Benin. Every activity took much longer than I expected. That year, I learned to whittle down my daily "to do" list to one action: buy groceries or go to bank or mail letters.

I handed Giroux three invitations, written in the formal French style dictated to me by Papa: *"Lynn HEINISCH a l'honneur de vous inviter à une soirée récreative et de retrouvailles."* As he headed to town to deliver, one of the guests rode up on his motorcycle, my colleague from the library, Paul Djihinto. As always, "Djipas" wore a jaunty tweed cap, a penchant he joked about, calling himself a Parisian.

After learning the computer, Djipas had gussied up the library with motivational signs ("Excellent!") and labels for the bookshelves. He aimed to instill order, as I tried to entertain the kids, teaching English, gymnastics, math quizzes, whatever I could think of to draw them to the library. Unfortunately, while my organization had managed to create the library and provide a computer, it had sent books donated by American publishers. The elementary students of Allada had a library full of college physics texts in English. I was glad to see that in the five subsequent years, the local school system had stocked the library with children's French books.

Djipas and I laughed about some of the mishaps of our year together, the countless moments in which I learned to live with ambiguity. Trying to reconcile respect for the culture in which I lived with earlier ideas formed in another society. The longer I stayed in Benin, the more I discovered how American my beliefs were;

178

the idea that everyone is entitled to opportunity; the belief that obstacles could be overcome. The idea that people willing to work hard should have a chance to succeed.

My idealism faced a lot of challenges. One was Emmanuel, the bright and hard-working student who loved to practice English, who told me his schooling would end after high school. There was no way for him to go to college, he said, he was poor. What about scholarships, I asked? What about a loan from the bank? He was surprised at my naiveté. We don't have those things, he said. I am not from a rich, well-connected family. I asked Célestin about Emmanuel. He had to drop out of school, he said. He had moved away.

Hervé and Prudent had formed a *"Groupe de Rap,"* which arrived at the Ahodis to discuss the party. The boys I remembered as a bit shy and earnest had grown into the *Groupe O.S.* (Original Sound), with an entourage, performing in French, English and Fon.

For a sound system, we approached Monsieur Zinsou, the director of the primary school. A jovial, round-faced man with a childlike laugh, Zinsou was also the minister at Célestin's church, the owner of one of the new internet centers, and a regular at Saturday morning workouts. Saturdays at 6:30 a.m., before the heat of the sun, everyone interested in exercise turned up at the high school field. One of my favorite times in the week was jogging around the dirt track, watching people kick soccer balls and do sprints, stretches, sit-ups and push-ups, those lucky enough to have shoes playing alongside those in bare feet. Zinsou was always there, joined sometimes by his wife and children.

My parents still talked about the Zinsous. Visiting me in Allada, they were amazed at the number of people who dropped by, day and night, to greet them. Guests arrived in their finest and bearing gifts. I had come to like the unscheduled visits. I had learned to abandon whatever I was doing and enjoy the spontaneous socializing. The Zinsous brought home-grown pineapples, papayas and mangoes. They arrived at the end of a long day, when my parents had collapsed in front of the fan, their capacity to chat depleted. And they were still there when Mom fell asleep.

Casmier and Célestin spent hours with the chickens: killing, plucking, chopping them into pieces and frying them. Giroux and I paid the beverage man to bring the cases to the house in his handcart. Gladys and Odile cooked the pâte rouge, billows of smoke blowing from a huge cauldron. Maman supervised the outdoor kitchen, while Papa directed chair arrangement in the school courtyard.

We iced the drinks in coolers, and my plan was for people to serve themselves. Five minutes into the party, Célestin's cousin Clement put a stop to that. At the rate drinks were disappearing, it would soon be over. Fiercely guarding the only bottle opener, he hand-delivered bottles and kept track of who had drunk what. Meanwhile, the guests took their places in the courtyard and Célestin and his friends dished out food.

"Do you remember me?" one boy said. "I'm Nicholas." Another spoke up, "I'm Armel." Same faces, in grown-up bodies. Mimicking the lessons I had taught, they greeted me: "How are you? Fine, thank you. How are you?" And, so the night went, the past blurring into the present. Honoring the protocol that always amused and sometimes irritated me, I took the microphone for a flowery speech. Midway, I choked up and had to stop. Papa saved me with remarks equally heartfelt, but more poised. The rappers then took the stage and we all danced together under that wonderful sky, celebrating our reunion. By 1 a.m., the drinks ran out, the guests said goodbye and the Groupe O.S. went off to party.

In a classroom, Célestin and his friends were stacking dishes. There was a knock and in walked Ambroise. I used to hear Célestin's older brother early mornings outside my house, working on beautiful wood carvings. I remembered a group of us discussing music when he announced he knew who had killed Tupac. I wasn't surprised he knew Tupac Shakur, whose face was on T-shirts all over West Africa. But I was shocked by the name of his killer. "Michael Jackson," Ambroise said, pronouncing it "Mikhail." Until the day I left Benin, I couldn't convince him otherwise. Now married, with a daughter, he drove a taxi in Cotonou. He had been to Mali, Niger and Burkina Faso.

Just when I thought it couldn't get any better, Célestin reached behind the blackboard. In a bucket, he had squirreled away enough drinks for the core party team. We toasted our great success.

I remembered going back to the United States after my year away, and the impossibility of answering the question "What was it like?" I didn't know how to explain, how to describe, how to do justice to the people of Allada. In a funny kind of way, it was like home.

Lynn Heinisch is a press officer with CARE, the international humanitarian agency. She has a master's degree in international relations from University of the Witwatersrand in Johannesburg, South Africa, and a bachelor's degree in English from Duke University. She has traveled to more than 50 countries, most of them in Africa.

Four Special People

Jerome Kilmer

I've taught at international schools abroad for more than a decade but the day after we hand out report cards I'm on a plane heading back to my parents' house in upstate New York. No matter where I live, part of me is still in my old bedroom looking out my window into the world and listening to the trucks rumble along Route 81 in the distance.

When I'm overseas I peer across the ocean into that window, filling the room with the knowledge I've gained from living and working abroad. I also submit articles to my local newspaper, knowing that Americans would benefit greatly by examining our culture from an international perspective.

Of the many disservices we do to ourselves and our reputation in the global community, one of the most unfortunate is allowing ourselves to be seen as abrasive and narrow-minded. More than a decade abroad, punctuated by encounters with four special people, has made me acutely aware of this problem.

The Deferential Doorman and Head-banging Cabbie

Teaching English in Japan is a common starting point for overseas educators. It's easy, fun, financially rewarding and any American with a bachelor's degree is eligible for employment at language schools throughout the country. So after completing my course work for my master's degree in English Education I spent nine months there, traveling by train, bus and on foot to companies and private homes in Greater Tokyo, working hard during the day, partying hard at night and becoming a Japanophile—a person enamored with Japanese culture.

Being a rookie expat, I arrived in Tokyo with just a few hundred dollars and a check from my brother for $500 in case I needed more cash. After a week I was running out of money so I entered Sumitomo Bank, foolishly thinking they would cash the check. When the teller refused, I cursed my situation, the bank, and even an old doorman, who just smiled, bowed and repeated some phrase I didn't understand as I stormed past him in a huff. I thought he was patronizing me, which made me even angrier.

Within the next few weeks I had secured employment at a language school and received $500 from home (my brother had to wire the money to me) so I was walking around in a much better mood. I had also learned essential Japanese: the two four-syllable words for "excuse me" and the ten-syllable phrase for "thank you," and to punctuate my speech with deferential bows. These polite words and gestures are used several times in all social interactions, and when Japanese are not familiar with a person, they are more polite.

After my first month of employment I entered the same bank and withdrew some of my salary. When I exited the same doorman gladly opened the door for me, smiled, bowed and said "excuse me" as he opened the door and "thank you" as I walked through, just the same as when I was so rude to him a few weeks earlier. He hadn't patronized me then, he had just responded to my gruffness the only way he knew how—with exceeding politeness. This time I understood him and I wanted to apologize but I couldn't communicate in Japanese well enough to do it.

On my last day in Japan I felt a huge surge of accomplishment. In addition to becoming a more chilled-out, peaceful person, I had paid off two loans and had enough money left over to buy a decent used car back in the States. I knew I'd miss Japan but shortly I would be back home in my own room, which was roughly the size of my entire Tokyo apartment. I was so elated that when I exited the cab which took me to the airport, I tipped the driver 1,000 yen (about $8 at the time). He gushed with surprise and appreciation. As I walked away, I figured I had paid my debt to the doorman. When I glanced back I noticed the cabbie looking at me, so I bowed. So he bowed—over and over! He looked as if he was smashing his head against the dashboard.

I've always cherished the lesson I learned from my first "Ugly American" episode about the power of politeness and the value of cultural gestures that show respect.

When I returned to my family in New York, I was glad to be home but reverse culture shock hit me hard; I became acutely aware of the caustic interactions in our daily lives and excessive violence in our media. Also, they seemed more interested in my views about geisha girls, sumo wrestling, and earthquakes, than any insights I had gained from the experience.

After only nine months in Japan, American society seemed foreign to me, so I opted for a teaching career overseas, which would allow me to experience many cultures while spending summers in the States.

The Guardian Angel

Fifteen years and three countries later, I'm married to an American teacher who grew up overseas. We live in Myanmar in Southeast Asia with our two young children, so when we travel we choose destinations close to home with nice hotels.

Two years ago we were graced by an extended encounter with a person who in the States would be an outcast or reside on the fringe of our society.

At Christmastime two years ago, when our daughter was three months old and our son an active two-year-old, we traveled to neighboring Laos, figuring that two weeks in the old royal capital, Luang Prabang, followed by a week in the capital Vientiane would be a warm, relaxing, low-maintenance way to spend our holiday.

Both cities attract many tourists. Beautiful, natural scenery; clean, inexpensive accommodations; internet cafes; great French bread and pizza and boat rides to interesting Buddhist temples, many built before the era of French colonialism in the late 19th century.

We figured we would hoist our kids onto our backs, glide through our daily excursions and pause when our toddler wanted to walk and wander or when our infant wanted milk. If we were lucky, it could even be restful. After just a few days, though, plan A changed to plan B. We soon realized that every culturally-stimulating outing ended in exhaustion. Lugging around and chasing after a curious toddler, coupled by Bev having to constantly breastfeed, had worn us out. We decided to trade turns, one taking Sam on daily outings while the other crashed in the hotel room. I, of course, got the better end of the deal; I couldn't breastfeed so I was either on my own or responsible for one child.

At night, feeling rested and rejuvenated, we went with the children to one of the many restaurants on the main boulevard. Our family received mixed reviews from the restaurant patrons; some were enchanted, while others, especially the younger backpackers, looked at us with please-don't-bring-them-in-here expressions on their faces.

On Christmas day, Bev slept in with the baby while I spent the morning taking Sam on a child-directed walk around the neighborhood. Some local residents greeted us with a friendly nod, others moved in to pinch my son's cheek, and others encouraged their toddlers to play with him. Hung-over backpackers wandered out of guest houses in search of a good breakfast while dogs, cats, chickens and roosters roamed freely, a common sight in any neighborhood in a developing country. The clanking of pots and pans and aroma of cooking oil also filled the air, creating a scene with so much sensory stimulation that I was reminded of my wife's comment, "It's like India without the abject poverty."

We then returned to the hotel and perused the many parked motor bikes. For a thrill I placed Sam for a moment on a Harley probably owned by an expat cruising across the country, Easy Rider style. We then walked to the pond in back, where Sam dropped little pieces of bread into the water for the little fish and carp. It was a fun, memorable Christmas morning, and when we returned to the hotel room I handed him off to my wife, who took the kids to brunch while I napped and joined them later.

When I arrived at the restaurant Bev looked at me with a weary glow. I asked what had happened. She replied that she had waited so long to be served that she was just about to leave. Then a transvestite waitress (we'll refer to her in the feminine for respect and clarity) whisked in from the street, graced our infant with a soft pinch on the cheek and kiss on the forehead, saying, "Merry Christmas, Baby." She then secured a table for them and took their order, paying full attention to my wife's keen need to be attended to. My wife finished her story with, "It was the nicest Christmas present I ever had."

Considered by South Asians to be good luck, transvestites are hired as singers and dancers to perform at a home when a new baby has arrived, or at celebrations like births and weddings. They also work in service or retail industries; we'd seen them selling clothes and perfume in shopping centers in Bangkok. But this was first time we had ever talked to a she-man.

Looking around (with my wife whispering, "Don't stare, be discreet!") I saw our special waiter in the back of the restaurant, and watched her as she waited on several tables around us.

She had obviously gone to meticulous pains to create a feminine look. Her figure was Q-tip thin, I guessed she weighed about 100 lbs; her pulled-back dark brown hair, dark eye liner and heavy blush tried to hide her square masculine jaw line; and her long, tight dress, high heels, and painted red toe nails completed the ensemble. Every time she walked past, her strong perfume wafted across our table. She looked stylish but not comfortable, in sharp contrast to my loose travel pants and sweatshirt.

About halfway through our meal little Lizzy started to shift and whine, and when we looked at her diaper it was clear she would squirm and scream if we didn't change her immediately. We saw a door with "restroom" spelled correctly, so Bev grabbed the baby and entered it, but returned immediately and said distraughtly, "There's not enough room in there."

No matter what country you're in, people in restaurants don't like messy diapers changed in their presence while they're eating. We exchanged an "Oh no!" look; realizing that we might have to cut the meal short and race back to the hotel room. Then our she-man appeared again and guided my wife to the corner of the restaurant behind the sales counter, remaining in the vicinity, smiling at the baby until she was wearing a fresh diaper and hugging her mother. Nobody in the restaurant took notice.

We finished our meal, left a generous tip and walked up to her and said, "Merry Christmas" while Sam waved. She responded, "Merry Christmas," then looked lovingly at our little Lizzy and said, "Bye Baby."

We talked about the incident a few times, noting that our she-man seemed to revel in coming to our rescue. Then we tucked our experience away in our wonder-ful-memories-from-abroad memory banks. Five days later we took a one-hour flight to the capital Vientiane, where we continued our routine of trading daytime duty and eating out at night.

We found a spacious restaurant with great French and Asian cuisine, an aquarium and big bathrooms, so we ended each day with a meal there. On our final night, we were preparing to leave, when I noticed Bev looking over my shoulder. She said that a person eating at the other side of the restaurant looked like "that nice she-man" from a week ago.

Expats experience coincidences like working with the same people on two different continents at different times, or running into someone they know at an airport, on a train, or in an obscure market place, but this would be extraordinary. She was facing us, but we were too far away to confirm her identity. She seemed to be glancing back at us and our kids, almost hoping that we notice her.

Approaching her table would have been inappropriate. She was sitting with a man, probably a "companion" who had hired her as an escort for a week. So I stared, squinted, and looked back at Bev, who said, "We have to know for sure." So we picked up the kids and moved behind the aquarium which was closer to their table, and peered out from the side of it. She gazed at us with a warm, glowing smile that

184

said, "Yes, it's me and I'm glad to see you." We smiled back and nodded, and when we returned to the hotel we agreed that it was the perfect end to our trip.

This story did not teach me the virtues of cross-gendering or cross-dressing. I may have some sort of seizure if my son decided he felt more comfortable in women's clothes. But after this episode with our guardian angel, I've lost my fear of those whom seem so drastically different than I. But when I'm home in the summer, I see the paradox between what we think of ourselves and how we behave.

We've been told since we were young that our country is "the melting pot" and that freedom of expression is a deeply rooted American value. But if tomorrow a transvestite, or someone from an ethnicity different from anyone else on the street, knocked on our door and introduced themselves as our new neighbor, most of us would bristle.

We are also told that "others" want to hurt us because of our freedoms, but anyone who turns on CNN or reads US newspapers sees US politicians and religious leaders taking a confrontational stance against alternative lifestyles. I wonder how many of them have ever talked to a transvestite.

The Appreciative Grandmother
One of the greatest perks of living in a developing country is being able to afford domestic help. Our beloved Htoola walked up our driveway on our first day in Myanmar seven years ago and has been our cook, housekeeper, and we now consider her third grandmother to our children. For more than 20 years she worked for expatriates from Singapore, Korea, and France, but according to her, the day we hired her she landed the best job of her life, working for Americans.

The other day, I asked her why. Here are some excerpts from her response:

"We love Americans because there is a truth like what they say... Americans give the people a good chance to give a good salary and buy for the house ...and they keep the time right."

To those who work in their homes, Americans are known for offering the most reasonable working hours and highest salaries, and in many cases even providing interest-free loans and paying for medical care. But most importantly we treat them as part of our family, and demand that our children do the same. In the wider expatriate community Americans are known to be honest, hardworking and generous.

So our hearts are strong and our character intact. But if we are to take an authentic leadership role in the 21st century, we need to smooth out our rough exterior and let those who live outside our country look into our windows. Then we need to listen to what they say.

Jerome Kilmer, freelance writer and veteran expatriate, teaches high school English at International School Yangon, Myanmar, and writes articles about living overseas for his hometown newspaper in Upstate New York.

Letters Home from Salone

Tracey Buckenmeyer

July 15th

Seke YO! Tope ander-a!
Kushay, ow di bohdi?
That's Temne and Krio for "Hey, there, how are you?"

I'm alive and living in Africa; West Africa to be specific and to be more specific, Sierra Leone (we call it Salone), a tiny oasis of obscurity on the coast of this Dark Continent. After two months of training I was sworn in as a full-fledged Peace Corps Volunteer on the 28th of June, a date that will live in infirmary (no, that's not a typo... read on!). I solemnly swore to uphold and to represent the US Constitution, apple pie and the American Way of Life-and all for about 875 leones (roughly $50) a month.

So now what? My assignment is in community health and I'll be living in a little village teaching best practices to unsuspecting innocent villagers. I know what you're all thinking. What does a just-graduated journalism major know about any of that stuff? But it's basic things like showing them the proper use and maintenance of wells and latrines (after convincing them they need both) and simple nutrition like putting groundnuts with their rice (protein!) and why it's good to use dish racks and clotheslines (to prevent the invasion of a certain critter known as the tumba fly, but more about that later).

Forty five of us flew over from Philadelphia where we had gathered for a quick orientation of which the theme was, in no uncertain terms, are you sure you want to be a Peace Corps Volunteer? After that question was put to us in a dozen different forms by a dozen different people, we were stamped with the PC seal of approval. The next thing I knew I was in a Boeing 747 singing "Puff the Magic Dragon," rose colored glasses firmly in place, headed across the Atlantic.

This same group (of which half would quit before the end of the two year assignment) underwent eight weeks of training in a village called Songo, about 20 very rough miles outside the capital city of Freetown, a period of time that seems so unreal now that I've been in the "bush." We were fed three times a day, had electricity (which meant lights and fans in this suffocating heat), plenty of activities to keep us busy and, well, each other. After those two months of living among 50 or so English speaking Americans I was unceremoniously dumped among 200 Temne speaking Sierra Leoneans about two weeks ago. Since my knowledge of that language consists mostly of the aforementioned greetings, there was a lot of nodding, hand shaking, smiling and *yo-seke-ing*. In fact, I'm pretty seked out.

I'm assigned to Mapaki; two miles off the main road, 25 miles from the nearest district Peace Corps headquarters in Makeni and 100 years back in time. I have my very own house, mud walled and thatch roofed, and my very own latrine. The thatch is supposed to be cooler than zinc pan and it's rather quaint and rustic looking but it holds water like a sieve. I awoke my first night here to rain dripping on my face, my bed, everything. Welcome to the toughest job I'll ever love.

Things are pretty rustic, actually catastrophic since, as you well know, I can't even cook on an electric range; here cooking means perching an iron pot on top of three stones and firewood. The food is rice and leaves, yes, you heard me, leaves; usually cassava that's sliced and pounded into a green goo and slopped onto rice. Remember how I complained about doing laundry? Show me the machine any day; here we wash (or *brook* as they say in Krio) clothes in the swamp by beating them on rocks. Indoor plumbing? HA! I haul water from a well a quarter mile away in a three gallon bucket I carry on my head, yes, on my head, and I use a cockroach-infested hole in the ground. I'm writing this by the light of a kerosene lamp and since kerosene is in short supply I will have to end this soon. "*Na foh bia,*" as they say here, which means "have courage" or "hang in there." I've a feeling I will be hearing that a lot…

My address is enclosed, use it! It takes about two months to get a letter here so send your Christmas greetings now. The mail system here makes the Pony Express look like fiber optic telecommunications. My kerosene is gone along with my energy … *nain dat!* (Krio for good bye).

November 28th

Hi all!

I've been here quite a few months now and I have to admit I'm fed up with being a host, especially to uninvited guests. You know the type-the ones who barge in unannounced and unwelcome and leave only when they are forcibly ejected; during their stay you are quite miserable while they enjoy themselves immensely, even thrive, at your expense.

I can only take so much, you know. After all, I'm only human (which is much of the problem as you'll see). I can put up with as much as anyone but there's a limit and when that limit is reached there is only one solution. To kill them. You may think that's a rather drastic measure to take to rid myself of such nuisances, but I've found it's the only way. Ignoring them doesn't work-they only become more insistent with their demands. Yes, to preserve my own health and sanity the only answer is death.

So I'm a murderer; yes, I know this must shock you. I've waged chemical warfare on these uninvited visitors, those unwelcome guests. I'm referring to those parasitic infestations that so delight in invading my inner anatomy. In the few months I've been in Salone, I've managed to acquire a tumba fly, giardia, malaria, amoebic dysentery, ascaris and uncinaria. My lower intestinal tract is becoming a 24-hour roadside motel with the comings and goings of all these critters.

The tumba fly had burrowed itself into my abdomen for two days before I noticed its existence. Being slightly past puberty, I didn't think I would be getting a zit on my belly (which is exactly what it looks like). The tumba is a nasty little creature that likes to lay its eggs inside human flesh. They get into your skin several ways,

187

usually from clothing. Sierra Leoneans lay freshly washed laundry on the ground to dry and the flies, which hover close to the ground, lay eggs in the clothes and when you put them on, the eggs get transferred to you.

Depending upon what article of clothing they decide to settle into determines which part of your body gets this 'guest'. (After my experience, I never again dried my bras or underwear outside!) And that's why, as I explained before, I'm trying to teach the people in my village to dry their clothes on racks up and away from the ground. But somehow the message didn't get through and I found myself with a reddish bump on my stomach. It was surgically removed with professional precision; you smear the spot with palm oil which suffocates the larvae, making it sticks its head out; then you squeeze until the entire worm pops out. Come to think of it, its removal does resemble that of a zit. That was only the beginning of my tropical maladies.

Before long, the unseen visitors arrived, those minuscule pests that infiltrate the human body in ways beknownst only to them; you become aware of their existence only after they have firmly imbedded themselves in your gut and the corresponding effects of such a residence have begun (which usually means a mad dash to the latrine).

As the tell tale burps of lingering sulphur appeared, I knew I had contracted a most unpleasant disease called giardia, which is some sort of parasite that lodges itself in your intestine and makes you most uncomfortable and unpopular as you can't control the tell-tale gas. I managed to carry this particular "guest" around for quite a while, for I didn't want to ingest the dreaded drug flagyl without being absolutely certain of what I had within me. The unassuming little amoeba or whatever it was that slumbered within my duodenum (or is it colon?) would rear its microscopic head at the most inopportune moments, if indeed, there ever is an opportune moment for such things, with unpredictable frequency and would send me flying or crawling to the nearest toilet, latrine or bush.

Yes, and those lovely, hot, hot, *pehpehs* (hot peppers) I consume in mass quantities at every meal reminded me of their rather potent existence every time the giardia germ struck. The searing sensation of fiery feces spurting out my backside is an experience of indescribable discomfort to say the least. Perhaps that's why instead of toilet paper everyone here uses water-cool, cool water.

One would think that after having such vile creatures as tumba slugs and amoebas I'd be running back to the States where such things are smeared on little glass slides and viewed under microscopes where they belong. Not a chance. As I said before, the Peace Corps is supposed to be the toughest job you'll ever love, and I'll love it till it kills me.

But that was before I got malaria (blood parasites) that had me writhing with a fever I wouldn't wish on my worse enemy; dysentery (more amoebas); ascaris and uncinaria (roundworm and hookworm). I didn't have all these at once, mind you, but one right after the other. As soon as I evicted one "resident," the next would move, or rather, slither right in. Don't ask me why I'm so popular; I treat my water, wash my hands, take chloroquine, wear shoes and get my shots on time. I can't figure it out but I've disappeared into the clinic toilet with a little paper cup more times than I'd like to remember. But now, at the moment, I'm free of all unwanted bacteria, all single and multi celled unwanted life. At least I think so. But one can never be sure, there's still typhoid, hepatitis, cholera and schisto; after all, there's a vacancy. *Na foh bia!*

June 5th

Dear Everyone,

I am now well into my second year "na Salone," and I am still asking myself why I left the comforts of the United States for the primitive (so called) life in a Third World country. What do I hope to gain? What am I looking for? What am I running from? Am I crazy?

John Lennon is crooning to me from a tape cassette I recorded a long time ago and have played a thousand times in a Sony tape deck rigged up to the battery of my motorcycle (the only power source I have since regular batteries are expensive, even if you can find them). See, it's not so primitive after all, the 20th century lives on even in stone age Sierra Leone, though that's not a fair description of the life I'm living. I've given up relatively few material comforts and have gained an invaluable perspective on life in the world in general, my own in specific.

Yes, I live in a mud hut with a thatch roof (that leaks terribly) with no electricity, no indoor plumbing and no wall to wall carpeting (in fact, no floor in some spots). But then again, there's no rent, no utilities to pay and no toilet bowl to clean. I live in a bush village off the main road reached by only a handful of dusty lorries and dustier people walking to other tiny bush villages further on. I live among a tribe of Africans called Temnes who speak their own tongue and not mine, nor I theirs. But with what I do know and what they know communication does manage to take place. That's what is so different from where I used to live and where I live now; a few superficial items easily overcome and adapted to. Some things, however, defy any assimilation or adaptation.

The aloneness. I am surrounded by new friends and "family," albeit ones with unintelligible chatter. But still alone. I feel eons away from these people who don't know that the space shuttle blew up; who can't imagine having too much food to eat; and eons away from you all back home, where you don't know that children who speak several languages will never learn to write or read a single one; who don't know women still carry out the same chores their ancestors did a hundred years ago.

Caught between two worlds, two universes of experiences unexplainable, untouchable to outsiders from either. I'm alone in the limbo of trying to jump the gap, to hopscotch from one universe to the other and at times it feels I've thrown the stone too far and I won't be able to stoop and pick it up again. Alone, because I can't communicate to anyone the things surging through my mind, a hurricane of impressions, thoughts, abstractions, not because of language barriers but because I can't put things into words in my own head. The feeling is there but the words are not.

A child died the other day and the mother mourns and aimlessly wanders to and from the gravesite. No one is terribly surprised and life, such as it is, goes on. It always does, doesn't it? A baby had died and a woman grieves but soon a child, yet another child, will replace the dead one. The dead are perpetually replaced through the pain of childbirth and the cycle continues.

So it seems there are a few major differences between the home I left and the place I've come to call home, the dull acceptance of death being one of them. Those are the things most difficult to adjust to; not squatting in latrines, hauling water and waging war on cockroaches or any other things you think of when considering life in a poor, underdeveloped country.

Africa. How can one talk about an entire continent when one is lodged in a fly¬specked-sized portion of it? One can't so I won't. I live in Sierra Leone and I can't even generalize about that, since another volunteer living 25 miles away can, and most likely will, have experiences totally different from mine. But I think we will all experience the essence of Salone the same, even though our reactions, of course, won't be the same.

Another difference from home is the people's acceptance of me, or perhaps, just my perception of that acceptance. At first, I felt welcome as a novelty, something to be stared at, cautiously approached and more cautiously touched. The "fishbowl effect" the recruiters warned us about, with me as the gullible guppy. Then I felt welcomed for what I could do for them-and the list is endless. From money lender to medicine dispenser to local transport to ticket to America, I am seen as the answer to what ails them. All of them! Obviously, this arouses not just a small amount of suspicion on my part; why do you want to be my friend, what do you want from me? The Sierra Leonean can be unapologetically opportunistic when necessary.

The difficulty for me as an American is the feeling of relative poverty. I mean, coming out of the United States with its fill'em up gas stations, supermarkets and super highways, seemingly unlimited everything and then going to a place where you have to bargain furtively with black marketeers for petrol; where milk, batteries and ink pens are hard to find; where even ice water is a luxury, one feels vital essential items have been taken away. Thus, while you are battling this feeling of deprivation, you are simultaneously besieged by a people of enormous, insatiable want and need. Once again you are caught in the middle, between the unconscious struggle to get your present level of living back to the level you were accustomed to while being begged for the few, as you see it, comforts you have left.

That's when the second battle begins, the battle against guilt. While you are collecting things to make your home more comfortable or send back home, buying imported food because one more grain of rice will gag you, buying petrol at 320 leones a gallon (when most Sierra Leoneans make 12 leones a day) just to visit friends, the guilt creeps in no matter how hard you try to ignore it. Guilt that you can do all these things, your life here can reach a "First World" standard while your neighbors languish in their lot, that of the so-called "Third World." You begin to feel incredible guilt at being healthy and rich and American, guilty with the knowledge that you can "go back," that is, leave this world of want and suffering and re enter the world of plenty while they cannot. Ever.

This deluge of emotion can harden you, make you turn a deaf ear to their obsequious pleas and demands, force you to remain aloof and untouchable so their suffering won't infect you, taint your existence among them. You hide in your house listening to something by John Lennon, remembering the luxuries of home while you escape into a good book.

Or the guilt can soften you, melt you into giving in and giving away all that you have and are. Their cries and outreached hands are filled with things from your life in an attempt to appease their incredible want and your insistent conscious. Too late you discover their want has no end and your things do. Too soon you are again listening to something by John Lennon and reading books, locking your door and trying to lock your heart against that want, that need.

Because you cared too much. Cared too much about the skinny kid next door who may die during the night, cared too much about the woman heavily pregnant with her eighth child and heading for a long day's work in the swamp, cared too much about the people filling your life. Because along with that caring comes an overwhelming feeling of futility, impotence, and not a small amount of rage that you can do nothing to change anything, nothing to stop the waste. Babies still die from measles, children still can't go to school; women are condemned to back-breaking work to put a few grains of rice in their children's mouths.

Aloneness. Guilt. Caring. That's the Africa I know. Oh, yes, I forgot something. Laughter. The capacity for laughter among these people is as great as their capacity to grieve. The children laugh with glee as they sing to the full moon that chases away the dark of the "bush" that terrifies them so. The women laugh and sing as they pound rice with their *mata odas* (mortar-and-pestle type tool to clean rice), with effortless rhythm, the pain in their backs and arms forgotten in song. Old men sharing a *booie* (jug) of palm wine, laughing over stories I'll never understand. Eleanor Smith Bowen, author of *"Return to Laughter,"* (Anchor Books, New York, 1964) said it so well. "In an en vironment in which tragedy is genuine and frequent, laughter is essential to sanity. Such laughter is neither callous nor humorous." It just is.

So, I'm learning to laugh. When the lorry has its fifth flat tire, taking five hours to go 100 miles, I can laugh. When I walk six miles to a village for a town meeting that they've all forgotten about, I can laugh. When I find cockroaches the size of pit bulls in my house, I can laugh (well, maybe not). Maybe things won't change. Maybe they are changing and I'm too involved to notice. Either way, life is here now, in all its glory, pain and joy. John Lennon is singing something about imagine...

Tracey Buckenmeyer was a Peace Corps volunteer in "Health and Community Development" from 1986 to 1988. The Peace Corps program in Sierra Leone, West Africa, remained one of the largest, with about 200 volunteers in the country at its peak, and ended only with the civil war that engulfed the region in the early 1990s.

Roots, Wings and Freedom

Katrina Sue Lehman

Roots

I grew up with my roots firmly planted in the rich farmland of rural Pennsylvania. I was raised as a small-town girl, where none of my relatives left for foreign lands except for missionary work. The daughter of a minister in a small, agricultural community of southern Pennsylvania, not far from Gettysburg, I was expected to stay home, get married, and raise a family. All my cousins did. All my aunts and uncles did. To this day, I'm not sure why I'm different from my 28 cousins or why I'm flying thousands of miles by jet plane to attend family reunions rather than driving over the hill in my Chevy.

In many ways, my childhood days were idyllic. The summers were hot and humid with droning bees on the honey suckle and Land O' Lakes butter dripping off the ends of home-grown Silver Queen corn. In the autumn the weather was crisp as we walked through the orange leaves downtown by the hardware store and by Cressler's grocery store. We canned our sour cherries for winter pies and our beets from the garden. We celebrated winter snow days, sang Christmas carols to the elderly at the rest home, made snow angels, and rode toboggans down Uncle's Bob's hill. Spring brought cherry blossoms on the trees in the front yard, brand new Easter dresses made by Mom on the Singer, egg hunts in the spring-muddy lawn, and crocuses peeping up through a late snow, harbingers of the green grass to come. Then summer again, with Sunday church picnics and river baptisms. Then fall. Then winter. Then spring. Then summer. Aunts got married. Cousins were born. Old folks died, and we attended their funerals: the cycle of seasons, the cycle of life.

I wasn't supposed to move away from my home town, and certainly not from the Keystone State. But I inherited the genes of my grandfather Lehman, a veracious reader. At many family reunions, I could be found in a corner, reading a book. Often, I would look up from my reading to see my grandpa with his reading glasses on the tip of his nose, his hearing aide turned off, reading *Prevention* or the Bible or Dickens in his rocking chair. Sometimes, we'd catch each other's glances and smile. My favorite pastime wasn't holding babies, but climbing the ladders to retrieve books at the local library. While other children were out playing softball or jumping rope, I would spend whole Saturdays in my room reading E.B. White's *The Once and Future King*. At night I would dream of King Arthur on his horse galloping through those Pennsylvania corn fields, his horse snorting in the summer air. I read books with settings in Spain and South America, and I'd voice those Spanish words until they rolled off my tongue like honey. I'd read books by Sir Edmond Hillary, and I fell asleep dreaming of Mt. Everest in a place somewhere near Katmandu. I dreamt of snow-capped mountains, blue-green oceans and scorching deserts.

I also inherited the traveling genes of my maternal grandfather, who, as a young lad, worked in the orange groves of Florida and took long road trips on his Harley Davidson. Because of his stories of being on the road, and by modeling the reading habits of my paternal grandfather, I donned my metaphorical traveling shoes long before I got my first car or took my first airplane ride to Georgia at the age of eighteen. And then I was hooked. Hooked by the clouds high above the earth. Hooked by the land below and how peaceful it looked from above. Hooked by dreams of living somewhere else, somewhere different. Hooked by the possibility of reinventing my life in another land.

Wings: "Way Leads on to Way"

My wings took me to Spain, where I lived and studied during my college years. I saw bullfights, ate my first paella, and drank my first sangria made from Seville oranges. Then, my wanderlust led me to a school in Honduras, where I taught English at a missionary school, snorkeled in the blue-green waters of the Caribbean, saw my first stingray, and hitchhiked to Lake Yajoa. Then I moved to teach in La Paz, Bolivia, the highest capital city in the world, where I lived two miles above sea level, climbed Andean glaciers and drove across the Atacama Desert to Chile. I kayaked in Lake Titicaca, camping on its shores near the Island of the Sun and the Island of the Moon. Now, I live in Myanmar (formerly known as Burma), home of the world's largest reclining Buddha and the Land of Golden Pagodas. The view from my apartment is of a temple covered with 54 tons of gold leaf.

T.S. Elliot once wrote, "…the end of all our exploring will be to arrive where we started and know that place for the first time." If traveling is this life-changing, choosing to live long-term as an expat has an even greater effect on one's life: the host country slowly, over time, becomes home. I remember flying into the airport in Tegucigalpa, glad to be back to the mountains of Central America. I remember walking across the bridge from Argentina into Bolivia, thinking "Ah, I'm finally home." Nowadays, I drive home from the airport in Yangon, Myanmar, and see the Shwedagon Pagoda winking in the evening sun. This, too, is home.

For going on nine years, I have made my home on four different continents. When we American expats gather in our host countries for Thanksgiving dinners or Fourth of July celebrations, the subject of home often comes up in conversations. Some of us come from small towns where few of our family members travel (yet alone move) to foreign lands. "What makes us choose to live overseas?" we ask. Some of us credit books we've read or latent traveling genes coming to life. Others say that seemingly insignificant events lead to the greatest life changes. More often than not, most agree that what was intended to be a year or two stint overseas ends up being a life-long career. As Frost so wisely puts it, "way leads on to way." My colleagues and I have lived in places like Tel Aviv, Beirut, Myanmar, Sumatra and Nairobi. We've experienced or witnessed bombings, states of siege, blackouts, kidnappings, tsunamis, and evacuations out of country. Yet, by choice, we continue to make our homes in distant lands, far from the country where we hold our citizenship.

193

Few of us could make it without our beloved house staff that cook our food, iron our clothes, and teach us the local customs and language of our host countries. In Honduras, Consuela (*Abuelita,* as I called her) made me the best flour tortillas in a cast iron pan. In Bolivia, Jacinta (an Aymara single mom) took care of me when I was ill by preparing local remedies like chamomile steam and menthol salve on the chest. Here in Myanmar, my 68-year-old driver U Thambe is my personal assistant: he has taught me local phrases and cultural practices, helped me to move apartments, driven me to the doctor when I'm sick, assembled my bike and offered me treats during Indian Diwali. Every other morning, he hangs strings of jasmine flowers on my outside door so that I have *paya* (holy flowers) to hang in my house. Known as "papa" by the other drivers of expats, U Thambe is a walking encyclopedia with a keen memory for dates, street names and the way Yangon (formerly Rangoon) used to be. He can find any shop, shrine, road or pagoda in town. Dependable, conscientious, kind, and diligent, U Thambe, like Consuela and Jacinta, is an indispensable part of my expat life.

For those of us who have chosen to live overseas, the holidays can be bittersweet. Family and long-time friends are far away, and the closest thing we can get to a turkey with all the trimmings is a broiled peacock over rice. Many of us live in Muslim or Buddhist countries, so it is quite strange to have November and December come and go without a carol, a Christmas tree or a gathering of the kin. As much as I bemoan the materialistic nature of the Christmas holidays in the United States, I miss the arrival of the Christmas season.

I remember one of my first holidays spent living abroad in Bolivia. After making a long-distance call to my grandmother for turkey basting suggestions, I stuffed and baked my first turkey. It was a delicious rite of passage. Although I missed not having my father around to carve the bird as I sat down to eat, I had to marvel at hearing four languages spoken at the table. All of us were far way from our immediate family, and as we sampled the potluck dishes from Italy, Germany, United States, Bolivia, and England, I was grateful for the connection I felt with my new, international family.

In each country I have lived, I have shared holiday traditions with my various, adopted overseas families. Here in Asia, for example, a German friend, an Australian friend and I decided to combine our traditions for the first day of advent. Compensating for the lack of pine, I used laurel leaves to make a large wreath. Then, after adding tiny red bows, a bell, and candles made in-country by a local women's cooperative, we carried the wreath outside and lit the first candle. In a red and green ceramic pitcher, my friends brought hot spiced wine (a German traditional holiday drink not unlike hot sangria) and homemade almond advent cookies, straight from the oven. Under the palm trees with a golden Buddhist temple in the distance, with the *Mariah Carey Christmas Album* playing on the laptop, and donning our Santa hats and scarves, we sipped the red hot wine and invited the neighbors and friends to share in our informal, yet meaningful, Christmas tradition.

It's a surreal world, the life of an expat. Though there are so many parts of our homeland we long for, including slices of pumpkin pie and the gathering of our family and friends around the table, we make do with what we have.

What we have, at home and abroad, is rich, indeed.

Freedom: A Paradox

Even after living in Myanmar for nearly two years, I still feel, at times, as if I were a tourist: that the external world around me is some sort of safari. From my truck on my way to school, I see the slow moving thronged feet of the Burmese people and the coconut palms and bamboo swaying in the breeze. Through my window, I watch the tricycle sidecars peddled by thin-armed men, trucks and buses brimming over with workers hanging on for dear life and the saffron-robed monks in their reserved seats behind the bus drivers. In front of me, as I wait at a traffic light, a truck full of children stares back at me. Some days, the cacophony of bird cries from a pick-up full of live chickens hanging by their feet wakes me out of a daze. From anywhere in the city, I can see a view of the pagoda thrusting into the clouds of the monsoon rains, or glinting in the sun, or glowing against the pitch-black sky. Everywhere, there are umbrellas, umbrellas, umbrellas, curious stares, smiles, the stench of durian fruit and open sewers, the sight of elephants carved from teak, markets, potholes, tea shops and clusters of yellow and green bananas at the fruit stands. Because my standard of living is high compared to most of the Burmese people, I often feel estranged from the daily life of Yangon. On the other hand, I realize that my life is just as strange to the Burmese with whom I work. Both foreigners and the local people are curious about the habits of the other.

Since the sight of one Westerner is sometimes enough to stop traffic, one can imagine what the sight is to the local folk of thirty or so expats as our walking/ running club makes its way through the huts and lanes in the outskirts of the city. We are a traveling carnival of sorts, a moving menagerie of critters, a caravan of freaks out for an afternoon stroll in our white Nikes. We cross wooden bridges, traverse dirt paths and pass lakes and villages and soccer matches being played in dirt fields. We see rice paddies and sleeping dogs and walk through bamboo factories and fish markets. Wherever we go, everyone stops their cooking, their washing, their eating, their games, and their bike riding—to stare. The best part of this whole experience is being greeted and followed by smiling children whose eyes are full of joy and curiosity. If they owned cameras, they would certainly take photos of us.

On these weekly walks, I should be thinking about freedom—freedom from the bubble of my daily life, the photocopying, emailing, conferences, lecture notes, faculty meetings, teaching of SAT prep classes and literature and computers, all that comprises my expat life in the air-conditioned biosphere of apartment-car-work-car-apartment. I am free, at least for the afternoon, from my bubble.

But most of the time, I'm not thinking about freedom. I'm thinking of cages. I'm thinking of zoos. I'm thinking of all the fish in my aquarium and how they must long to swim free without running into a glass wall. I'm thinking of the three goats that I pass that are tied to the tree, their necks rubbed bare by the rope. I'm thinking

195

about the empty, wooden Chinese cage at the tea shop with its little door open and tiny yellow feathers rested on its floor. Where are the canaries? Are they flying up there with the ten red, square kites that bob and dance so high above us? I'm thinking about how the borders of a country are sometimes a cage and of the giant, heavy hands of its zookeeper. I am thinking about how those of us who live free so often create our own prisons in our minds. I am thinking about how those who are jailed or under house arrest, like Aung Sung Suu Kyi in this country, can choose to have the freest minds of all.

Katrina Sue Lehman is an English and technology teacher, a poet, a writer and world traveler who has lived and worked in Central and South America, Asia, and Europe. She has lived in tents, geodesic domes, cabins, underground homes, and straw bale houses. Her favorite place in the world is Taos, New Mexico. She presently lives in Myanmar, formerly known as Burma.

A New Perspective

Upon my first visit to the Swedish Embassy, I noticed that it had one additional feature not present at the super-secure Fortress USA across town, and that was the presence of a snoozing cat lying just in front of the door.

David Wade

Flowers and candles had been placed as close as possible to the barricades and overflowed onto the neighboring sidewalks. We approached and laid our flowers down. Overcome by emotion, Brigitte and I stood there silently, watching the crowd.

Laura A. Mancini Chan

The first thing Americans ask, even before leaving the Zurich airport is, "Why are these people so thin?" Thus, I find myself trying to explain why Europeans are thin without making it sound as though Americans are overweight.

Bonnie Burns

I join a survival class. It is not called that by the Navy, which instead entitles it something like "Gateway to Living," but it is a survival course nonetheless.

Deborah Fulton Anderson

Webster's dictionary defines expatriate as "someone sent into exile, someone who has left his country." I never liked this word much ... perhaps it was the "ex" that triggered a sense of missing something truly fundamental to my person ... my home, my family, my friends, my language ... and my country.

Joy Toulemonde

Superpower and the Snooze-a-Cat Gap

David Wade

During 1998-2000, when oil was a mere $18-$22 a barrel, I worked as an assistant professor of biochemistry at the Faculty of Medicine of Kuwait University, in lovely Kuwait. At that time the former dictator of Iraq, Saddam Hussein, was still in power and was a constant worry to everyone in Kuwait. Whenever I had the occasion to visit the US Embassy in Kuwait, I was in awe of the elaborate security precautions in place. The Embassy is a massive complex of buildings located on the edge of a residential area and almost completely surrounded by open, undeveloped, flat land where any intruder could easily be spotted within a quarter-mile of the facility. Early during my stay there, a battery of Patriot missiles was installed in an empty field behind the Embassy.

A visitor's first encounter with Embassy security is on the main road that pases several hundred yards from the buildings complex. This outer perimeter security consists of a guard and a metal device designed to stop vehicular traffic from entering a side road that leads toward the Embassy. After the visitor satisfies the guard that he/she has a legitimate need to visit the Embassy, the vehicle is allowed to proceed to a parking lot located outside the Embassy's buildings complex. As one gets near the Embassy complex, there are concrete barriers on the road that are strategically located so as to make any approaching vehicle slow down enough to negotiate its way around the barriers. Upon reaching the parking lot, non-Embassy personnel must get out of their vehicles and walk to the Embassy complex.

As one approaches the complex on foot, one encounters security zone number two, which consists of a guard tower on stilts. All vehicles intending to actually enter the Embassy complex must stop at this guardhouse and undergo a vehicle inspection. Early during my stay in Kuwait, this checkpoint was also manned by a Kuwaiti military vehicle topped with machine gun and soldier. Pedestrians, and automobiles that pass inspection at security checkpoint two, are then allowed to proceed to security checkpoint three, which is located at the complex of buildings comprising the Embassy proper. The building complex is surrounded by a high wall, topped with barbed wire, probably electrified, which contains a built-in guardhouse and a gate for passage of vehicles. Mechanical devices are installed in the road that passes through the gate in order to prevent the entry of unwanted vehicles. Pedestrians must identify themselves at the guardhouse, where they undergo a personal and baggage inspection, complete with metal detectors.

Visitors who pass this inspection are then permitted to enter the grounds of the Embassy, but are only allowed to proceed to the particular buildings which are related to the purpose of their visit. In my case, this always meant that I proceeded to the consular building, and entry into this building involved a fourth security check, with metal detectors and baggage checks. If one succeeded in passing all four security checkpoints, then one had gained entry to the interior of the Embassy complex.

At that time the university did not have the resources to provide equipment and supplies for research by temporary professors, presumably due to the fact that the price of oil at that time was only around one-third of its 2005 level. Thus I had to spend my summer vacations wherever I could find space in a laboratory to do research. Colleagues in Sweden and Finland graciously provided such space, so my summer vacations were spent doing research in Stockholm and Helsinki. On one occasion I had to visit the Swedish Embassy in Kuwait to obtain a visa for this summer work.

In contrast to the US Embassy, the Swedish Embassy was located within a residential area, nestled on a small residential property among a row of similar properties and only a few feet from the main road. Like the US Embassy, the Swedish Embassy had a wall on the property, which separated it from a very small parking area just in front of the Embassy. However, the wall, more properly called a fence, was no more than three feet in height, probably did not surround the entire property, and was painted a nice blue color—the kind of wall not uncommon in residential areas. After parking just in front of the Embassy, one had to walk a few feet to the opening in the wall/fence, walk a few more paces up a path leading to the house's porch, and then up a few steps to reach the front entrance to the building. The only reason one might suspect that the building was anything other than a regular residence was that the front door was contained within a small glass enclosure that had an intercom enabling visitors to announce themselves prior to being allowed through the front door.

Upon my first visit to the Swedish Embassy, I noticed that it had one additional feature not present at the super-secure Fortress USA across town, and that was the presence of a snoozing cat lying just in front of the door. After announcing myself through the intercom and being buzzed through the outside door by the receptionist, I had to give the snoozing cat a little gentle persuasion with my foot in order to move it from its position blocking the front door.

After my visit, I wondered if the snoozing cat was all that it seemed, or if it might not be a special type of Scandinavian cat trained to intercept potential troublemakers by, perhaps, biting their toes. Ah, those clever Swedes, I thought! In this post-9/11 era of heightened security, it might be prudent for the diplomatic security service at the US State Department to consider installing similar snoozing-cat devices at Fortress USA facilities around the world. Although I heard no discussion of this matter during the deliberations of the 9/11 Commission, I can only hope that our nation's security does not fall victim to a snooze-a-cat gap.

David Wade is a biochemist and native of Somerset, New Jersey, USA. He received his Ph.D. from the University of Medicine & Dentistry of New Jersey, and he has spent almost eight years doing postdoctoral research and teaching outside of the United States, including Canada, Sweden, Finland and Kuwait, where he met the cat. Wade's postdoctoral experiences include training with 1984 Chemistry Nobelist, R.B. Merrifield, at Rockefeller University, New York City, and with former chairman of the Nobel Committee for the Medicine Prize, S. Orrenius, at Karolinska Institutet, Stockholm, Sweden. Wade currently teaches in community colleges in central New Jersey, and does peptide-based research at the Wade Research International/Foundation (http://www.wade-research.com).

An American Experience in Berlin

Laura A. Mancini Chan

It was a clear September morning in Berlin, and the sun was glinting sharply off the River Spree as I crossed the bridge, hurrying towards the nearest elevated train station. Once again, I was rushing to get to the office on time. I boarded the train as usual and passed by the heart of Berlin's government quarter, hardly taking notice of the ever-increasing number of buildings under construction. When the train finally trundled into Friedrichstrasse Station, in former East Berlin, I exited and walked down what has become one of the city's most fashionable streets. My office was located in a nearby side street, not far from the parade of expensive shops.

"Guten Morgen!" I called out to the receptionist, as I entered the building.

"Morgen, Frau Mancini Chan," she replied. We were not yet on a first-name basis, even though I had worked there for two years.

Upon reaching the third floor, I hastily got a cup of coffee from the kitchen and settled in at my desk.

My colleague, Dagmar, greeted me as she entered the room. We chatted about yesterday's meeting as our computers booted up. Soon, we were engrossed in our e-mails and the files on our desks. The morning passed quietly enough, and I was pleased that I had managed to make a dent in my inbox. Later, I returned from a late lunch and found the phone ringing in my office.

"Laura, a plane just crashed into the World Trade Center in New York!" my husband exclaimed, as soon as I picked up the receiver.

"What!? Was it an accident?" I replied, not quite digesting his words.

My husband worked in the trading room of a local bank where the TVs were always on, and he assured me that this was breaking news.

"How could this happen? Planes aren't allowed to fly that close to the city," I countered. Having lived in New York before moving to Berlin, I recalled flying alongside the city from a distance, but never crossing over it.

"I can't believe my eyes; another one just crashed into the other tower!" my husband interrupted me, "Don't you have a TV in your office?"

"No, but I'll try CNN on the web. Talk to you later."

I hung up and tried to access CNN, but the site was overloaded. By now, my colleagues were also aware of the situation and were trying to find out what was happening.

"I'm onto the Yahoo Germany site," called out Martin from his office down the hall.

A group of us joined him, watching his computer screen in horror. No one yet understood what was happening. When we heard that a plane had crashed into the Pentagon and that another one had gone down in Pennsylvania, I returned to my office and hastily placed a call to my parents in Pittsburgh.

"Morning, Dad," I said when he answered the phone, "Have you turned on the TV yet?"

"What? No, I just picked up your mother from the hospital," he replied, as she had undergone thyroid surgery the day before.

I asked about my mom, and reassured that she was fine, I explained to my dad what had been happening.

"You're kidding? Planes are going down? Are you sure you've got the news right over there?" he said, in shock, and I heard the TV being switched on in the background.

"Just be careful today," I advised him, "Maybe it's better if you two just stay at home."

"Don't worry about us. I'm not going to tell your mom right now though. She's resting. Let's talk later."

I put down the receiver and was unable to concentrate for the rest of the afternoon. I couldn't help wondering if this would go on all day around the country, and I feared for friends and family. I tried to call the cell phone of my childhood friend in New York City, but it was impossible to get through. Eventually, I returned home and spent most of the evening watching the unfolding news coverage. Local friends called me, and everyone seemed to share my sense of shock and outrage.

The next day, I was sitting in my office, trying to concentrate on the never-ending stream of e-mails that demanded attention when Brigitte burst into the room. A lively, middle-aged woman, this time her blond hair was in disarray and tears stained her cheeks.

"Has the world gone crazy?" she asked me, obviously full of anger, "Who would do this to *my* America?"

Brigitte was bearing two bunches of flowers and put one down on my desk.

"Laura, come with me, let's go to the Embassy," she said and clasped my hand.

Although the main US Embassy complex was on the western outskirts of the city, the US government also had a building in central Berlin that was not far from our office. As I left the office with Brigitte, I recalled a story she had told me months ago. She grew up in divided Berlin and to her the Americans represented what was good in the world. Even now, more than ten years after the Berlin Wall had fallen in 1989, she refused to ride the elevated train, called the S-Bahn. When I asked her once why she would go out of her way, taking buses and underground trains to avoid the S-Bahn, she had replied that the S-Bahn was *Ost* meaning east. Even when the city was split in two, the East German government had retained ownership of the S-Bahn stations in West Berlin. This meant that they were left to crumble, and renovation work wasn't begun on them until after the wall had fallen. To Brigitte, the S-Bahn symbolized the entire system that she had opposed growing up.

Brigitte visited the United States on holiday whenever this was feasible. She told me of the wonderful trip she had taken with her daughter, when they rented a car and drove around much of California and the West Coast. She talked of the beauty of the country and the wonderful shopping malls.

"In America, that's where you can really *shop*," she once told me. "It's not like here where the shop assistants size you up first depending on what you're wearing and determine whether or not to treat you well. No, in America, it's 'May I help you?' and 'Have a nice day!'"

Years ago, Brigitte had succeeded in securing a multiple-entry visa to the United States that was valid indefinitely. But eventually it came time to renew her German passport. Upset at the thought of losing her visa, she had visited the American Embassy and asked what to do. They had told her to return with both her cancelled passport and the new one, and they would transfer the visa into the new passport.

"Now we have the visa waiver system, but I still kept the old passport with the original visa all these years anyway," she told me.

When Brigitte and I reached the US government building, we saw that a security blockade had been erected that kept the crowd at a distance. A tank and several armed guards stood nearby. Flowers and candles had been placed as close as possible to the barricades and overflowed onto the neighboring sidewalks. We approached and laid our flowers down. Overcome by emotion, Brigitte and I stood there silently, watching the crowd. Eventually, we turned and made our way back to the office.

"Thank you for bringing me here," I said to Brigitte, touched at the depth of her feelings.

Just after September 11, there was an outpouring of support for America in Germany, as in much of Europe. Television shows were aired depicting Berliners talking about "their" New York and showing photos from their stateside vacations. After the major rescue efforts were completed, a firefighter from New York appeared on television and was presented with an oversized check representing donations from the people of Berlin. Although there was largely a feeling of support for America, the perceptions of my German friends differed as they watched events unfold. I recall seeing President Bush's televised visit to Ground Zero. At one point, the rescue workers and firefighters assembled around him began to chant, "USA! USA!"

"Why did they do that?" a German friend asked me, shaking his head in wonder.

I read an article in the newspaper that included the responses of several people in Munich to this televised event. One woman described it as *'beklemmend'* meaning that she felt this display of patriotism was oppressive. It was difficult to explain American patriotism to my German friends, who through their historical experiences have learned to be deeply mistrustful of such national sentiments. On the whole, I found that people tended to display a sense of identification with their hometown or region, rather than a sense of national patriotism. Perhaps, aside from more recent history, this is also a reflection of the fact that prior to unification in 1871, Germany was made up of many independent principalities.

President Bush's measured response and building of a coalition that supported taking action in Afghanistan did not give the impression of America being a reckless superpower. But, as the months rolled by and Iraq's flaunting of UN inspections came to the fore, opinions in Germany began to change. It became harder for me to defend the actions of my country, as it became increasingly evident that the United States and Britain would go to war in Iraq. Demonstrators in favor of a peaceful solution marched through Berlin frequently. I was asked if I planned to participate, but I could not. Even though I was personally in favor of a peaceful solution, something held me back from demonstrating against the policies of my home government in a country that, although it had become my home, was not my native place. Perhaps it was the same sense of spirit that caused the rescuers to break out in chants of "USA!" that held me back. It was a feeling that I could hardly put into words, but I knew that I could not openly demonstrate against the policies of my country while living abroad.

By the time the United States invaded Iraq in March 2003, I had spent five and a half years living in Germany. I felt that I had adjusted and that Berlin was home to me. But the experience of living through the tense situation of the invasion threw my American identity into sharp relief. I began to think more seriously about the beliefs and values that formed my mindset when I was growing up. Although my immediate family has been fortunate to travel a fair amount, most of my relatives have rarely, if ever, left the United States. When I first moved abroad, some of them questioned my decision with comments such as, "Everyone wants to come here because this is the best country in the world. Why do you want to leave?" When going back on visits, I would sometimes be asked, "What's so great about 'over there' that makes you want to stay?" My experiences formed a gulf between my relatives, others who had never been abroad and myself. I could tell stories about life in Berlin and try to explain that I didn't see either place as inherently 'better' than the other, just different, but that explanation was usually met with a shrug. I found that if someone had never been abroad before, it was much easier to relate to them by discussing whatever was current where they lived. Not talking about my experiences actually put me back on a sort of level playing field. Otherwise, I definitely sensed that my apparent 'worldliness' was viewed either as eccentricity or placed me in the category of being a bit of a snob.

My ties to Pittsburgh, where I grew up, are becoming ever more tenuous. My parents have retired and moved to Arizona. My brother and sister both call the West Coast their home. The United States exists in my memory in the sort of timeless way one recalls the key elements of their youth. Events like starting my first after-school job, passing my driving exam, long summer vacations spent at the community pool, vacations at national parks, football games on crisp fall evenings and finally going off to college particularly stand out. These are some of the signposts of growing up in America that I still retain within me. These memories illustrate in myriad ways the ideals I was brought up to believe in, such as egalitarianism, a sense of patriotism, a belief in God, hard work and optimism. I've noticed that Europeans sometimes view the American sense of optimism as naïve, but it has carried me through the challenges of my life.

205

It doesn't matter how many years I live outside of the United States, or how much I adapt myself to my surroundings, some parts of this core will always remain. The ability to view events from multiple perspectives that I have gained is akin to holding a prism that reflects light in all colors and directions. It illuminates aspects of the world that are not visible when looking through a single pane of glass. Yet, I have learned that the ability to be flexible and see things through the eyes of others is not the same as giving up what one holds dear. Rather, it presents a choice as to how to act and how to respond, knowing both sides.

One day, not long after the United States invaded Iraq, I was traveling by train from Berlin to Frankfurt on business. A well-dressed, elderly gentleman sat opposite me. As I pulled out an article to read, preoccupied with getting some work done, I noticed him looking at me intently. When I finished the article and placed it on the table between us, I caught his eye, and he immediately took the opportunity to start a conversation.

"May I ask," he said politely, "if you are a foreigner? I've noticed that you were reading something in English."

When I answered in the affirmative and stated that I was American, he asked me how well I knew Berlin. I explained that I had been living there for several years, and that I had first visited the city in 1994.

"I used to know Berlin very well, in my youth," he went on to say, "but I have lived in Bielefeld since the war. Actually, I was a prisoner of war held by the Americans."

I was surprised to hear this, and when he told me his age, I realized that he must have been about nineteen when the Second World War had ended. Fearing the worst, I braced myself to hear the rest of his story.

"One day, the Americans asked if any of us could speak English, and I replied, 'A little bit,' because I had taken English class for a few years in school," he went on to explain.

After that, the Americans gave him a job translating in one of their offices. They treated him with respect, and he received better meals and clothes. Eventually, he was transferred to an area administered by the British and moved to Bielefeld. There, he had married, started a family and remained.

"If it weren't for the Americans and the British, I never would have had the opportunity to have this life," he said, finishing his story.

Given the negative images of America that were prevalent in the media at that time, I was deeply touched that this man was willing to share his story with me. Listening to him, I felt as if the thread of history were stretching across the years to connect me to the experiences of Americans from that time period. As I got off of the train in Frankfurt, a thought crossed my mind. I desperately hoped that in fifty years' time, an American might be taking a train somewhere in a rebuilt, prosperous Iraq. Perhaps an Iraqi would sit down across from this American and tell him or her a similar story. If that could become reality, then America and her allies will have prevailed.

Laura A. Mancini Chan grew up in Pittsburgh, Pennsylvania. As an undergraduate, she spent a year in China. Laura worked in international human resources in Berlin, Germany where she lived for nearly six years before relocating to London in mid-2003. In addition to her current work as a freelance intercultural trainer, Laura is pursuing an MA in Chinese Studies and working on a book about her travels through China.

The Greatest Country on Earth

Bonnie Burns

My first glimpse of Europe was from a tour bus window on one of those seven-countries-in-twelve-day-tours. Even my journal was a blur. Like most people who travel abroad for the first time, I assumed my first trip to Europe would also be my last. After that trip, by scrimping in other areas of my life, I managed to take a vacation abroad every year or so, but I always felt as if I was leaving something behind when it came time to go home. The obvious way to travel more was to live closer to foreign countries, but the idea was absurd. It was the adult version of dreaming the Beatles would come to Kansas to perform in the summer of 1965. Paul McCartney would spot me in the audience, call me up to the stage, fall down on one knee and beg me to marry him.

Like many corporate Americans, where I lived was at the discretion of my company. "Go get your paycheck," they said. Kansas City, St. Louis, Dallas. Then a temporary assignment in Zurich, Switzerland came along and changed my life. While I was there, I was offered an unexpected, modest early retirement.

No longer beholden to a company, for the first time I was free to decide where I lived. Nothing in my life had prepared me for such dizzying freedom and I was positively paralyzed with indecision until it dawned on me that my choice need not be permanent. I could pick where I lived and for how long. That was when I decided to live in Switzerland. At least for the time being.

Over dinner with my Swiss friend, Denise, I said, "I've heard adapting to a foreign culture is like removing layers of an onion; it must be done very slowly, one layer at a time." Grinning, she said, "Layers of an onion is what we Swiss say about getting to know new people. If you are lucky, you meet an onion; but sometimes you meet a potato."

That was not the first time I heard a saying used differently in another country. Passing some men digging a trench in China, I mentioned to my Chinese guide that when I was a child, we used to say if we dug deep enough, we would reach China. This startled him, because as a child he heard if *he* dug deep enough, he would reach America.

Another time, in Potsdam, Germany, I asked a man born in East Germany about his experience when the Berlin wall came down.

He said, "No one knew what to do or what it would mean. It was a time of great uncertainty. One day we heard we were free to travel to the West. The next day, people on both sides started tearing down the wall with their bare hands."

I asked, "Didn't you want to travel before then?"

"No," he said. "The idea of travel never occurred to me. For my entire life, there was a wall. They told us it was there to keep the people behind the iron curtain from coming over to attack us. It was there to protect us from the barbarians in other countries."

I said, "Did I hear that right? You thought Americans were *behind* the iron curtain?"

"Yes," he confirmed.

"Oh no, no, no," I said, tick-tocking my finger at him, "*You* were behind the iron curtain, not me."

Then we both started laughing and agreed it no longer mattered.

Living abroad irrevocably alters your life. Everything shifts to adjust to the new situation. Your interests and opinions change. You strike up friendships with people who share your experience and you drift away from those who no longer do.

Visiting Americans ask me to explain Europeans. Conversely, Europeans ask me to explain Americans. It is a no-win situation that satisfies neither nationality because it is not possible to pick apart a single thread in the fabric of society.

The first thing Americans ask, even before leaving the Zurich airport is, "Why are these people so thin?" Thus, I find myself trying to explain why Europeans are thin without making it sound as though Americans are overweight. I say they eat smaller portions, they cook their own meals and eat virtually chemical-free food and they exercise as part of daily life. No matter what I say, it sounds suspiciously as if a judgment is lurking in the wings.

One of the many cultural adaptations I made living abroad was to accept that general references to Americans didn't mean "me." Americans have been taught that stereotyping is discriminatory and must be avoided unless you want to be a bigot. Unfortunately, we also ignore statistical facts in the interest of political correctness. A factual statement like, "Americans don't know much about geography" will cause many to protest: "Oh, that's not true and besides, who cares where other countries are located?"

Living as an American overseas during the Clinton era sex scandal was embarrassing. My continental friends needed no explanation why Clinton did what he did. That much was obvious. What they could not understand was America's insatiable appetite for the sordid details. Try explaining that to people who think that privacy is paramount. Weird as the whole thing was, I long for the good old days when that was big news.

Issues today are far more dangerous. When America went to war in Iraq, with Bush's famous line about being either "…with us or against us," European friends asked why Americans did not care what the majority of the world thought. Instead of spending a minute trying to understand the international community's rationale, they came up with "Freedom fries" and other childish taunts, as if grade school tactics could convince a nation to disregard its fundamental beliefs.

As a child during the Cold War, I was shown in every way possible that America was the greatest country on the planet. In every way possible, I believed it. Aren't we lucky to live in the greatest country on earth? No wonder everyone wanted to move to America.

When I started traveling internationally, my perspective shifted. It began when I saw countries with freedoms I wouldn't mind having. Freedom from violence and crime. Freedom to take a coffee break, lunch hour, or vacation without fear of being the next downsized piece of deadwood. When I found out millions of people wanted to migrate to Europe instead of America, I was flabbergasted. I'd never heard that on the news in the greatest country on earth.

Living abroad, your perspective changes if for no other reason than exposure to opinions and information unheard in America. Although, with access to internet and worldwide television coverage, it is inexplicable that such educated people lack basic curiosity about other points of view.

One thing I know for sure, news presentation is different between the continents. In Europe, people still have freedom of expression without running an "apology-check" between brain and mouth. You may disagree with what was said, but at least you don't have to wade through the politically correct-speak that often leaves you unsure where the speaker stands.

Like days gone by in America, European newscasts don't have non-stop, in-depth analysis by so-called experts. People are left to think for themselves. Nor is news endless speculation; news is reported as it used to be in America: after the fact and not before.

They do things differently over here in Europe. They do them more slowly. I am sitting here at the table sticking frying pan decals on a card. When I get all thirty spaces filled, I will walk down to my neighborhood grocery store and pick out free cookware. There are only a few spaces left; I should have the card filled in a week or two. Already, I am debating whether to get the skillet or the saucepan. Living through the second green-stamp era of my life delights me to no end.

The simplicity of European life suits me. Not long ago my father came to visit. It was his first time in Europe and I wanted to show him Paris, the city considered by some to be the most cosmopolitan place on earth.

One afternoon, we went to a grocery store nearby the hotel. Back in the meat section, a small crowd had gathered. Out of curiosity, we wandered back to see what the attraction was. There, a woman was holding a long stick of bamboo with a string tied to one end and an "S" hook tied to the end of the string. Standing behind a little barrier, she was fishing for a rubber-roasted chicken. I could not have walked away for love or money.

Clustered all around her, we customers shared her struggle. The French ooh-la-la'ed, my Dad and I ahh'ed, and everyone fought back the urge to whisper advice. After several heart-thumping close calls, the hook held firm and she carefully retrieved the rubber chicken. Pleased for her, we clapped quietly as she accepted her prize. Holding a plump packaged roasting chicken up in the air for all to admire, you would have thought it was an Olympic medal. My heart went out to her, the sponsors of the contest and everyone in the meat section.

My turn was next and it was not as easy as it looked. Although I firmly held my end of the pole, the bamboo wiggled down at the end where the string was. Bamboo is not very sturdy. I got close to nabbing one a couple of times, but alas, I walked away without a chicken. When I relinquished the fishing pole to the monsieur next to me, the French crowd nodded and nudged in the direction of my father.

Dad got closer than I did, but still no chicken. As we left, the other customers gave us the French version of "well, you tried" shrugs and smiles. Despite my disappointment, it was easy to be a good sport. What would we have done with a raw chicken in a hotel room? Paris may be the cultural and artistic center of the universe to some, but to me it is where I went fishing for a rubber-roasted chicken.

If I feel as if I am living in the past, my surroundings confirm it. Medieval walls just outside my door surround the *alt stadt,* the old city. Everything is within walking distance—the butcher, the bakery, the grocery, the library, the post office and the drug store. For the first time since high school, my own two feet are my primary means of transport. At first, my legs balked, groaned and ached. The real surprise came the first time I broke out in a spontaneous run to catch a departing train. My steps seemed too close together, stuttering and rather girl-ish. It was no wonder. The last time I ran, I had *been* a girl. Since living in Europe, my endurance has improved, but people using walkers and canes still sometimes pass me on hiking trails.

Several times a day in the Swiss village where I live, church bells ring out from the old bell tower. By closing my eyes, I can visualize huge bells swaying heavily back and forth. All too soon, the sound fades away, as if the bells are just leaving for the next town.

Typical in Europe, my village's community life centers in the cobbled town square. Since medieval times, people have gathered around the water-well for social interaction. Once a week for the farmers market, orange and brown striped awnings cover stalls where fruits and vegetables are artfully displayed. The secret is simplicity. If you have fifty eggplants, you heap them in a pile. If you have twelve, you arrange them. Like life itself in Europe, less is best. It took me a long time to appreciate the concept that fewer things in smaller spaces make a better life.

The farmers' market is charming like nothing else and is on my list of places for my visitors to experience Swiss life. Once a week I go back to a time seen only in movies or paintings. Armed with my wicker basket, I lean in to inspect the various produce before carefully deciding. When I moved to Europe, I had not expected to see foreign vegetables any more than I expected to see dogs who understood German. But I must say, some of the produce looks computer-generated—all spiky and strangely colored. Others I still can't name look as if they were yanked unwillingly out of the ground. I can almost see their grimaces as they lie there on the table.

Each season brings with it a change in the wares at the farmers market. Today, autumn arrived with bushels and bushels of apples just plucked from family orchards. And joy of all joys, they had the tart, homemade apple juice I remember so fondly from last year. They sell it right out of a giant glass container through a red rubber hose with a clamp on the end.

"Bitte, eine flasche," one bottle, please, I said as she released the frothy golden juice into a plastic bottle. With a cheerful smile, she bid me *"Aufwiedersehen."* To be sure, she will see me again. I will go back next week to buy another bottle,

because in a few weeks time they will not make more until next fall.

I come from a land of plenty. Switzerland is also a land of plenty, but just not plenty of all the produce grown on the planet all year round. Oh sure, you can buy exotic fruits and vegetables grown on other continents, like avocado or pineapple, but they are in scant supply and you pay dearly. If a hundred thousand pineapples are shipped to mainland USA, they send two dozen to Switzerland. The idea is less dependency on foreign imports and a healthy balance of trade, a page out of my childhood life in America.

Another concept I recall from my childhood was seasonal limitations of produce, but that ended long ago with foreign imports. When I arrived in Europe I thought, "What do you mean I can't have asparagus year round? Asparagus is my favorite vegetable. I want to have it in spring, fall and winter, too." Finally, after ten months of asparagus deprivation, I experienced my first asparagus season and it was a positive celebration of asparagus. Stores stack displays of asparagus steaming pots and vegetable peelers with handles shaped like asparagus. Restaurants put out a special menu: asparagus soup, asparagus with hollandaise sauce, fat green asparagus, tender white asparagus, asparagus tied with ribbons. Never have I enjoyed asparagus as much since I can't have it all the time.

They say distance gives perspective and it has certainly changed mine. But despite everything, I love America in general and lots of Americans in particular. My American ties seem not to hold my expanded views against me. As well, my European ties don't hold American political decisions against me. The difference between the two is the Europeans want to discuss American political and social rationale and Americans simply don't ask. Apparently, part of living in the greatest country on earth means you do not care what anyone else thinks. I suppose growing up in the greatest country on earth colors your view, but then again, Europeans think they know a bit about that, too.

In the end, we should teach our children that most countries are wonderful places to live and the people living there lead happy, fulfilled lives and don't all want to move to America. We should make our children understand there is no such thing as a "world's greatest" contest with a gold medal for first place and the rest of the world as losers.

The international community is not far away anymore; it is as close as our computer screens. People living in America, the world's leading nation, have a responsibility to listen and to understand other's points of view and in particular, the underlying rationale. That is, after all, true leadership.

Bonnie Burns, *a lover of all things that travel, is a Kansas native. Nearing early retirement, she accepted a two-month overseas job assignment. Eight years later, she's still not back. One of these days, she will return to the country of her birth but until then, she loves living the expatriate life. Ms. Burns presently resides in Abu Dhabi, United Arab Emirates.*

Crossing the Street

Deborah Fulton Anderson

April 1965: In preparation for International Day at Carrie Stern Elementary in Greenville, Mississippi, the students are each assigned a country. We are to dress in a costume befitting that country and memorize three interesting facts to present on stage for the entire school. I get Italy and am greatly disappointed. I'd hoped for Holland and the wooden shoes. My girlfriend Caroline got Egypt and her mother was letting her wear black eye-liner and sandals à la Cleopatra.

My classmates and I are as white as Sunbeam Bread and mostly Protestant. The Catholics seem to prefer their own school and we won't get our first Black students for another year as most schools are still segregated. We have two quiet Japanese students but no Hispanics, no foreign exchange students and not even a first generation immigrant kid.

International Day is the closest we come at Carrie Stern to recognizing the world beyond our rather bland mono-cultural borders. Most of our expectations seem as predictable as those of our brothers and sisters. The kids who sign our birthday cards at ten will be the same ones we'll take to the school dance at fourteen, graduate with at seventeen and maybe take down the aisle when we wed.

I open our encyclopedia to "I" and am daunted by the huge section of text devoted to Italy. We haven't yet studied the Roman Empire. *Pompeii and Pliny* are as foreign to my ear as *espresso or antipasto.* My understanding of the culture is limited to pizza, spaghetti and the green cans of parmesan in our cupboard. I turn on our Philco and watch reruns of "I Love Lucy" instead. Inspired by an episode, I show up on International Day in peasant-like dress, with apron and kerchief, and paint my bare feet passion purple as if I'd been stomping grapes.

June 1973: My roommate in college invites me to spend the summer with her and her family in Germany. Her father is in the Air Force, and the family lives on a huge military base. I soon realize I have left America to come to another America. Families work, live, shop and play within its confines. There are Armed Forces television stations, supermarkets and movie houses. I hear the term "base rat" and understand its meaning. Outside its guarded walls, we visit a postcard Germany—castles and crystal, organized tours to American-friendly recreation spots. I leave after three months and realize later I haven't learned anything. I might as well have been on a tour bus, observing the scenery as it drifted by my window, safety belt secured. I am determined not to make the same mistake again.

December 1983: I arrive in Naples and am part of the last batch of "military dependents" allowed in the area because of the shortage of housing. There are few habitable spaces because of the earthquakes—something that none of the library books I'd read about the region had mentioned. The earthquakes, a local phenomenon of "bradyseisms," are adding even more disruption to the existing chaos of the region. Ancient buildings are collapsing and questionable cracks are appearing in even "modern" residences. As a result, arriving military families are forced to stay in small, claustrophobic hotels for months.

Stepping off the plane, I had expected mild Mediterranean temperatures and the welcoming garlic-sauced aroma of the Italian kitchen. Instead, the first thing that slaps the senses is the noxious stench of sulphur, the screech of car alarms, a chilling rain and the whining tears of American children begging to go home.

I married a guy who happened to be in the Navy, but I wasn't prepared for the accompanying labels and expectations of being a "dependent spouse." In the States, my husband's job hadn't been the *sine qua non* of my identity—just one piece of the overall picture. Like most women I knew, I'd always worked. Now, in Italy, detoured off the career loop and disconnected from my network of friends outside the navy "family," my world seemed to be growing increasingly smaller— imploding in ever narrowing circles. It was ironic that what I had naively thought would be an adventure—a reaching out, an opening up, an embrace of another culture—was for me, in those first months abroad, a shutting down. I watched the laborers outside our hotel trying to patch the facades, pushing arcane wheelbarrows of mortar and cement, shouting and laughing in a circus of dust and urine, and felt that I was the one under construction.

January 1984: I join a survival class. It is not called that by the Navy, which instead entitles it something like "Gateway to Living," but it is a survival course nonetheless. In one week, it teaches new arrivals the basic phrases to eat and shop and the essential non-verbal language of the street. We spend an entire day learning to cross the street.

The Neapolitans love to drive but do not recognize traffic signals. Any attempt at traffic order, in fact, seems to be treated as a pesky bureaucratic rule that is to be ignored as any government imposition on what, in their experience, is a perfectly workable system. This distrust of imposed order applies to pretty much everything. The challenge, for the foreigner, is deciphering the code. We start with the basics— crossing the street. Our teacher is a huge African-American guy named Jackson. He wears a red leather coat, has one blue eye and one brown eye, and I am about to trust him with my life. He is perfect for the crossing-the-street class because he is a curiosity to the local drivers who slow down to stare at him and at us.

Jackson stands out because he is Jackson. We stand out because we are dressed in our American uniform—jeans, tennis shoes and sweatshirts, polyester and nylon—clothes no Italian would ever be seen in for a stroll in the city. The Italian women I see are in leather and wool, scarves elegantly tossed around their shoulders. The men are smoking, walking arm in arm with each other, deep in conversation. This is not a wealthy culture, but the residents all seem beautifully dressed. I spot a pregnant woman who is about to cross the street. I position myself to her right, so she is between me and the oncoming traffic. As she makes her move into the street, I keep to her side. The cars stop for her. I know this is cheating, that I cannot always count on finding women *incinta,* but this is survival after all.

July 1986: We are on "home leave" in the States and are stunned by simple, subtle things. The size of cars and parking spaces. The size of supermarkets. The size of Americans in general. Observing groups neatly lined up waiting for Whoppers and enormous sodas, how orderly we look in our casual, united sameness. I marvel at the convenience and choice, the 24-hour availability the efficiency of getting cash, mailing a letter, sending a fax. In Naples, we had learned to feel satisfied accomplishing only one of these tasks in an entire day. In the States, we drove and shopped, drove and ate, drove and visited friends, drove and crossed items off the "to do" lists with amazing speed.

It was in the air-conditioned bubble of the new mall, the Muzak-reverberating maze and lack of fresh air, where it struck me how impersonal and sanitary it all seemed. In our little commune of Arco Felice, I knew the olive man, the cheese man and the bread lady by their first names. In our *salumeria,* I'd see the owner, Enrico, signal to a certain customer (an elderly *nonna* who always had her granddaughter in tow), a simple gesture that spoke of an intimate understanding. I finally asked Enrico what the gesture meant, after years of observing this ritual. He told me that if the *prosciutto* was too salty the little girl would drink too much and be up half the night, keeping her nonna awake. The signal was to let her know whether to buy the ham that day or not.

These cultural comparisons are not always welcome or understood by friends and family. They are often interpreted as a kind of snobbery. Back at my sister's house, we show pictures and try to explain our lifestyle in Italy. They are polite, but after a while their eyes glaze over and they look bored—a look that I would see often-repeated on these home visits. They think that we are somehow living on an extended vacation, a routine apart from the "real world." My mother says that it all sounds very interesting but when are we coming *home?*

May 1990: We begin a second "tour of duty" in Italy after realizing, quite simply, that we love the country. This time we are in La Spezia at a small NATO research facility. I'm re-learning Italian as the Ligurians do not understand the street dialect I have picked up in Naples. I take private lessons and the process is easier this time because I have lost the fear of sounding like an idiot in order to communicate. I've learned that this reluctance is a great hindrance to many expatriates, especially in a culture that seems to patiently take our language misuse so graciously. I now realize that it is not necessary to understand every word, but, as my teacher advises, to let the words "flow over me like water" and to try to get *il succo delle parole,* just "the juice," the basic understanding, instead of feeling frustrated.

I feel confident enough now to converse actively with my neighbors (who love to gossip or debate endlessly which method yields the best *sugo di pesto*). I can

215

argue and bargain. But most importantly, we've become less of a curiosity in the community and more, I think, a part of its whole.

December 1993: A group of about fifteen British women, who have lived in La Spezia since they came over as young girls, married Italians and had their children, have supported each other through all stages of cultural adjustments. Each December they organize a charity bazaar and enlist the help of the International Women's Group, that they founded, which includes the "short termers"—other English-speaking expatriates who find themselves, for whatever reason or chance, living in Italy.

The British women tell me that they have noticed a pattern in their twenty-five years of observing "expats." They divide us into three groups. The first kind are only abroad for three years or less, learn little of the language, travel extensively and return at regular intervals to their home country. Then there are the expats who stay for over three years, make some friends but never truly settle in because they are never sure exactly how long they can extend their employment overseas. These two groups are quietly tolerated by the long-term Brits but are not generally included into their close alliance. The third group are the true residents. They buy homes, keep their children in Italian schools (as opposed to sending them away to English private schools), and when they speak of "home" it is not their country of origin. It is here.

I see this pattern as well. What initially appeared as exclusionary snobbery of the long-term English-speaking residents toward the other expat groups, is in fact a kind of emotional protection. The British women who reside permanently in La Spezia keep their bond with each other as a link to the culture and language they left behind. And they know they won't leave each other.

July 1995: I am saying goodbye to one of my closest American friends. Their work contract couldn't be extended, so they are leaving after five years in La Spezia. Their daughter was born here, and she will carry an Italian name and passport when she leaves. These are more than just souvenirs. This family wept when they realized it was time to return to the States. I am weeping too.

There is a special bond between friends who have shared the frustrations and blessings of living abroad. It doesn't always happen. In fact, after twelve years of living in Italy I find I often avoid other Americans, and not just the tourists who flock here (often loud and boisterous and mocking of the culture). Instead, I align myself with those who take the time to learn the language and study its politics and history. We realize, without saying so, that through the relationships we develop with our Italian neighbors, we make the strongest impression they will have of America. We are America's ambassadors.

January 1996: My husband's own NATO contract in Italy cannot be extended and we have a choice. Retire now and return to the States or stay in Europe and

216

move north to Luxembourg? We already know the answer and don't even need to discuss whether we are finally ready to return "home."

May 2000: We are back in the States for my mother's funeral. I have been back frequently in the last two years, trying to help her through chemo treatments, organizing her will and the many sad, necessary decisions that need to be made. Caring for one's parents is difficult enough in the same geographical zone. Add six-thousand miles to the equation and the resulting sum is often enormous guilt. There is a terrible scale that weighs devotion on one side and practicality on the other. When my father became ill, I stayed for six weeks during the hospital and hospice care. Exhausted and needing some emotional sustenance of my own, I flew home to Italy and a few weeks later he was dead. I did not return for the funeral and am still agonizing over that decision, despite its "practicalities."

At my mother's funeral my sisters, brother and I are drawn together in grief and nostalgia. We have tried to arrange regular family reunions because it meant so much to our mother. Now, I think we will see less and less of each other as the practical side of the scale weighs in again. My nieces and nephew, now grown and in college, are also at the funeral. I have seen little of them in the last 18 years, and I wonder how our relationship might be now if we hadn't lived so far away.

September 2001: On the morning of September 11 we are launching a project that has taken our concentrated effort for more than eighteen months—a 400-page guide for expatriates moving to the Grand Duchy of Luxembourg. I am co-editor of the book and am very proud of this effort to assist newcomers to the area. When we arrived in Luxembourg from Italy in 1996, the transition was tough—a new language and a new set of cultural lessons to learn. Being part of the "Living in Luxembourg" guide is a way to give back all the support we ourselves have received. The book celebration lasts until early afternoon.

Many of the Americans I know are driving home from that celebration when our mobile phones start to ring. The messages are pretty much the same: Go home and turn on the television. I call the women I know who do not have English-language television and try to explain what is happening. Some are already in tears. They see the images but they can't understand the French or German newscasts. We call our families in the States and watch together, miles apart, the horror of the same film footage, over and over.

January 2005: We make plans to attend my niece's wedding in London. She is marrying a Greek, and this will be the first intercultural marriage in our family. She has worked in England for only a year, and probably never uses the term "expat" to describe herself. This is all an adventure and she is optimistic about the choices ahead.

I am full of questions about work permits, sponsorship, passport stamps, qualifying for health benefits, visa requirements and how her fiancé feels about frequent trips to the United States, in what country he would like to permanently reside, and even what language their children might speak? She answers with the same polite optimism, but I note there are many questions she cannot answer.

She hasn't asked for my advice any more than I would have asked my relatives when I was her age. Her experience, especially in a bicultural marriage, will have its own set of challenges quite apart from my own. They've already chosen neutral ground to start their marriage and the fact that neither is on home turf gives their situation balance.

I wonder if one of them will feel the tug of "home" and convince the other to return there. I wonder when and how the realities of the decisions they are making now will come to tug at their hearts. I wonder if my niece's present optimism and curiosity will sustain her through the years of disconnect with this once-familiar place called America.

I remember the terror of that first traffic lesson in Naples. After all the advice about how to cross the street safely, there came the time when we just had to trust and breathe and step into the chaos. I write to my niece and once again wish her *Buona Fortuna, Bonne Chance* and smile as I realize that even if I saw "good luck" written in Greek I wouldn't recognize it. I'm sure she will, though.

Deborah Fulton Anderson is a freelance writer who has spent over twenty years living in Italy and the Grand Duchy of Luxembourg, her current residence. She is an active member of the Creative Writers Consortium and has several short stories published in their anthology, Writing from a Small Country. Deborah is also program manager for an English-speaking radio program and is currently working on a project inspired from the American Folk Life Center of the Library of Congress and the collective story initiative "StoryCorps."

The Mysterious "EX"

Joy Toulemonde

Webster's dictionary defines expatriate as *"someone sent into exile, someone who has left his country."* I never liked this word much … perhaps it was the "ex" that triggered a sense of missing something truly fundamental to my person … my home, my family, my friends, my language … and my country.

I came to France twenty years ago and although I have been living here as long as I have lived in the United States, I realize that "home" will always be the American soil. Do not get me wrong, I do not feel as if I was sent "into exile"; I chose to come here. My intent was not to lose anything, but rather to gain from the experience. The past twenty years have enabled me to take a different look at this "ex."

It all started when I was little. Something in the French language moved me. I guess it was due to my father playing Edith Piaf at dinnertime on Sunday evenings. I would dance around the table singing words I didn't know, but the music of the words felt mine. When given the choice in Junior High School, I decided to take French as an elective. The more I learned, the more I realized there was to learn and that the only way I could truly comprehend the language would be to integrate the culture.

After finishing college, I threw on a backpack in the fall of 1984 and headed east… way east from California… to Paris, France. The first couple of weeks I spent finding a place to live and signing up for French classes at the Sorbonne (the justification to my parents for spending a year abroad).

I loved the city, its hustle and bustle, the beauty of the multicolored leaves falling from the trees (something I had never experienced, coming from California), and the smells, the mixture of perfume, Gitane cigarettes and fresh baguettes. This was my first contact with "ex": *ex-cited* to be in this romantic city I had dreamed about for so long.

I hung out with other American students and we spent our free time discovering Paris and all the wonderful things it had to offer. I felt happy. However, I soon realized that we were seeing Paris through a window and had no contact with the people on the other side. Although we watched them in admiration, much as we basked in the beauty of the Eiffel Tower and the Arc of Triumph, they took no notice of us. We were no more part of their life than the trees lining the banks of the Seine River. To my great dismay, I had not integrated their culture nor could I understand the way they thought.

A few months later, my perspective changed when I met and became involved with a French man, who later became my husband. As neither of us mastered the other's language, communication was difficult at first. Words often led to misunderstandings and disagreements. Our first fight involved the word "special." When I told him that I didn't feel special in his eyes, he ascertained that I was not! Hours later, I discovered that this word means "weird" in French. I was not only dealing daily with a new language, but was also becoming aware of my next "ex"… which is, just how *ex-tremely* different cultures can be.

For some strange reason, I naively believed that people were the same everywhere throughout the world. Simplistically, we all have the same needs, don't we? Perhaps this is true, but how we choose to fulfill those needs may vary. There are many ways of getting from point A to point B and the French have their own routes. At first, I did not understand their routes and, rebellious by nature, refused to take them. I thought I could continue to do things the way we do in the States and often imperiously felt as if I were the only one driving the right direction down a one way street. Unfortunately, I was really only beating my head against a wall. Slowly, but surely, it got the best of me. I was eventually forced to adapt in order to survive.

My first trip to the *boulangerie* was the precursor. I watched the people in front of me each ask for a baguette as if they were giving an order to their dog: No "thank you," no "if you please." Yet, the bakery woman so kindly wrapped the baguette and handed it to them with a smile and a "thank you sir." A callow child, I decided to show her how polite we Americans are. I mustered all my courage to utter more than two words in French, and asked her "to please have the kindness to sell me a baguette," followed by a courteous "I thank you very much, madam." To my amazement, she glared at me and threw my baguette on the counter, with no "thank you" or "have a nice day."

Believing that perhaps she had not understood me correctly, I worked on my accent and checked my grammar (which was not difficult in a sentence composed of less than ten words). My efforts were to no avail. Her attitude did not change. Then, one day, I decided to behave just as harshly as those in the line in front of me. Surprise! It worked! The woman actually handed me my baguette, thanked me and wished me a good day.

As much as the French citizens rebelled against the monarchy in the late 1700's, there remains an inherent attraction to the distinction between social groups and classes. It's as if they are saying: "Act like Louis XVI, but, in all fairness to others, live like Oliver Twist!"

Another strange behavior can be seen in their driving manners. For example, if you want to merge in front of another car on the freeway, you can be sure the other driver will pretend not to see your car and speed up, reducing the room between him and the car in front, so that you cannot squeeze in.

After months of frustration, I finally figured out why. It is what I call, the "movie theatre line theory." Everyone in France knows that lines were made to be cut. Nobody waits behind anyone else. They all pass in front, funneling toward the entrance by pushing and shoving the people on all sides. If you wait your turn, you will, at one point, notice that you have not moved forward and that all the people behind you are already inside the show. The worst is that by the time you reach the ticket booth, there will likely be no more seats available!

It takes only once, for any intelligent person to reckon that survival in this country requires doing the same as its people. Still to this day, I feel *ex-acerbated* by this and hate having to push, shove, and treat others with disrespect. In this case, my "difference" became my weakness and I had to change my behavior in a way that conflicted with my fundamental beliefs.

Fortunately, as time passed, I discovered that my "difference" could also be an asset. As I became more fluent in the language, I was able to find work in my field of marketing. For the first time since my arrival, I found that being different from the others worked in my favor. People were interested in what I had to say and sharing my thoughts gave them a new perspective on situations. Suddenly, what I thought had been my weakness, became my strength and I began to feel I had a place in this country, and thus *ex-celled* to a new level of integration into their society.

A few years later, my husband and I began our family, probably the hardest thing for a woman to do in a foreign country. Without my mother or family around to help, I again felt disadvantaged compared to other young mothers of my age. While they were able to rely on family support and daily encouragement, I had only myself to rely on. At first, I felt defeated by the tremendous task that lay before me. Then, I became driven by the overwhelming desire to succeed at raising my children as open-minded, "bicultural" human beings.

Here again, I foresaw my "difference" to be an advantage, and set out on a long mission, one which proved to be a unique *ex-perience* in life.

Raising a bicultural child is not "automatic" because of his/her genes. It takes a lot of effort and requires true motivation. It means reinforcing the American language skills through a cultural awareness (the reason I first set out for France). It means acknowledging that your child will never be completely like you, for he lives in a different country. However, he will never be exactly like his French friends either, for he has a parent like you!

Just as I have felt different from others in this culture, and uneasy at times with this difference, I had to accept that I was reproducing a similar situation for my children. Fortunately, as I have watched them grow, I have seen the benefits of this "ex" developing within each one. I believe they, and myself, to be *ex-traordinarily* lucky to have had this opportunity.

They are used to seeing things from various perspectives and have learned to accept diversities rather than judge them. I have heard them say:

"How should we eat our fries in this country? With our hands or our forks?"

"That language is different." Instead of, *"That language sounds weird."*

"Do you think that everybody sees the same color when they look at the color green?"

"That woman has difficulties." Instead of, *"That woman is retarded."*

Today, I am a high school teacher in a small town outside of Paris. I teach French

221

children history in English. For 60 minutes, twice a week, I take those children on a voyage to my culture. My goal is to help them leave their "standards" and "judgements" back home and try to see things through the eyes of another. To understand *is ex-ceptional*. To accept is *ex-emplary*.

With all due respect to Mr. Webster, I would like to add a new definition to the word expatriate as *"someone who may not be physically present in his country, but who continues to ex-ude its culture, while ex-ulting the one in which he now lives."*

Joy Toulemonde is a mother of five children (ages 5 to 13), married to a French man, and has been residing in Meudon, France for the past twenty years. She came as a student and never left. With her family she returns to the United States every year for the months of July and August and every other Christmas. Their purpose for returning is to see family and friends, as well as to transmit American culture to their children, all born and raised in France.

Order Form

Fax orders:	Send this form to +41 (0)22-340-0233.
Email orders:	Go to www.aca.ch and select order form.
Postal orders:	American Citizens Abroad
	5 Rue Liotard, 1202 Geneva, Switzerland

Please send to:

Name:_____

Address:_____

Address:_____

City:_____ State:_____ Zip:_____

Country: _____

Telephone:_____

Email address: _____

Number of copies:_____ **Price per copy: US$ 25.00**
Shipping and handling charges (economy rates)

	For first book	**For each additional book**
	US$	**US$**
United States	5.00	2.00
Switzerland	5.00	2.00
Great Britain	5.00	2.00
Rest of Europe	7.00	2.00
Rest of World	9.00	2.00

Total purchase (including shipping and handling) US$ _____paid by:

☐ **Direct bank transfer** made on: _____(Order date) to:

American Citizens Abroad US$ account with UBS, Geneva, Switzerland

IBAN account number: CH74 0024 0240 2008 0660P • Swift UBS: WCH ZH 80A

Bank transfer order made by: _____

(please print name in block letters)

Or

Credit card: ☐ Visa   ☐ MasterCard   ☐ American Express

Card number:_____ Expiry date: _____

Name on card:_____

(please print in block letters)

Signature: _____   **Order date:** _____

Printed in the United Kingdom
by Lightning Source UK Ltd.
108737UKS00002B/1-63